The Anthropological Imagination

The Anthropological Imagination

MURIEL DIMEN-SCHEIN

MCGRAW-HILL BOOK COMPANY

New York St. Louis San Francisco Auckland
Bogotá Düsseldorf Johannesburg London Madrid
Mexico Montreal New Delhi Panama Paris
São Paulo Singapore Sydney Tokyo Toronto

Book design by Paulette Nenner.

First McGraw-Hill Edition.

1234567890MUMU783210987

Library of Congress Cataloging in Publication Data

Dimen-Schein, Muriel.
The anthropological imagination.
Bibliography: p.
Includes index.
1. Ethnology. I. Title.
GN316.D55 1977 301.2 77-6658
ISBN 0-07-016986-1
ISBN 0-07-016985-3 pbk.

To the memory of my parents,

Dora Zauzmer Dimen
Alfred Dimen

Acknowledgments

The insights and struggles experienced by all students in all twenty-five sections of introductory anthropology that I have taught over the last seven years stimulated the considerations which have shaped this book. Indeed, I am now grateful, as I once was not, to the curricular vicissitudes of Herbert H. Lehman College, City University of New York, which forced me to teach the introductory course so often, because in order to keep myself interested, I had to rethink the entire discipline and therefore to grapple with its unsolved problems. My field research with the Navajo and Greek peoples who allowed me to study their cultures, presented to me contradictions—in anthropology's premises and in its relation to the world, and in my own relation to anthropology and the world—which over the years also made me rethink anthropology. Tom Lewis' suggestion that I write a popular introductory book first inspired me to put all this experience to good use. Stanley Aronowitz, by proposing this book to McGraw-Hill, and Joyce Johnson, by accepting it, gave me the chance to do so and the opportunity of saying whatever I wanted and needed to say.

Many others also have helped me to think about and to write this book; any errors in theory, fact, or style persist in spite of their good advice. Nancy Foner and Robert F. Murphy read the original draft of Chapters I through III and gave me needed early direction, while Stanley Aronowitz's trenchant criticism of a late draft of the same chapters enabled me to eliminate some misconceptions. Kevin Dwyer corrected inconsistencies in my discussion of symbolic structuralism in Chapter V. Karen Armstrong's reading of Chapter VI, and our discussions about surplus-value and modes of production, helped to sharpen that chapter's focus. Eric Delson and Carol Kramer remedied my ignorance of physical anthropological and archeological material, respectively, in Chapter VII. I wish to thank the members of the Anthropological Field Methods Seminar, Spring 1974, for allowing me to use their research in Chapter III: Michelle Barrett, Bernice Bennett, Lucia Forbes Désir, Victoria Fraina, Alvin Gonzalez, Kathleen Grandpierre, Susan Jacobs, Palangadan Kunhikannan, Norman Ponce, Gregory Severin, Patricia Stern, and Judith Zara. Joyce F. Riegelhaupt and Eric R. Wolf read the first draft of the entire manuscript, and I am grateful to them not only for noting factual errors but for criticizing my general approach in a way which kept me honest. Carol Lefcourt's and Laura Martin's reactions to the second draft showed me where my ideas and writing had to be clarified. Joanne Dolinar's sensitive eye and light hand made the editorial process a pleasure. Madeleine Lewis rescued me during the final proofreading. Carol Lopate's reading, commentary, and generous encouragement have sustained me since my first thoughts of writing this book. Finally, I am indebted to Seth Schein not merely for his careful reading of all versions of the manuscript, but also for his unceasing support for my work and his unquestioning confidence in my ability to write the kind of book I wanted to write.

Contents

Introduction xi

I. Western Culture, Social Science, and Human Nature: Between Mind and Matter 1

II. What's in a Name? The Paradigm of Culture 19

III. Why is the Sky Blue? Theories and Explanations 55

IV. Separations and Connections: Kinship, Marriage, and Households 99

V. Symbols and Sensibility, or "You'd Better Go See a Doctor" 137

VI. Energy, Work, and Power: From the Frying Pan into the Fire 179

VII. Space, Time, and Process: Cultural Evolution 229

Suggestions for Further Reading 267

Index 281

Introduction

I came to write this book after several years of teaching introductory courses in cultural anthropology to college students for whom this might be their only acquaintance with the subject. My experience showed me that, even though Margaret Mead and others had made anthropology's core concept of "culture" part of the mainstream of American thought, anthropology had additional unique and distinctive ideas to offer a general audience—not merely the idea that people can live in many different ways, but rather that anthropology's contribution to public knowledge is a particular point of view, a way of looking at the world, a synthesizing theory of human beings and human culture.

The fundamental perspectives of an academic discipline too often go unmentioned in textbooks. Texts aim to present orderly answers to every question and final solutions to every problem. But fundamental perspectives contain unsolved problems and unanswered questions. Such perspectives are difficult to articulate because the elemental ideas they contain are both extremely simple and extremely complicated. Basic perspectives and ideas are also the most controversial ones and therefore the most exciting ones. Because of this, they are precisely what should be available to the nonprofessional. In anthropology, they are views of and ideas about cardinal concerns of our own culture—the nature of human nature; the difference between theory and fact, or knowledge and beliefs; the connections between love and marriage, or scarcity and surplus, or power, honor, and glory; the relationship between individual will and the laws of the cultural and natural universes.

I have, therefore, written this book for the person who, in or out of a classroom, has perhaps heard of anthropology, does not really know what it is, and would like to find out. I have written the kind of book I myself would like to read to learn about an unfamiliar discipline.

I write about fundamental perspectives because they are the framework for theory, and, as I say repeatedly, only through theory can people see, grasp, make, and remake their worlds. To shape our lives as we see fit, we need to be able to shape our perspectives on them, to know and name what we see and what we don't see. Theories, though seemingly abstract and irrelevant to real life, in fact are no different, in principle, from everyday thinking, for both derive from what we do in everyday life. In a sense, this means that what I say here pretends to have some practical import. I am firmly committed to the human use of human knowledge to liberate minds and society. Knowing how to create understandings of the world can help to make us free.

But these are grand concerns. I would not presume that what I say here can do more for anyone than what a glimpse of social theory did for me. My first contact with it was like a crash of lightning that lit the darkness. In my first year in college, I suddenly found, in the work of the French sociologist Emile Durkheim, one way to make some sense out of a painfully confusing world. His view gave me the hope that the fragments of social life might indeed fit together to form a coherent whole. I saw that between people there were real relations that structured their lives, and that could explain why people did what they did. A little later I read some of the works of Karl Marx and began, in this formalizing of my liberally oriented upbringing, to develop an ordered sense of why and how not all the pieces actually interlocked as securely as Durkheim's theories supposed. I began to think that I might one day understand some reasons for the overwhelming chaos in my own life. Finally, I read the archeologist V. G. Childe's Marxist-oriented sweep of human history, which inspired my hope that I, too, could participate in the creation of a grand view of cultural evolution into whose processes I could integrate my life and my society.

I chose anthropology over other social sciences for two reasons. First, I was drawn to its moral emphasis that our own culture was not the best or only way to live, and that alternatives existed. I found this debunking deeply satisfying, given my profoundly unsatisfying adolescence in the suburban conformist culture of the late 1950s. Secondly, even before I learned (only in college) that there was any such thing as anthropology, I had been fascinated by the human past. This sealed my choice, for the study of the evolution of human beings and human culture lies at the heart of American anthropology.

Perhaps here I ought to say what anthropology is. It may be defined as the study of human beings as they live in groups and as they have come to be what they are. It has four fields. The one on which this book focuses is cultural anthropology, the study of contemporary cultures and their operation. A second, archeology, is about the evolution of culture; archeologists investigate sequences of extinct prehistoric and historic cultures. A third, physical anthropology, is the study of the biological evolution of human beings, through the examination of fossils, living primates, and contemporary hereditary physical variations among human beings. The fourth field, anthropological linguistics, is about the structure and social functioning of human languages, and the history of language change. The theory of evolution unifies the four fields.

In graduate school, I specialized in cultural anthropology, though I studied all four fields and have always tried to keep a sense of their unity. This book reflects these concerns. Unlike a textbook, it does not cover every single concept or subtopic or classical case-example of cultural anthropology. It aims, rather, to convey the sense of method and approach without which one cannot know or do cultural anthropology.

I have decided to discuss all the kinds of data that a cultural anthropologist wants to know about any given culture. These usually fall into three categories: The first category of information includes ways of making a living (the *techno-economic* and *techno-environmental* base); the next is *social organization,* including social life and power structures; and the third is *ideology,* or systems of ideas and beliefs. The categories are related to one another in that the direction of causality, and therefore of explanation, goes, over the long run, from first to third, from the bottom-line material facts of life up to the mental.

Although I once espoused this order of explanation, which introductory courses and texts often follow, I now think that it does not quite work, at least as far as it goes. It aims to explain change, and therefore evolution. But by omitting reciprocal interaction among the categories, either from top down or some other sequence, it denies the effect of ideas on human action and therefore begs the question of the relation between individual and culture. I therefore use a different sequence in this book.

The chapters proceed from basic concepts (I–III), to that which is to be explained (IV–VI), to that which explains (V–VII). Chapter I gives a philosophical and methodological overview of the book and field. Chapter II explores the concept of culture. Chapter III analyzes the problems of theorizing, focusing on three prominent theories in cultural anthropology. Chapters IV–VI continue this concern with theory, but they also introduce data from a few specific cultures to illustrate the concepts they present. Chapter IV describes concepts relevant to understanding domestic and social life: I begin with this portion of cultural data because, in the first place, it concerns us most in real life and we therefore want to explain and control it; secondly, its concepts logically precede others, and a grasp of them must therefore be primary. Chapter V discusses secular and religious ideas and beliefs, symbolic systems, and the relations between individual and culture. I try to demonstrate the interplay between ideology and structure. Chapter VI describes not technology or economics per se, but modes of making a living in the context of both human and non-human environments, economic structures, and the configuration and distribution of power; it emphasizes interactions between politico-economic arrangements, social relations, and ideational systems. Chapter VII is about change and evolution. But it is not primarily about the future. Rather, it details the kinds of processes that characterize the human past and appear in the present; I leave the reader to use these processes in making up the future. At the end, I provide in Suggestions for Further Reading some main works relevant to each chapter.

Although I hope this book is sufficiently general to include that which is common to all anthropologists, I am aware that it nevertheless contains my particular view of the field and my biases. For example, not all anthropologists focus on evolution. My emphasis on it comes from my graduate training at Columbia University, which was oriented toward neo-evolutionary and ecological theory, both influenced by Marxism. At the same time, I also studied French structuralism, as well as Continental and North American sociological theory.

My background is thus mixed, if not self-contradictory. I finished graduate school with a quite rigid, materialist, determinist view of culture and human evolution, parts of which still influence my thinking. But during the succeeding half-dozen years, my intellectual and personal development showed me the importance of some questions that this view cannot answer within its premises. In particular, it cannot account for or explain how cultural ideology, through individual consciousness or subjectivity, results in the individual action, socially conceived and performed, which transforms the objective, material base. Although we cannot make the world out of ideas, we can do nothing with material substance unless we understand its relation to ideas. In a sense, this means that no social theory can be adequate unless it takes account of its own emergence and effect on the world. And no person should be satisfied with a social theory until it explains what she/he is doing holding that theory in this particular world. This does not mean that culture is the sum of the separate minds of its individual members, or that culture and individual personality are distorted mirror images of one another. Nor do I espouse an idealism or mentalism. I merely insist that we have more to take into account than the tangible, observable, countable, material world.

I decided, therefore, that my view needed revision. My considerations led me to investigate other theories whose influence will also be seen in the following pages: that of the Chicago school of symbolic structuralism, which adds the dimension of meaning to potentially arid structuralism; psychoanalytic theory, including both Freudian and recent object-relations schools of thought; the dialectical Critical Theory of the Frankfurt School of social theory.

In some ways, then, my approach is idiosyncratic and unorthodox. For instance, in Chapter VI, my discussion of economic systems departs from the beaten anthropological track. I use the Marxist concept of *mode of production,* since anthropology has developed no viable concepts for production systems as it has for systems of exchange. This, in turn, entails some discussion of surplus production, and its elusive, hotly debated role in culture and evolution. In Chapter V, I speculate about a universal human psychology, a subject about which little is known. Throughout the book, I express my personal, feminist, and political concerns, and my views on the economic and political inequalities that inform all our lives.

My approach, therefore, is critical and questioning, and has political and moral import. This is entirely appropriate, since anthropology, like all knowledge, bears the mark of its culture, of the interplay of human minds and material conditions in which it has grown. Anthropology contains value judgments, for social science is one part of the ideology of industrial society. Like all ideology, it can obscure as well as reveal; it can function to justify as well as to condemn the current social order. Moral and scholarly honesty therefore require us to keep a continuously self-critical eye on the ideas we create, in order to be aware of their distortions and our own blind spots. Indeed, I think it incumbent on social theorists to go beyond the theory with which they start; it is our job to transform what we have received so as to question its social bases and eventually the society in which they are found and from which the theory emerges. This is why I also discuss the sociology of anthropological knowledge.

There is much we do not know. There are many questions to which we have no answers (and undoubtedly many questions we have not thought to ask). It has been difficult to resist the temptation to force an answer, to try to work things out before they can be worked out, and to attempt new explanations of interest only to professionals. If there are no answers, I usually have left the questions open, since good questions are more satisfying than weak answers. In the few cases where I have risked new solutions, I say so, just as I say when I assert something disputed or not generally accepted by the community of anthropological scholars.

If there is one elemental idea I want to drive home, it is that of process. Though events happen and things exist in concrete space, life is lived only in and through time. This makes change a fact of life. Human beings change through culture, and culture changes through human beings, so that the fullest development of one is contingent upon the fullest development of the other. These processes, like all human ones, are continual and never complete: Our culture represents a point in evolution.

Similarly, this book represents a point in my development. Since we never can move entirely outside our own ideas so as to view them as clearly and critically as we would like (or, at least, we ought), we need others to criticize what we say. I expect my ideas, as do all ideas, to change in time, and I hope they will be helped to do so by people who, in correcting my errors, have come to see the world more clearly. I hope that what I say will help to enlighten some people about anthropology, provoke them to new thoughts, and give them a sense of the degree to which their world does and does not lie within their control. Perhaps then they can go on to create the ideas and theories that will permit them to make order out of chaos by envisioning and creating a better world.

This book is part of a journey as yet barely begun.

I.

Western Culture, Social Science, and Human Nature:

Between Mind and Matter

Human Nature

Very often, in the course of trying to determine what is "really human," we conjure up an experiment in which we would isolate a human infant and allow it to mature by itself. How would it feed itself? What language would it speak? Would it be basely aggressive or simply peaceful and loving? As we concretize this image of a helpless baby, the experiment begins to seem faintly ridiculous (as well as cruel). No infant could possibly survive under those conditions.

Well, then, perhaps we could set an older person down on a desert island; would we then finally discover what human nature is? In the twentieth-century novel, *Lord of the Flies,* the writer William Golding allowed a group of twelve-year-old boys to be ship-wrecked on an island; earlier, the eighteenth-century novelist, Daniel Defoe, placed an adult Robinson Crusoe on a lonely isle. To some readers of these novels, the heroes' behavior reveals innate human traits. But others disagree with this inference, since it disregards the effect of the characters' prior experience on their island behavior: Before they arrived, they had learned how to live; they had learned languages, techniques of food-getting, and the social rules of order (especially, in these cases, the rules of dominance, subjugation, and obedience to authority).

The experiment seems frustratingly difficult. There is no way we can conduct it: The infant would die, for it is, naturally, unable to care for itself. And, just as naturally, older children or adults would retain many of their already formed characteristics; having begun to learn a particular way of life, they would bring it with them and it would inform the way they set up their own new society. What are we to do with this stymied inquiry?

In an ideal sense, scholarly or scientific thinking never has any failures. We use our mistakes to learn more about our subject, our methods, and our theories. For example, the results of a scientific experiment are not wins or losses; they merely confirm or disconfirm the ideas, or the particular theories or hypotheses, that underlie the experiment. The results then raise or lower confidence in the particular ideas which we, the experimenters, hold about how the world works. If expected results occur, the hypothesis underlying the test has been verified, and its underlying theory has received support. If something unexpected happens, then either the hypothesis was wrong (and its generating theory weakened), or the conditions of the experiment have been faulty; we have to reexamine both. What went wrong with our experiment?

Since it was imaginary, we need not worry about its conditions. What then was wrong with our hypothesis that an abandoned infant could grow up by itself and exemplify the fundamental features of being human? The infant would die because of basic biological facts: A baby has the physiological and neurological ability only to breathe, eat, sleep, and excrete—and to begin to assimilate and transform the approved ways of performing these functions. It needs an adult to give it food, provide a place to sleep, clean it, teach it, and love it. This conclusion is eminently commonsensical, but if we look deeper, it tells us something not so obvious. The hypothesis was faulty because it broke a natural law: The human infant can surive and therefore grow only if it receives care for several years after birth. Beyond a certain minimum number of years, the amount and kind of care a baby is deemed to need vary according to the way of life it is born into, as do the number and kind of care-takers, and the definitions of child and adult.

The implications of this universal necessity for care constitute basic premises of anthropology. The care involves each baby with one or more adults, and this involvement means that the baby immediately begins to learn a distinct way to live. For example, it learns how to be either male or female, since the behavior, demeanor, and work expected of females and males, and the social standing to which they are assigned, differ around the world. Depending on its sex and on the meaning which sexual identity, or gender, has for its care-takers, the infant will be touched, played with, talked to, and thought of differently, from the moment of its birth. It will learn to expect and respond to this differentiated treatment, and simultaneously absorb the tacit, perhaps inexpressible attitudes of its parents and society about femaleness and maleness. These attitudes reflect the varied life-chances assigned to gender in each society.

In other words, the care that each infant receives is not only care but also communication about living. The baby learns, for example, whether it is to be fed by breast, bottle, or both. Of course, the infant is not consciously aware that one object is called breast and the other bottle, but since they are different kinds of objects, its experience of them, and therefore of the world, will be different. Some infants, then, have no chance to know so early in life that manufactured objects can replace a body; others will never feel the sensuality of nursing at the breast. Still others learn that their food may come from the bottle at one feeding and the breast at another.

In many ways child care is contingent on the world outside the nursery. For example, people other than the biological mother may care for the baby. If, in the baby's society, only relatives are considered friends and all nonkin are seen as enemies, then only relatives will be its care-takers. In a class-structured society, the "latch-key" child of a working mother returns to an empty home after school, but a wealthier child may be in the hands of a full-time governess until boarding-school age. Whether or not all children share the same experience of care, each learns to accept as self-evident ("natural") its present and perhaps future experiences of nurture.

These conditions subtly but indelibly influence its psyche and behavior. The infant learns that to get something it wants it must deal with other people, and do so in certain ways. Perhaps it must smile for its parents or, when older, be gravely respectful toward them. Among many non-Western peoples, it may have to behave in one way toward its mother's relatives and in another toward its father's; it may share name, community membership, and property with the former, and (eventually) get spouses from the latter. The infant may begin to learn that because of its parents' position in society, it may want things which it can never get, whereas others, because of the circumstances of their birth, get pretty much what they want.

Whatever pan-human or unique characteristics each normal infant has, these are soon molded, distorted, or elaborated by what it learns. Our hypothesis broke another natural law then: We cannot be born without learning a particular kind of life whose pattern and meaning are transmitted by even the most basic acts—the way a baby is fed and cared for. The hypothesis neglected the universal impact of determinate ways of feeling, thinking, and behaving on each human being. It neglected the fact that the relation of humans to the cosmos, to nature, and to each other is indirect; it is "mediated" by culture.

Finally, our hypothesis that we can discover the essence of human nature if we let a child grow up on a desert island broke a third law: The life of every human being is lived in the context of particular relationships. A child is not a child unless there is an adult. In our culture, it is said that you do not become an adult as long as there lives someone who remembers you as a child; in other cultures, one becomes an adult as soon as one has a child of one's own. The definition of adulthood thus comes from a connection to another person or other people.

Human beings carry out their daily lives in ways which spring from such connections. For example, housewives keep house, as their name indicates, but whom they keep it with, and for whom they keep it, determine what housekeeping is like and what it means. In twentieth-century North America, a housewife usually has her own home as the wife of a man who is supposed to go out and earn money. Her position means not only that she will behave differently from, for example, a woman with a career, but also that she will be treated differently. In nineteenth-century Yugoslavia, a housewife lived and worked as a member of a larger group of women to whom she was connected by marriage, her sisters-in-law and her mother-in-law; the work each did varied according to her age and seniority among the women. Unmarried women also belonged to the work group, though their position was always lower than that of married women. Their husbands, brothers, fathers, and sons worked in similar, all-male groups.

In our daily work outside the home, we are employer or employee; we have coworkers, foremen, and shop stewards. In other times and places, there were lords and serfs. In agricultural economies today, people may help each other harvest their corn because they are neighbors or kinsmen, or they may do so only in return for some kind of compensation—in money, kind, or promises of future aid. We have friends, acquaintances; and we have enemies, those who treat us with hostility, or whom we treat with hostility, because of differences in physical form, language, beliefs, customs, wealth, or power. In some places, every human being expects to have the same life-chances; in others, there are rulers and ruled, those with wealth and those without.

Our hypothesis, and its underlying idea of the lone human being as the exemplar of human nature and the source of our knowledge of human nature, ignored the fact that if we live, we live with other people in a structured society. The activities we perform and the jobs we do are all connected to what specific others do. Our acts and relations are determined by the patterned relationships of individuals and groups to each other that constitute the whole of society. In turn, we define others, and they us, in terms of our jobs, positions, and mutual relationships.

These are facts of structure and social existence, and they are beyond our will; they are part of being human. Our hypothesis was inadequate because to isolate human beings contradicts the way we find them existing in their natural state.

However, the experiment has taught us something about the nature of the raw material, of human nature: We cannot live, physically or mentally, without being social. Sociality is a condition of human survival and this basic tenet of social science is also a way of thinking that is essential if we are to understand society and culture.*

SOCIAL SCIENCE AND WESTERN CULTURE

Yet somehow we, in our culture, object to this. Having thought about and absorbed these ideas, something in us cries out to set up the experiment again, because something has been left out. In inquiring after the nature of things, we must heed not only our hypotheses and methods of research, but also our hunches. Let us see what our omission is and whether it is important.

I seem to have said that society submerges the individual, that human nature is only social or cultural nature. Yet we also know that the individual is not merely a photo-reduction of her/his society. Just as the society is not simply a collection of individuals but is also structured, so the individual, though unavoidably part of society, is also different from it. We are physically separate beings, and a part of each one of us is always emotionally, intellectually, and spiritually alone, in spite of or perhaps because of our perpetual interaction with others. We know our inner and outer physical boundaries; we can sense empty stomachs and acid ones, we can feel our skin and nails. Our psychic separate-

* I have so far defined *culture* as the facticity of the mediation of human existence, and *society* as the integrated, recurrent sets of relations, or structure, within which people live. Both terms connote something encompassing the individual, and in this sense, I use them interchangeably. Chapter II contains a more extended discussion of the concept of "culture" and its problems.

ness is harder to know or sense, partly because it develops through social life. However, though we fit into recognizable personality types or character structures, we are each, through chemistry, body form, and life experience, different and unique.

I am saying, then, that there are two simultaneous but different orders of phenomena, the sociocultural and the individual. Though connected, each also has its own characteristics, and if we wish to understand either, the one should not be taken for the other. The individual has a brain and a body, a circulatory system, and a structure that reminds us of its historical descent from other life forms; it can be studied as a biological organism. But its brain and its psyche also require us to study it from the perspective of psychology. The society, on the other hand, consists of groups of people with differentiated obligations, prerogatives, and relationships. It can be described in terms of the number and kinds of these groups and by various demographic and economic statistics. It has mechanisms which enable it to reproduce itself, through its relation to its environment, its education of its young, and its means of enforcement of its rules. Sociologists and anthropologists study, for one thing, the way societies function at a moment in time, and theorize about how those societies maintain themselves.

Each society can also adapt to changes which impede or facilitate its functioning; in so adapting, its form inevitably alters. Societies or cultures thus have, within them, the potential for evolution, for undergoing, over time, transformations toward more integrated forms. This means that each society has a past and present form that we can study. From one perspective, cultures have beginnings and ends, but from another, each imperceptibly shades off into other forms. One of the major interests of anthropology is the study of the processes that underlie such transformations, of the evolution of society and culture.

The theoretical separation of the individual and society creates intellectual pitfalls because now, having set them apart, we have to put them together again in order to replicate reality. This process generates a paradox. We now ask: How does the society manage to exist despite the multiplicity of personalities, each with its own strivings, fantasies, and solitariness, and how does the individual personality remain individual despite the strength of the sociocultural forces? Like any paradox, this one is but a product of our usual way of thinking. We have, for certain scientific or intellectual purposes, abstracted two separate entities from the living reality. But we must not mistake these abstractions for what really exists; in reality, individuals live in society or culture, and society or culture is lived through individuals.

More directly, our hankering after the lone individual outside a culture is a subtly compelling part of our own culture. It is not just a detached assessment of a faulty hypothesis, or a mental reflection of differences in levels of phenomena. The questions we ask and the knowledge we seek emerge from our background, which sometimes perversely obscures what we want to find out. Our scientific experiment parallels Defoe's novel because both arise from the Western obsession with the individual's ability to survive, to surpass, even to transcend society and the material forces that hamper the achievement of personal goals. We pit the individual against the society. We celebrate lone heroes like Odysseus, and rugged individualists like the pioneer. Taken literally, Genesis begins with the creation by one lone god of one world and of one human being, out of whose body came another; the individual becomes the source of all other individuals and things.

With the weight of our history and tradition of the individual on us, it is no wonder that the concept of a society or culture, the other part of our paradox, becomes too enormous to grasp. Yet the dead weight of our past is not enough to explain our resistance to sociological analysis. For our myths do include the society as well as the individual, even if we are not conscious of it. Adam and Eve created a family, and their children found nonincestuous spouses with whom to reproduce (even if only from "the Creation in the next county"). Odysseus voyages so that he can return to home and family. The frontiersman spent much of his time producing goods so that he could make enough money to buy the goods that others produced, and his life was molded as much by Native Americans and by the railroads as by his will. We continue to elevate the individual despite the great body of social thought found in the Western tradition, from the writings of fifth-century Athens through the massive tomes of nineteenth-century European social theorists.

Why does our everyday thinking obscure the social interrelatedness of our heritage or relegate it to sacred, unknowable status? In part, it is because our most immediate, and therefore surest knowledge comes from our own individual maturation, so we easily reason out from our personal experience to the life and growth of a society. But though we are not always aware of it, we also know that there is more to our lives than our inner and outer boundaries. Unique as we are, our individuality is molded by our experience, by our interactions with others in social relationships.

These relationships are what society consists of and are the context of the life of any individual. There are relationships between people, such as friendships, and between people and things, such as ownership or craftsmanship. Outside the individual there are also other powerful but less immediately felt interactions. There are, for example, relations among the way we organize our work (self-sufficient family homesteads or interdependent wage-laborers), the kind of crops we grow (wheat or rice), and the kind of tools we need (tractors or irrigation canals). Spatial arrangements of people and buildings (clustered huts in a forest, isolated homesteads on the prairie, or densely packed high-risers in cities) pace and shape our lives. Individual behavior flows grandly or tightly depending on the means of communication and control (whether we hear drums, read the printed word, or see newscasts; whether social order depends on the immediate strength of face-to-face contact or the threats of jails and the military). The distance between hopes and achievements narrows or widens with the distribution of power among different individuals and groups (whether we have job mobility, whether we can influence domestic laws or foreign relations). As we have seen earlier, human life is social life, and that social life has specific and therefore specifiable, analyzable forms. If we can know them, then we can understand that on which our individuality is predicated.

Yet, our cultural tradition makes it difficult to trust, describe, and talk about the notions of relationship, society, and culture, and to see the society/culture and the individual as simultaneously separate and connected. Individuals are visible, their relationships are not. Whereas individuals can remain as they are whether they stay in one place or move from here to there, relationships are fluid. We can measure changes in individuals' sizes, weights, and so on, but it is hard to know if relationships have changed or if they are the same as they were ten years ago. Our intellectual traditions of positivistic empiricism (which trust only sensorily perceived "facts," such as individual actions, and not inferences from them, such as relationships) and our culturally valued materialism (which believes only what it can touch and measure) lead us to emphasize individuals.

Indeed, when we try to study culture, these traditions tempt us to treat it as if it were tangible and measurable. In the process, it, like the individual, comes to be seen, erroneously, as an object, as a thing with clearly defined edges and a center. As such, the individual and society become conceptually easily separable from each other: In describing ourselves and our society in the terms given by our cultural tradition, we treat the society as outside ourselves, and ourselves as outside the society. In so separating them in abstract thought, we put each out of the other's range of influence and, significantly, out of our own control. If our theory conceives them as separate, we think they are separate, and act accordingly.

To treat individuals and culture as if they were unconnected is to treat them as things. Thereby, we also "thingify" ourselves and obscure our relation to, and control over, culture. That is, we reify ourselves and society or culture. This reification emerges automatically from our way of life and taints all our ideas about ourselves and others. Our economy depends on the creation and refinement of new machines, and in it, all people, acts, and goods become things. People "improve" themselves as they would their tools; they "work on" relationships. Our social system fosters a kind of thinking in which people, social groups, and ways of living become timeless entities; indeed, we often feel like fitted parts of a machine whose meaning consists of their momentary functions and purposes.

This reification has two consequences: The first occurs often among people who are not social scientists. Intuitively realizing that people and societies are not objects and assuming that all theories reify, they contemptuously dismiss all theory and affirm that one can understand the world without understanding society and culture; in this view, one needs, for example, only a commonsense, everyday-life understanding of human nature. The second consequence occurs among social scientists: We forget that people, social groups, and culture have fluid boundaries, that they are alive, and that they change. Our theories therefore became static, and do not encompass change. Such constricted thinking somehow seems at variance with the notion that it emerges in a rapidly changing society, but is congruent with the fact that our society has not changed fundamentally in the last hundred years.

But the social sciences need not reify. Following the tradition of Western science, they try to eliminate the supernatural as an explanatory device and instead attempt to discover, or formulate, naturalistic laws and principles. Like other disciplines, then, they tend to objectify and classify, arousing inordinate distress and anger when they do. I would maintain that it is, at the outset, necessary to take people and society as objects, as if only their external boundaries and present form were important, in order to define them and to discover their similarities and differences. In this way we can understand them as natural phenomena, explicable by the principles and processes which order all life. This means that when we observe human beings, although we may feel for their joy and pain, we must, at the same time, treat them with the same dispassionate, detached attitude with which we would treat gasses, rocks, trees, and fruit flies.

However cold-blooded this attitude may be, it is not inhuman(e), for it is, in fact, what most people do anyway. It comes from the very processes which constitute the daily lives and thoughts not only of Westerners, but of all people. For instance, in deciding to invest money, to tell someone off, or to change jobs, we usually back off from the situation to get some perspective on it before we take action. In other words, we look at it in a detached fashion. "Witch doctors," or magicians, in our own cultural past or in non-Western societies today, perform the same operations. They take the natural world, including people, as objects, with the aim of analyzing how they function, in order to understand or control them. On the basis of their findings, they are then able, if they wish, to make the best possible decisions about what course of action to take.

Cultural anthropologists, like some other social scientists, live with the people they study and, in order to gain an immediate understanding of their lives, try to behave like members of the community at the same time that they observe them. When everyone sits silently at a religious ceremony, we too keep still; if we don't enjoy their food (e.g., sheep's eyes in Greece or Turkey), we try at least to eat it, and if finally we refuse, we can then do so from personal preference, not cultural disdain. We inquire into minute details of the functioning of everyday life. We watch a wedding, a birth, and a funeral with equal detachment and equal involvement. We ask tiresomely repetitive questions, cross-checking the answers, and we hover constantly, observing all action and listening to every conversation. We attempt to figure out relationships between people, to categorize the groups in the society and describe their connections, to glimpse the processes that give life and support to the structure, and to determine how the people, their society, and culture are products of past and present historical circumstances.

Such dispassionate observation of human beings may frighteningly seem to eliminate all feeling for the people under study. But this fear assumes that detachment and involvement cannot coexist, when in fact they do. The dichotomy between empathy and cognition, like our earlier dichotomy between individual and society, is partly accurate, for they are different processes, but it is also partly false, for they occur at the same time and affect each other. Our culture may indeed impel us to choose one reaction or the other, and not both, but this means neither that we can, nor that we must, do so.

One may also fear that, in this process of observation, human beings seem to become senseless, will-less objects, moved around by "invisible hands" and anonymous forces. I think this fear is misplaced. It is more likely that we fear the actual power that controls and reifies us in our own society, rather than the supra-individual structures and processes that must exist in any society. Our cultural ideology self-protectively inhibits us from naming or defining these actual controlling powers, for we might act against them. In other words, our particular sociocultural experience may condition us to believe that something is out of our power, when in fact it is not; it is a result of a particular historical time and place and is not universal and immutable.

But simply because we begin our investigation by treating organisms and groups of organisms as if they were objects, we do not have to continue to do so. After abstracting, we must return social groups and structures to their living context. For people do not live in some universal, abstract Society, but rather in societies that have specific form and content, histories and circumstances. They may be nomadic or sedentary, egalitarian or hierarchical, dependent on the power of machines or of human labor, organized by kinship, vassalage, or commodity relations. Whatever their characteristics, they are contingent. They come into being under certain conditions, can continue to exist only under certain other conditions, and change or disappear as those conditions alter. To ignore the specificity of our culture is to flee from the freedom to change it.

Social science theory must specify those characteristics and their conditions. In so doing, we depart from the mythical but expected scientific stance of objectivity. Objectivity usually implies that we observe our data and record them "for what they are" with no preconceptions. In this sense, no scientist, no person, is objective. We always begin with some preconceptions. For example, we begin by separating organic and inorganic matter into different categories, for although they are both matter and therefore subject to the same laws, their behavior also differs and they undergo different processes. We distinguish our own biological species, which we call *Homo sapiens*, from other, quite similar species. Apes and monkeys, our nearest nonhuman relatives, resemble us in body form, mental abilities, and ways of living; like us, most of their behavior is learned and their survival possible only by virtue of social cooperation. Because there are differences between us and because we think that there is something special about humans, we single ourselves out for particular study. We recognize that within this species, among human beings, there are different languages, ways of living, and ways of relating. Such preconceptions organize our perceptions. In a sense, they create our data. We must therefore make them explicit, and we must state and explain the reasons for them. In short, we must have theories.

Theories state what it is that we are looking at. They categorize the real world of things and events. They express our expectations of how categories are related to each other and how these relationships change. They contain reasoned conjectures or hypotheses about why certain relationships and events and not others occur. Theories guide the formulation of hypotheses and the setting up of investigation. Does this mean that if one has a theory one will find only what one is looking for? In a sense, yes. For theories select only some things, out of a whole range of phenomena, for investigation. It is not possible or even desirable to look at everything.

The process of investigation, however, involves continual testing of the strength of the hypotheses against the data that are supposed to verify them; upon the receipt of invalidating information, the hypotheses are reformulated or, if necessary, rejected. This is the essence of specific method, practiced routinely in the laboratory and in field work. A second process intervenes, or is supposed to intervene, to prevent self-fulfilling theorizing. Theories specify the relationships between the subject matter they include and that which they omit; they thus do not pretend to include everything. A theory may specify relationships between itself and the other theories about the excluded subject matter. Additional, even competing theories may catch facts that the chosen theory lets slip away.

If I say, then, as I think, that particular historical circumstances produce particular societies and cultures, I am making a theoretical statement which says that concrete social forms appear under specifiable conditions and that they are not created merely because people have dreamed them up. In addition to our dreams and plans, these conditions include material forces—ecological, technological, and economic ones—and social forces—the distribution of power, or control over people and things. They determine the structure of society; they cause people to act and interact in some ways and not in others by limiting the possibilities of choice. This theory also asserts that social and cultural systems vary and that they change and evolve as conditions vary and evolve.

BETWEEN MIND AND MATTER

It is only through an understanding of evolution, through a theory of the causes and conditions of social and cultural forms, that the paradox of the individual and the society can be resolved. Unfortunately, our theories of change and evolution are weak, although they have been one of the major, original, and continuing concerns and contributions of anthropology. Much traditional and current social theory focuses on the analysis of societies as they function at a moment in time. Such functional theories are necessary if we are to understand the structure and the operation of social systems, but they tend to be mechanistic as well as static. The notion of process, which we lack in social science theory, is the clue to the solution of our problem. *Process* is a vague notion, but it is meant to recreate in theory the actual fluidity of the relationship between the individual and society, the actual imperceptibility of the steps by which change takes place, and the ambiguity of both.

The essence of sociocultural process is the interaction between natural environment, individual, and structured relations between individuals. Each of these elements constitutes a distinct level of reality, a separate system that we can isolate and whose coherence we can discover. Thus, as I have said already, the individual and the society are two separate systems; here I have added the environment as a third. There are interactions between each pair and among them all together that are complex interplays of harmony and conflict, causality and feedback, determinism and creativity, stasis and change, such that together all form one perpetually changing system. Although human beings "by nature desire to know," we also desire to create. One of the clearest characteristics that sets us apart from other animals is our continual, inevitable transforming of our environments, both social and natural. Other organisms do this, but we do it more and better. This creative action is not only a permanent feature of our existence, it is also necessary to our survival. Change is thus embedded in both society and individual. In the individual, the core of aloneness, which coexists with social interaction, is what enables us to observe dispassionately, to comprehend the society even though we can't touch it, and eventually to change it. The power of reflection permits us to develop theories and is a necessary, though not sufficient, condition for change and evolution.

As part of our power of reflection and observation, we also make judgments. We create systems of morality to guide our actions. This moral sense enables us to take people and societies as objects, all the time realizing first that they are not objects, and second that we also treat them in terms of their natural fluidity. For all our desire to see what would happen if we performed the experiment with which I began this chapter, we would not do it. It would be illegal, but it is also immoral. Perhaps some feel that even the thought of putting a baby alone on an island is immoral. What is immoral is not the thought, but the absence of a second thought about the implications of one's findings for the health and well-being of the infant.

As observers and analysts of social groups and human cultures, we are subject to the same moral sense. In fact, we cannot avoid it. Because we live social lives, we have feelings about what we see and opinions about what ought to be. In the process of observing, we have to be conscious of these feelings and not allow them to blind us; we cannot ignore what we hate in what we love and glorify only the good. But the choice of what we study is a moral one, as are our methods and the actions we take after our studies are done. What we do and what we discover bear on the lives of the people we study, as well as on our own lives.

The postures of the humanities and science toward the world have often been portrayed as opposites, the former as an emotional, aesthetic, moral evaluation, the latter as a robotlike, amoral curiosity. As inaccurate as these stereotypes are, social scientists have been bounced back and forth between them; some have themselves debated whether they are of the sciences or the arts. But such efforts are clearly futile. Social science does not have to fit preexisting categories, nor can it. Neither is it a blend of opposites. Quite simply, it is another, distinct way of looking at the world. If the humanities study mind and the products of mind, and if science studies the material conditions and products of the world, then the social sciences study the interaction of mind and matter, use the combination of technique and inspiration found in all scholarship, and partake of the morality of the culture in which they are situated.

Our subject matter is perhaps the most difficult, since what we examine is both inside and outside of us, and since we simultaneously participate in that which we observe. It is a product of that which it aims to explain, and it can change that which produces it. The subject matter of anthropology is the continuous creation by human beings of their lives, of culture. We study the events of evolution, the transformations of people by nature and of nature by people. And we are interested in how determinate groups of people take the limited possibilities of their lives and try to realize their desires through them, thereby making their own history out of what they have received. We focus, then, on processes of creation, of transformation, and of becoming. We look at the interplay between necessity and choice, between material reality and mental interpretations of it.

I believe that we cannot realize our desires and make our own history without a social theory that specifies the conditions on which a desirable life depends and thereby directs us toward what we must change. Since change is realized through, though not caused by, the action of individuals, I also think that such changes require a theory that shows how ideas become transformed into action and how, since ideas are products of material and social conditions, these conditions affect the individual consciousness. I do not think that most social science theory, as it stands, can do this; its tendency to reify the individual and the society, and its silence on the mechanisms of evolution, hamper its utility for guiding our actions. But I think its potential is enormous. In particular, anthropological theory contains a totalizing view of the world that replicates the fully integrated quality of life as it goes on at any given moment. The implications of this holism need to be explored, and this is one aim of the following chapter.

II.

What's In a Name? The Paradigm of Culture

Three Meanings of *Culture*

Anthropology has traditionally specialized in the exotic. Indeed, to get a Ph.D. in anthropology, students have usually had to do a year or more of field research, in one of those cultures labeled primitive, simple, or peasant, which contrast with our own, which has been called civilized, complex, or industrial. Anthropology's identification with the primitive and exotic partly reflects the academic division of labor, for each department in the university must have its own intellectual reason for existence.

Sociology and anthropology share many interests and ideas, but they are conventionally separated by subject matter. Their intellectual divergence, reinforced by present bureaucratic constraints, has also grown from different pasts and rests on different theoretical bases. Both fields have their most recent origins in the nineteenth century, in the speculations about the nature of society and the path of cultural evolution that preoccupied social thought during the development of Euro-American industrial capitalism and imperialism. Sociology came to focus on the latest of the evolutionary forms; it based its theories on inquiries into the character and functioning of industrial, or complex, society.

Anthropology stayed with the earlier forms of society, and remained concerned with the evolutionary process. Anthropology took shape as a field of inquiry when expanding industrial capitalism met on its frontiers obstacles to its goals, the indigenous inhabitants of North and South America, Africa, and the Pacific. In North America, for example, in the late nineteenth century, Lewis Henry Morgan, a founder of American anthropology, became intrigued by his Native American neighbors, the Iroquois, in upper New York State. He thought that it would be both interesting and useful to learn about their way of life, since it differed so profoundly from his own. His studies led him to believe that their culture represented a form of human society that had preceded his own. He therefore incorporated his findings into an evolutionary framework much like the abstract, speculative schemes constructed by other American and European social theorists, such as Sir Henry Maine or J. J. Bachofen. These schemes placed cultures or societies in chronological and formal sequence, from earliest times to the present, and from simplest to most complex.

Morgan and other nineteenth-century theorists were also interested in the fact that customs varied so widely around the world. The reports of explorers and missionaries told them of fascinating oddities, such as the simulated capture of a bride by her groom in wedding ceremonies, the tracing of descent through females, the ability of people to survive on wild game and vegetation, and beliefs in animal ancestors. Using logic and guesses, they tried to discover the meaning, origins, and interrelations of such phenomena.

Morgan, for example, sought data to verify his theories of cultural evolution by asking missionaries and government officials in remote outposts in exotic lands, to fill out questionnaires about the terms which people used for their blood relatives and in-laws, and about their rules of kinship and marriage. He also hoped to record and preserve this great cultural variety, which, he correctly thought, the assimilative power of European and American expansion would rapidly obliterate. The desire to salvage any remaining cultural variety has impelled much anthropological research ever since.

In the early twentieth century, American anthropological interests shifted away from speculative theorizing about evolution and from the study of nonindustrial societies as representatives of earlier stages of our own cultural evolution. They turned instead to the study of other cultures in and of themselves, for their own sake.

Franz Boas, who established anthropology as an academic discipline in the United States, like his contemporary Bronislaw Malinowski in Great Britain, insisted that data be collected first hand about such societies; students went to the field, lived with the people they studied, and tried to act as much like members of those cultures as possible. The information that they brought back was later to be analyzed and used to confirm or negate the hypotheses which earlier theorists had created. Some researchers traveled overseas to do this ethnography. Others stayed in the United States and did what is known as salvage ethnography, in which they interviewed aged Native Americans in an attempt to learn what life was like prior to its disintegration due to the spread of industrial society and the placement of native Americans on reservations.

Salvage work has often been associated with or emanated from a romantic sense of the long ago and far away. It aims to capture something that cannot actually be captured, the living-out of ordinary life by people long gone. Even the *ethnography* of extant cultures—the study of their lives here and now—smacks of romanticism, since we often study people who not only are geographically distant, but whose life is so alien that we can barely comprehend it. This "search for the primitive" is perhaps a kind of wistful attempt to regain a way of living that we have lost. The desire to record and thereby immortalize these ways of life may spring from an unrealizable wish to rediscover Eden —society in its pristine state, before it was forever soiled by the coming of modern society. Perhaps what we, as outsiders, perceive in other cultures is a wholeness, or organic unity, which is absent from our own lives.

This quality of wholeness has an analog in anthropological theory. Holism, as it is called, is the core of anthropology's concept of culture, and has informed much of our research methodology. It appears in the classic definition of culture, as given by another founder, Sir E. B. Tylor:

> Culture, or Civilization, taken in its wide ethnographic sense, is that complex whole which includes knowledge, belief, art, morals, law, custom, and any other capabilities acquired by man as a member of society.

Culture, then, includes everything. It does not refer just to "culture" in its ordinary meaning of great art, literature, and music. In the anthropological sense, there are no people who are uncultured.*

Culture commonly has a third meaning as well, one that is the source of the meaning of *high* (or *elite*) *culture*. This is the symbolic dimension of human existence, encoded in and created by language, in particular, but by other means of communication also. This domain is especially expressive of values, moral systems, and intellectual interpretations of the world. It includes the rules by which *institutions* (or organized constellations of people and objects, like the stock market, marriage, or government) operate, and the social values attached to the institutions.

There is not one agreed-upon definition of culture for all intellectual disciplines. Marxist theory, for example, separates culture from *socio-economic formations*. The latter refers to the

* The facts that we, in our culture, distinguish some works of art from others, and that we accord prestige to those who know about those masterpieces and withhold it from those who do not, are themselves contingent, appearing in particular kinds of culture. As such, they merit scrutiny. Indeed, one of the most important questions we can ask is: What are the conditions under which "high culture" comes to be a distinct behavioral and intellectual category? What kinds of economic and political systems produce such exclusionary distinctions among works of art and people? For not all cultures do so.

structural base on which daily economic and political life is carried out; that is, socio-economic formations are the more concrete, behavioral, or empirical aspects of sociality, in contrast to the culture, which term Marxists use for the rather intangible representations that people make of social reality.

Sociologists define "culture" similarly, but use their core concept of *society* to mean the self-equilibrating, autonomous system of interaction among people who share a common land, government, and identification.

This discussion raises an issue I have been carefully skirting, the difference between culture and society. I will continue to skirt it here, since I shall return to it in Chapter III. But I do want to indicate what is at stake in it. One concern is the split between material and mental, and another is the related split between observable, hard data and indirectly inferred, soft data. *Social* anthropologists in the United Kingdom (like E. E. Evans-Pritchard, Raymond Firth, Meyer Fortes, S. F. Nadel) follow a distinction similar to the Marxian-sociological one: They reserve the word *society* for the observable interactions among people, and the word *culture* for the intangible symbols, rules, and values that the people use to order and define themselves. These theorists particularly want to keep mental representations, or culture quite distinct from those conditions of social life that can be perceived by sense organs (especially eyes) and that they consider to be their legitimate subject matter.

Some North American anthropologists, however, focus on the culture part of this division. *Symbolic* anthropologists like Clifford Geertz and Victor Turner study ideology, such as the multiple meanings of words and things, and the role of symbols in ordering social life by unifying opposing meanings. *Ethnoscientists,* or *cognitive* anthropologists, like Charles Frake and Ward Goodenough, are interested in the rules for speech and thought that structure people's perceptions of the world and, therefore, their behavior in it; they think that if observers learn how people order their universe linguistically, they can learn to behave almost like members of the culture.

Some of the foregoing anthropologists object strongly to what they consider other American anthropologists' myopia on the material, technological, and economic aspects of human existence. They criticize the ecological, cultural materialist, and neo-evolutionary schools (which include Morton Fried, Marvin Harris, Marshall Sahlins, Elman Service, A. P. Vayda), who continue to insist on the wholeness inherent in Tylor's definition, but have not (with the recent exception of Sahlins) systematically treated that which the third meaning of culture connotes—the intellectual, psychological, and subjective dimension of life. They thereby omit the relation between individual and culture from their otherwise valuable global theories. Reciprocally, they criticize others for being myopic when it comes to material reality.

Insofar as this debate involves not a battle among claimants for the title to American anthropology, but rather intellectual stakes, it is important. I sympathize with any criticisms of nearsightedness, but not with narrow solutions that unrealistically segment one part of culture (in the Tylorian sense) from another. It seems to me that American anthropology's decisive contribution to social science is its emphasis on wholeness. This emphasis realizes one implicit aim of the nineteenth-century social theory from which contemporary social sciences developed, to create a theory that accounts for and encompasses the seamless joining of all parts of human life as it is lived.

Traditionally, anthropologists do take every instance and aspect of human behavior as their field of study: people's actions, thoughts, and feelings, as well as the complex connections among them. We are not interested just in oddities, nor in discrete customs or traits. Quite the contrary. If we are looking at everything, that everything includes all those everyday things that people do as part of ordinary existence, as well as the structures and ideas that hold these things together. Prosaic activities constitute the bulk of all our lives; so that what anthropologists (and sociologists like Peter Berger or Erving Goffman) find fascinating, most of the time, is the mundane.

Nevertheless, the concept of culture, conceived as everything, has problems. First of all, it is a vague and diffuse concept that continually threatens to escape our mental grasp. It purports to make everything accessible and clear. But how can one observe, record, and explain everything (or even claim to do so)? One can't. Given that, the concept of culture (like the concept of society) serves not to explain all, but rather, like the concept of life in the discipline of biology, to mark off a domain of study. It refers at once to the fact that culture is a panhuman phenomenon, and to the fact that every human being lives by or in a particular way of life or culture.

That is, the concept can be and is used at two different levels of abstraction. One level is that of the human species, whose means of adaptation or biological survival is culture. The other level of abstraction refers to each particular culture, as when we speak of "the Iroquois," "the ancient Greeks," "the Bedouin," etc. On the panhuman level, culture presents a paradox. It is based on biology, but is itself nonbiological. It could not exist unless human beings had certain physical and mental characteristics; no other animal has culture. Conversely, because they lack certain biological characteristics that other animals have, humans could not survive without culture. In other words, the neurological and morphological structures of *Homo sapiens* both presuppose and permit the existence of culture.

The very few, general instincts that human beings have are insufficient for survival. Humans must consequently learn nearly all of their specific behavior, and the expansive intelligence of their large, complex brains makes this possible. Slowed by their bipedal gait, with their vital organs exposed by upright posture, human beings are physically weaker than other animals. But this erect, two-footed stance frees from the business of walking the characteristically human hand. The thumb's opposability to the other four fingers makes the hand flexibly capable of many precise tasks. Precise, creative, and intelligent coordination between brain, eye, and hand enables human beings to envision and fashion the tools and weapons with which they build their cultures.

Humans create their own cultures, and therefore themselves. Like other animal species, they perceive relationships between objects, and between themselves and objects; they act on this perception, and depend upon it to survive. But unlike other creatures, humans transform their nonhuman environment and structure their human environment so that, in effect, they produce their own environment in the course of trying to stay alive. Thus, they alter branches to make bows and arrows, and shape stone into arrowheads; they plant wheat to make flour and build ovens to bake bread. In addition, human beings reflect on their acts, themselves, and their relationships to other people. By infusing these conscious observations with meaning, they interpret the world around them and through speech communicate these representations of social reality to one another. They can then generate and express rules of behavior that coordinate the actions of diverse human beings in social, or group, living. In other words, humans socially establish a human environment in the midst of, and articulated with, a "natural," or nonhuman, environment in which they survive. This sociality compensates for the physical inadequacies of *Homo sapiens* by enabling the young, the old, and the weak to be fed and protected. In turn, sociality requires that each person born be moral according to the terms of the culture, learning how to live within the structure, to abide by its rules, and to submit to "enculturation," to be taught and to learn by word and act.

At the panhuman level of abstraction, then, culture is not so much a collection of things to be acquired, as Tylor's definition implies, as it is the social creation, by members of the human species, of ways and rules of feeding themselves, reproducing themselves, befriending and defending each other, and explaining themselves. It is not something that we could refuse to create if we so willed; it is as natural and inevitable as the neurological structure of *Homo sapiens,* who would not exist without either. In the anthropologist A. L. Kroeber's term, it is *superorganic;* in that of the anthropologist Leslie A. White, it is a unique phenomenon *sui generis*. Culture is not an individual creation and it is not merely a mental one. It is produced by the action of human beings living in groups in particular circumstances, and by their perception and evaluation of themselves and their lives. This means that culture is always "busy being born."

What's in a Name?

Tylor's definition, though easily grasped, also easily becomes abstract and distant from concrete historical circumstances. My elaboration of it is perhaps slippery because it presents culture as always in the making; like all natural things, culture is constantly changing in interaction with other natural systems. But this definition, in emphasizing creativity, restores to the concept of culture the focus on symbolic systems without losing its grasp on the material facts of life. Symbols imply subjectivity, and so lead us to the relation between individual and culture. In so doing, this new definition also avoids reification; it makes us look at the relation between people and the conditions of their lives, and at the actual situation in which the creative process works itself out.

It thereby brings us to the second, more situational level of abstraction. In this sense the term *culture* means the particular way of life of any given group of people, society, or population. In every specific culture, one will find determinate arrangements of people and things into an economic organization, social structure, political order, and ideological system. Here, culture and society become more distinct, the latter being the structured interaction of a population which perpetuates itself over time through breeding and socialization (or enculturation). But culture might also be said to include society here, for even if one took it to refer to representations of reality, these representations would be as much of social reality as of any other.

The actual content of cultures ranges widely but not infinitely. Thus, there are different ways of getting a living, which vary from the reaping of the productions of the nonhuman environment by foragers of wild game and vegetation, to the control of the reproduction of plants and animals for food in agricultural and pastoral societies, to the near-total creation of food by the combination of domesticates and synthetics in our own economy (e.g., diet margarine). Everyday life is structured by diverse basic social units, such as the nuclear family, or the community of kin, or the secular neighborhood, and by the different relations, egalitarian or hierarchical, political or economic, among these units. People confront and interpret the natural and social worlds variously, by worshipping spirits, ancestors, or gods; by being caught in the spin of millenarian religious movements expressive of sociopolitical discontent; or by creating systems of common sense, or cosmologies, or philosophies, or academic disciplines.

The thrust of the culture-is-everything concept at the first level of abstraction often pushes us to make a "laundry list" of what it connotes at the second level (screwdrivers, automobiles, PTAs, churches, city halls, psychiatry, etc.). At least as significant is the fact that the items on the list are not randomly associated. Rather, in each particular group of people we study, the means of livelihood, the structuring of social relations, and the translation of experience into a view of the world will be connected to each other in specific ways. They may interlock neatly: Thus, the family or household structure may be finely attuned to the needs of the work process. Or their relation may be contradictory, and conflict-ridden: The economic system may make demands that continually strain household relations. In either case, the observer can, by study, understand the logic of their association.

Metaphors like "the fabric of society" or "patterns of culture" reflect this logical integration. They imply the wholeness, the integrity, or the unity of parts of a way of life. However, these notions also connote faulty ideas as well. They do not mean, for example, that a particular culture is sufficient unto itself or that it provides everything its members could possibly want. Nor when we speak of the wholeness of a way of life does this mean that each culture is "wholesome"; the American involvement in Southeast Asia has not been especially salutory, yet its existence and form make sense in terms of the needs of our economy, international politics, and masculine ideals, each of which is in turn related to the other. Again, the idea of integrity connotes honor, but although the ideology, history, and socio-economic structure of Nazi Germany were integrated with one another, the culture was inhumanely out of control. The notion of the unity of parts tends to imply a kind of harmony or resolution. But a culture may contain opposing groups, conflicting structures, or ideas that lag behind ongoing social life. The oppositions, conflicts, and contradictions come out of relations between parts of culture and can be explained in terms of them. Thus, black power and other revolutionary groups emerged in the United States in the 1960s in the context of unkept cultural promises and structured inequality in the distribution of wealth and power. The context implies conflict, which may itself characterize U.S. culture—or perhaps all culture, for a culture without conflict and contradiction may "be busy dying."

Race, Nationality, Ethnicity, and Language

At the second level of abstraction, then, the concept of culture has two major senses: It sums up something unique about and peculiar to a particular way of life lived by a particular group of people or population; it posits that the parts of this way of life can be meaningfully understood in relation to each other. In our everyday parlance, we use other words and phrases, such as *race, language, ethnicity, nationality,* or *religion,* to express similar ideas. However, the meaning of these terms only partly overlaps with that of culture, and the terms themselves have conflicting theoretical presuppositions and implications. In order to clarify the meaning of culture, let us examine these terms and see where they lead us.

Race is the one that traditionally worries us the most because of the skeleton of slavery hanging in our national closet. It is a biological concept, and denotes within a species genetically determined physical differences that may be adaptive for survival. Colloquially, people assign membership in a race according to traits like skin color, hair form, etc., which characterize the large continental populations technically labeled geographical races. Such traits are popularly assumed to cluster and to be transmitted together, though they usually vary independently. Recent research by physical anthropologists has revealed other "racial" variations of single traits like blood differences, which crosscut geographical races and which may be more significant for human biological evolution. Sickle-cell anemia, for example, confers adaptive advantages in malarial regions, for it is linked with immunity to the disease; it occurs in Africa, the Middle East, southern Europe, and the Far East. Another example is the variation in adult ability to produce lactase, an enzyme necessary to digest milk. Present in Euro-Americans and some East Africans, this trait is normally absent among other Africans, Afro-Americans, Native Americans, East Asians, and Pacific Islanders, that is, everyone else in the world.

While such phenotypic variation, i.e., the observable expression of genes, may mean life or death for most life forms, it is less vital for human beings because we survive less by bodily adaptation to our environments and more by the intelligent transformation of them.

Race, then, does not determine the things we want to explain. If it did, cultural patterning would derive from genes; we would then have to look to biology for the source of culture and its various concrete manifestations. But specific cultural forms are not genetically determined, even though the human capacity/need for culture are interdependent with human biology. Race and culture vary independently. On the one hand, different cultures exist within geographical races. In Africa, the Negro "race" contains both the agricultural Bemba people of Rhodesia who trace their descent through females, and the cattle-raising Nuer people of the Sudan who trace descent through males. On the other hand, similar cultures have appeared among different "races." Both Mongoloids (Han China, 226 B.C.–A.D. 220) and Caucasians (Great Britain, eighteenth and nineteenth centuries) established empires whose powerful centralized bureaucracies controlled the domestic populace and encroached on foreign territories. A committed genetic determinist might argue that imperceptible genotypical differences underlie cultural variation, but this would leave two logical problems: Since the genotype of each person varies, each individual would then belong to a different culture; this is manifestly not true. Secondly, if genes determined cultures, how could one explain how an individual or a group of individuals, could, without changing their racial affiliation, shift from one culture to another within a single lifetime, as immigrants to the United States have been doing since the beginning of American history?

What's in a Name?

Now, it is true that all the members of one culture may indeed be of the same physical type. This can happen in geographically or otherwise isolated places, where inbreeding will stabilize the genetic makeup of a population. It can also happen where marriage rules encourage or require people to mate only with those of the same skin color. Because these rules often are part of a system that contains additional rules like racial segregation in schools and neighborhoods, race and culture covary. An observer can then wrongly infer that race and culture are brought about by the same forces.

But what such a racist system has created is *social race,* a cultural, not a genetic, association between physical form and behavior. On the basis of segregation, people have created subcultures. But the separation of biological and cultural forces emerges clearly, if we observe cultural process over time: Human behavior and neighborhoods, for example, change in the course of a lifetime; slums can become posh if their inhabitants become rich, and their culture consequently alters. When mating crosses racial boundaries, interracial offspring learn to live in the neighborhood and culture of either parent. Finaly, the rules that create social races and the conditions that create racism also can disappear.

The concepts of *nationality* and *ethnicity* come closer than race to the idea of culture. But they apply only to certain kinds of cultures, to those with large, heterogeneous populations, diversified economic bases, and a centralized political structure. *Nation* implies a political structure that takes and maintains territorial boundaries, and a code of law that justifies and regulates the state's sovereignty over the land and people within the boundaries. Since the concept of nationality directs us to look for structures and mechanisms of political-territorial control, it logically excludes those populations that lack the notion of territorial sovereignty and the power to control a territory to the total exclusion of others.

Furthermore, national boundaries may not in fact coincide with cultural boundaries. For example, the populations on either side of portions of the United States–Canada border are so similar in their daily lives that one would think they had the same culture if one did not know about their political division. Now, a nation may create a distinct culture on the basis of its political power and territorial limits. The United States, it seems to me, is engaging in such a creation, by building a uniform environment (fast-food and motel chains, Muzak); by consolidating the social structure (the entrenchment of class and ethnic divisions); by developing an ideology and mythology of a unified tradition (TV soap operas and advertisements with their continuing cast of characters; George Washington and the cherry tree); and by adopting unitary symbols (the flag and the dollar sign). Nations can become culturally distinct, but their political separation does not necessarily guarantee this distinction.

A common religion can integrate a nation-state and may in fact be part of the definition of nationality. To be Greek means to be a Christian Greek or Greek Orthodox, even though there are, for example, Greek Jews. Religion can also be an organizing principle of a culture. For example, a religion like Judaism or Islam orders a way of life by ruling not only on beliefs and ceremonials, but also on such mundane matters as the food one eats, the clothing one wears, the people one marries, and the elders one respects and obeys. But although religions can overlap with nationality and/or culture, they can also exist separately. Until 1948, when the state of Israel was created, Jews for centuries had no state of their own and adopted the culture and nationality of the countries they inhabited (as many still do). Finally, our notion of religion is too narrow to include all kinds of supernatural belief. Derived from our own traditions, it implies an articulated set of monotheistic beliefs, a hierarchy of specialist clergy, a lay population, and weekly rituals of observance. Like nation, the concept of religion would lead us to ignore other integrated, but ideologically different societies.

Groups like the Jews, which share customs, name, tradition, and often language and exist within a larger political entity, are *ethnic* groups. *Ethnicity* implies many of the same things that culture does—residential unity, distinct patterns of economic survival or mutual aid, specific forms of social relations, a self-definition by the group as a distinct entity, and structural integrity. But although ethnic groups may form the basis for the future creation or development of a culture, they first appear in human history only when complex societies or nation-states develop. In other words, they are not socially or politically or territorially sovereign, and it seems to me that the notion of cultures, like that of society, implies at least one of these kinds of autonomy. A foraging society like that of the /Kung, or Bushmen, of Botswanaland's Kalahari Desert, would exemplify social sovereignty, that of the United States political or territorial sovereignty.

Ethnic groups, in contrast, emerge in situations where people of many different traditions and cultures meet under the aegis of an overarching, integrative structure. They may come together in a city, in a centralized political state, in a religious center like Jerusalem, or in a market town on the borders of regions that produce and therefore exchange different crops and products. Occupational specialization, country of origin, or language may distinguish ethnic groups, but the conditions and purposes which underlie their coming together link them in a more diffuse system of social relations. Their identification as distinct groups crystallizes in the course of their dealings with, and in opposition to, each other. They do not exist without there being another, different group and without the economic and/or political structures that link them.

These structures are usually integrated with a specific culture and give to that culture the power to dominate others. One example would be middle-income, middle-class suburban American culture; another, the Turkish culture of the Ottoman empire. In this context, ethnic groups form subcultures, which structurally parallel the cultures of social races that I discussed above. Ethnicity, then, is sometimes the product of economic and cultural imperialism. Yet, by emerging in opposition to such domination, ethnicity also protects its members who become very reluctant to see it change and fiercely defend its validity.

The last of the concepts alternative to culture that I want to discuss, *language* or *linguistic group,* is perhaps the most complicated, if only because what we are explaining and the tool we use to explain it are the same: We use language to explain itself. Also, its sweep is broader than culture, as when we speak of the "Slavs" or "Latins," "Bantu" or "Semitic" peoples. Such language families cross national as well as cultural boundaries, and our popular labeling of them implies a shared style and temperament (e.g., moody, authoritarian Slavs contrast with hot-tempered, independent Latins). Such linguistic categorizing attributes the cause of these similarities to language and thus, like race, also raises the question of the causes of culture.

Let us first establish what a language is: It consists of a set of sounds that can be put together according to certain rules to make meaningful utterances. Each language forms a system with its own internal parts, relationships and logic. Each language has descended from earlier forms, and is usually related to other similarly derived languages. The processes of language formation and change conform to solely linguistic principles.*

But language and culture do have a relationship. One part of it is that because they are different orders of phenomena they can vary independently. For example, the Greek and Albanian languages come from two different branches of the Indo-European family, but on the common borders of Greece and Albania, the quality of life, or culture, is very much the same. Conversely, the cultures of Jamaica and Great Britain, in both of which English is spoken, are different. Cultural process can, nevertheless, effect linguistic change: Jamaicans speak English because Jamaica was a British colony; the maintenance of national boundaries, in combination with economic and geographical isolation, has kept Greeks and Albanians speaking different languages.

Conversely, linguistic process also affects culture. Anthropologists learn the language of the culture they study because it is an important social institution as well as the major human means of communication. As members of our own cultures, we speak to

* I shall not discuss these principles. The study of linguistics is highly technical. Anthropological linguists generally specialize in unwritten languages; others keep to written ones. In Chapter 5, however, I shall discuss briefly the social and symbolic dimensions of human communication.

each other (and ourselves) through language whose rules and logic we must follow even though we do not do so consciously. In fact, we are probably even less aware of linguistic rules than of cultural ones. Like culture, language is acquired or learned; it transmits culture, and is itself transmitted by cultural means. When born, not only are humans biologically equipped to learn whatever language their parents or care-takers speak, they are ready to learn it. Normal infants begin to learn to speak without formal teaching or prompting. But, as adult and child communicate through language, the adult simultaneously teaches the child how to behave, feel, and think.

The child thus learns language and culture simultaneously, and, as these influence each other, they also shape the learner's cognitive and affective processes. Vocabulary and grammar, for example, make us see things in some ways and not in others. In English, we cannot speak of someone in the third person singular without saying "he" or "she"; in many languages (e.g., German and Italian), one can speak of neither people nor objects without indicating whether they are masculine or feminine or in some cases neuter. The world becomes sexually compartmentalized for the speaker, because the languages categorize the whole world according to gender, and the classification fits socially ordered sexual attributes, roles, and behavior. Both language and social structure may, then, subtly shape the emotional or personality correlates of socially assigned gender.

In other words, on a very general level, a systematic relationship is likely to obtain between culture, character, and language. But the nature of their interaction, the tightness of their integration, and their specific covariation remain mysterious and require exploration; any firm statements on this point are shots in the dark. For example, the language groups, like those of the Slavs, to which we popularly assign a unity of temperament and culture, usually are geographical neighbors. The similarities among them, then, probably arise from a combination of factors, environmental, linguistic, and political, and not from any one alone.

Language is more generally and fundamentally constitutive

of culture than are the other phenomena I have just discussed. But linguistic phenomena still are not the same as cultural ones. Linguistic structures help form our cultural world view, but they do not create it. To take a final example: A new verb entered the American language in the 1960s, "to Xerox." Its referent—multiple, rapid reproduction of visual material—is, it seems to me, the product of intertwined developments in demography, technology, and social relations: The growth of populations and the attendant service professions and bureaucracy involve paperwork. Political integration depends on the increase of social cohesion through high-speed transmission of information by mass media. Under those conditions, the production of duplicating machines became possible because they filled a need and began to yield a profit. Individuals in these circumstances become accustomed to immediate gratification of the need for multiple copies and begin to plan their work time around the speed with which photo-reproduction can be accomplished. The Xerox machine and the knowledge of its capability make the speeded-up, paper-worked world more manageable, and the word *Xerox*, symbolizing at least this, comforts each of us that we have some handle on such a world.*

THE SOCIOLOGY OF ANTHROPOLOGY

I wish now to turn to the sociology of anthropological knowledge. How do we account for these alternatives to "culture" which I have just discussed? Like words for technology (such as "xerox"), popular and specialized terms for social groups also come from cultural conditions. The popular usage of the words *race* and *ethnicity* is provoked by their great contemporary economic weight; our cultural emphases on linguistic affiliation comes out of our own literary tradition, that on religion, from its role in the development of Western cultures. Given the specific

* And the Xerox Corporation has a handle on our minds and dollars. Being the first to market profitable copiers, its own brand name became, like Kleenex and Saran Wrap, a generic term that made secure its early monopoly. Only recently has IBM caught up in this field.

historical circumstances of the United States, with its recent slavery and immigration, the linguistic, ethnic, and religious affiliations of any given group have often actually coincided, so it is natural that we link them conceptually. But if at times the affiliations overlap completely, at others they shift, much to our conceptual confusion, so that we don't know if blacks are a race or a subculture; we speak of white ethnics; and we call Jews a race even though some are quite dark and others blond and blue-eyed. We are suffering again from our cultural compulsion to reify our concepts and pin our world down to a stable street map.

The concept of culture itself also has social origins, but it is potentially freer of them. The notion that each way of life is unique, forms a coherent whole, and has meaning and validity for those who live it, is an old one in our tradition. But its codification into a technical concept is a direct product of recent history: Anthropology developed in certain nation-states concurrently with their attempts to control all those regions of the world that their expanding economies could utilize. The idea that one concept can embrace a whole way of life and all ways of life may reflect the imperialist idea that one polity can control all the rest. But this totalizing concept has an opposite side; it is dialectical, in that it also creates that which it reflects or that which creates it. Like the totalizing framework of anthropology itself (and of other nineteenth-century theoretical systems, such as those of Charles Darwin or Marx), it may also reflect and, perhaps make possible, the emergence of the politico-economic bonds of a genuine world culture, as Eric R. Wolf, a prominent American anthropologist, suggested several years ago.

The concept of culture approximates an idea shared by many peoples. In nearly all known societies, people feel their own way of life to be unique and whole. They commonly split the world into "us" and "them." The "them" can refer to one or many undifferentiated peoples, and the "us" are clearly defined by their familiar beliefs, habits, and attitudes. For example, the Native American Cheyennes refer to themselves by a term that means "The Human Beings;" no one else is a "human being" in their eyes. In the little mountain village that I studied in Greece, people continually emphasized how different they were from residents of other nearby villages and from other members of their own ethnic group. We make similar distinctions about our own towns, cities, ethnic groups, etc.

But whereas the Cheyenne classification makes the Cheyenne a qualitatively different kind of creature from other people, the anthropological concept of culture explicitly means that all humans share basic physiological and mental capacities and can therefore be understood by similar theories and principles. Whereas the Greeks used their concept of "us-them" to elevate "us" and derogate "them," the concept of culture enjoins a moral commitment to the equality of all human beings, even though the concept took its present shape in the context of great political inequality. The Cheyenne and Greek concepts of "us-them" resemble our popular concepts of ethnicity or nationality in unreflectively taking what they represent for granted. The concept of culture, in contrast, is quite consciously self-examining because it is embedded in a scholarly discipline which demands its continual refinement. This makes it a conceptual tool for research as well as a moral classification. It is generally applicable, because it treats both the familiar and the exotic as instances of the same processes. Therefore, we can study and analyze cultures not to evaluate them, but to understand how they work.

Of course, in studying another culture firsthand, we usually experience things and acts that we like or dislike. Through enculturation and our own personal histories, we have learned moral systems by which we judge events and experiences. For example, we may, predictably, be disgusted by the Chinese use of human feces as fertilizer. But this is irrelevant to what we want to find out about the culture, such as the techniques of the collection and use of feces, its contribution to increased production, the ecological and socioeconomic conditions under which people must use a potentially toxic substance for fertilizer, and so on.

In other words, when we study another culture, we observe with detachment and also react in terms of our own feelings and morality. The observation and the moral reaction really happen successively, but they often seem to occur simultaneously. In order to understand what is happening and to perceive the meaningfulness of people's own behavior to themselves, we have to separate these two processes, very often temporarily suppressing our personal reaction. All people practice this separation of observation from evaluation from time to time, but it is a strain to sustain it, whether we study an alien culture or our own. The tension created demands discharge, so anthropologists usually leave the field site periodically to relax (and, incidentally, relieve the people they study from their constant presence), and later return at least aware of their feelings if not (ideally) unhampered by them.

In other words, we cannot avoid making value judgments, even though one tradition in social science claims that we can be value-free. Our dislike or disapproval comes from the fact that we can conceive of another, preferable way of doing things, be it that of our own culture or of some private utopia. The belief that one's own way (or vision) of life is better than others' is universal. It is often accompanied by the idea that one's own culture is the only conceivable and therefore rational one. The universality of this attitude, which is called ethnocentrism, hints at its utility for the survival of any culture: In the enculturation process, the acceptance of one way of life is facilitated if all others appear impossible. Thus, many of us know how painful it is to imagine a better way of living, to try to create it, and to fail, or to see success recede. So we learn, not necessarily correctly, that it may be easier to forget our visions than to try to live with them. In an angry about-face, we fiercely grab at what we have been told is best, and become ethnocentric.

Ethnocentrism is thus a universal, culturally learned attitude which we must continually watch out for in order to understand our own as well as other cultures. For ethnocentrism, in suppressing the wish for a better way of life, also inhibits the detachment necessary to examine any way of life. It constricts our imagination and precludes our full comprehension of the ethnographic fact that other ways of life are both possible and viable. Ethnocentrism is so powerful that, although we may acknowledge cultural variation in the abstract, we can only accept its reality through immediate experience. The shock of being an outsider in a new cultural environment forces the explosive recognition that life can really be successfully organized in another way and that this way is as eminently reasonable to the people who live it as our own is to us. (And, although many of us think that our culture is quite unreasonable, our objection is itself a cultural fact which we accept as valid, sensible behavior.)

During field research, we get to know the people we study not merely as objects of research but also as human beings who are as (ir)rational and (un)aware as we are. We accept that although we are the same kind of being, our lives and ways of thought have different moral and material premises. I think that this is a very confusing experience—at some times making perfect sense and at other times, none at all. In coming to terms with this confusion, and with the fact that each alternative way of life is self-evident to those who live it, we realize that no way of life, not even ours, is in fact, self-evident. If there can be so many different ways of doing things, then there is no reason why things necessarily must be organized in any one particular way. Finally, and this is important, we therefore infer that our own culture could have been different, and, since it is not, that there must be some explanation of why it is the way it is.

The beliefs, values, and morality of each culture form contingent parts of a larger system, varying according to multiple factors. The attitudes and acts of individuals make sense in the context of that system. None of us can say, for example, that we would not hold some abhorred value if we had been reared in circumstances which sanctioned it. If, for example, I were a Greek woman, I would probably think it reasonable for the mourning rules to differ for males and females. If my brother died, I would have to wear black clothing for three years; if I died, he would wear a black armband for a month. Indeed, this custom is so self-evident to Greeks that when I asked them why there was a difference, either the question made no sense to them or they could find no answer. For they took the custom for granted. My questioning of it reflects a different culture, one that prompts me to question what others take for granted in order to pursue my profession. But neither could I answer why I so automatically note any differential treatment according to gender; the importance of potential male-female inequality seems self-evident to me, as it did not to the Greeks to whom I spoke.

This is what is meant by saying that all customs, values, and ways of life are relative. The attitude of *cultural relativism,* that as observers we must accept the contingency of customs and values, has a complicated place in anthropology. Its methodological directive seems to me simple and important: Since cultures vary according to circumstances, we must discover what those circumstances are and what pattern they produce. But cultural relativism is also a Western moral position that is more difficult to sort out. It keeps us humble by reminding us, quite reasonably, that our own way of life is not the only or the best way to live. But, it has also been taken to imply that, since all values are relative, there is no reason not to do anything one wants. A humble aphorism becomes an unsavory morality: If it is all right for, say, the Jivaro of Ecuador and Brazil to be headhunters, then according to this reasoning we can exploit members of our own and other cultures and carry on geopolitically expansive wars. According to a culturally relativist morality, each culture is its own justification, since no one can deny to any culture the right to do things in "its own way."

The metamorphosis of cultural relativism from methodology into moral system shows how social science can, consciously or unwillingly, support its own culture's ethnocentrism. Cultural relativism can allow the individual to abandon personal and cultural responsibility, because one may reason that one cannot, after all, change one's enculturation and that one's culture lies outside of one's control. It assumes a uniformity within each culture and an absence of creativity within each individual. It depicts each culture as having "its [one] way"; therefore, no variation or change seems possible, and the culture becomes a homogeneous, static object. The use of cultural relativism as personal morality objectifies the individual by assuming that each of us is immutably, rigidly programmed in the image of the culture.

But each culture really contains variation or, at least, it must do so, if it is to be able to change and adapt. A culture consists of ever-shifting relationships between things, people, groups, and ideas, and of the processes regulating these relations. Individuals can choose on the basis of these possibilities. Some choices are more difficult to make than others, for, as we have seen, cultures usually discourage alternatives. But although we can explain the fact that people choose some alternatives and not others, or indeed choose not to choose, explanation is not moral justification.

Finally, cultural relativism contains moral and methodological premises about cultures, not about individuals. It cannot be used as a moral blueprint for individual behavior, because it says nothing about the conditions of choice, which is an individual act. Our casual stereotypes (the "ugly American," "the inscrutable Oriental") are caricatures, and no more. No one can personify a culture or represent a culture in and of oneself, but only in the course of relating to another individual, thing, or group. In so doing, different, shifting dimensions of self and society appear. Because the individual is also a distinct level of organization, or a system different from a culture, with separate originating and maintaining conditions, he/she contains possibilities not prefigured in the culture. Specifically, we, as social individuals, can create new moralities, particularly those that critically replace the dominant moral codes. This means, of course, that we must criticize not only the code, but also its supporters. To do so means to abandon the moral relativism in which each individual's behavior is as good as anyone else's and therefore immune from criticism. I think that cultural relativism becomes a morality because it is easier to swallow it whole than to work these problems out, especially since it satisfies our need to accept our problematic culture.

How then can we reconcile our culturally given ethnocentric morality with the anthropological demand for detachment? First, we can separate detachment and involvement because, in fact, they occur separately. Next, it seems to me that the greater one's detachment, the easier it is to come up with alternative, happier visions of culture, to remember those we have forgotten, and also to be truly relativistic about cultural variation. If we understand that cultures can differ and that the object of one's ethnocentric love can change, we can also infer that a culture can change. These realizations correct our natural cultural biases, for we know, all the while we observe, describe, and analyze, that our ideas are contingent on our culture and on the one we study. Our ideas shift with shifting culture, and when culture changes, so will knowledge of it.

CULTURE-TYPES

Cultural relativism also poses a problem of methodology and theory by implying that since each culture is relative, it must be explained only "on its own terms," that is, in terms of the particular circumstances in which it exists. A general theory of culture and types of culture thus appears inherently impossible. Many anthropologists in the 1920s and 1930s adopted this position. Many also thought it impossible to determine when or in what ways one culture could be said to be like another. They felt that to type a culture would obscure its unique qualities, and perhaps, dehumanize its people. The dominant theory of those years, *historical particularism,* was that culture varied tremendously, partly because of the genuinely malleable potential of human beings to learn any culture into which they were born.

However, two related factors gradually forced anthropologists to be aware not only that it was possible to generalize about cultures, but also that it was necessary to do so. One factor was the conceptual framework of culture that anthropologists used for field research, and the other was the information that resulted from the use of the concept of culture. Many twentieth-century anthropologists have believed that they conduct their research inductively, without theoretical bias (an attitude exemplified by Ruth Benedict's work). However, as I have indicated, I do not accept the deductive-inductive split. Though I respect Baconian, inductive canons of evidence, I know that when we look at the world and try to discover what it is, we do not do so with blank minds. Even if we do not reason deductively from an abstract scheme of first principles, at the very least we have unconscious cultural categories that structure our perceptions. Thus, despite their antitheoretical stance, anthropologists have in fact gone to the field with certain preconceptions. At a minimum, the concept of culture has framed their thoughts and guided their observations and questions, specifying then, as it does now, that one will study people who, by their own definition or by ours, constitute a separate, isolable group with a distinct way of life whose parts are all interconnected.

In other words, the concept of culture makes a theoretical assumption of the integration of parts, though it does not specify the nature of the integration. The concept becomes a research tool because it instructs us that when we look at one aspect of culture, we must look also at others. For example, we cannot adequately describe or explain economic organization without at least a reference to the rest of the culture. If we study the cattle-raising Nuer, the ways that they react to and treat their environment become germane because their pastoral economy will be very directly affected by climate and natural resources; since their economic success will be affected by activities of neighboring cultures, their conduct of intersocietal or foreign relations will also be relevant. This cross-referencing among parts of culture is distinctive of the anthropological way of thinking, replicating the actual process of life in which everything does indeed affect everything else.

The concept of culture generates questions about the cultures we study. It leads us to the specifics of each particular cultural item, such as the details of engravings on the ceremonial spears of the Tiwi of North Australia, or the rule among the Yanomamö of Brazil and Venezuela that a woman and her son-in-law must not meet. It also prods us to ask about the relations between such traits or customs—whether and how, for example, marital customs are symbolized in works of art or validated in mythology.

Armed with the idea of culture, then, anthropologists collected more and more data that began to show that, contrary to expectations, the number of possible cultural variations was limited. Certain forms of kinship (such as rules of descent in which relationship is reckoned through either males or females, of which the former is the more common) recurred, as did certain religious systems (such as the worship of animal ancestors or totems). The suspicion that such recurrences were mere artifacts of the observers' theories is allayed by the fact that the nineteenth-century anthropologists who, as we have seen, had different theories, also noticed them. Despite these earlier observations, however, the detailed field work of the twentieth century was necessary to verify their authenticity and frequency.

Anthropologists also realized that two or more traits might also regularly recur in association (this had, again, been perceived, but not verified in detail by earlier anthropologists). For example, a subsistence base of collecting and hunting wild game and vegetation usually requires seasonal population movement and would therefore be associated with social relations structured to minimize the friction experienced when basic social units, like nuclear families, had to separate and rejoin seasonally. One might also expect to find that people in such a society would owe their strongest loyalties to their own nuclear families.

As more was learned about particular cultures, essential similarities in structure and patterning appeared. We now know, for example, that all cultures have some form of kinship, of linking people to each other on the model of biological relationships. There are also regular ways in which societies differ. If we consider the distribution of power, for example, we find that egalitarian social structures have a limited occurrence and that the monopoly of wealth and coercive force by one section of a society against the rest appears in some cultures but not in others. We do not expect to find an elaborate priestly hierarchy and monumental architecture in a foraging society, but do in one with an agricultural base and a multicommunity political structure. In other words, cross-cultural regularities in the types of connections between parts of culture appeared and began to call for explanation. As long as culture is accepted as limitlessly variable, there is no need for explanation. As soon as we perceive regular differences in conjunction with regular similarities, we cannot help but ask why they exist.

Hence, in the 1940s, anthropologists began attempts to deal

with this issue by creating typologies, theories, and explanations of culture. Typologies make the world of phenomena easier to manage by condensing data and observed regularities into single terms. To classify, we select some characteristics of things as relevant and exclude others. For instance, people have often categorized cultures according to their means of subsistence, e.g., agricultural or pastoral. But while this criterion conveys some important differences (like the effects of a settled or a nomadic lifestyle), it may gloss over similarities. Thus, pastoral agricultural societies may have very similar political structures, such as the powerful chieftainships of the sheepherding Basseri of south Persia and of the sedentary agricultural Zulu of East Africa. Also, this classification refers to the presence or absence of traits, but ignores the nature of the relations among traits.

Other typologies rely on the structure of social relations. Lewis Henry Morgan posited three evolutionary levels—savagery, barbarism, and civilization; each expressed something distinctive about, in turn, economic organization, social groups, political institutions, and beliefs. Emile Durkheim dichotomized societies according to the kinds of relations within and between social groups. One type was *mechanical,* if the major connections between people and groups were based on likeness in form and function. The Nuer society, organized into structurally similar villages, is one example of mechanical solidarity. The other was *organic:* people and groups were linked by their differences and therefore by their interdependent need to exchange with one another. The ancient Inca empire, with villages and towns, peasants and craftsmen, producers and middlemen, exemplifies organic solidarity.

Twentieth-century anthropologists have been, however, less interested in developing evolutionary models than in summarizing similarities and differences of extant cultures. The most common typology consists of two categories, labeled by terms which have been in use, if not in favor, for a long time: *primitive* and *civilized* (or *advanced*). Despite their evolutionary import, what these terms mean to convey is a difference in the overall structuring of social life. A primitive culture has a small population and a homogeneous tradition enshrined in oral literature and history;

the bulk of work is done by human labor enhanced by humanly propelled tools and is organized by age and sex; social groups are multifunctioned; kinship systems are complicated; each group is relatively self-sufficient; and social orders are egalitarian, or if they are stratified, everyone in them at least has enough to eat. A civilized culture depends greatly on nonhuman energy sources, complex technology, and much specialization of labor; highly interdependent social groups are many and diverse; a powerful structure of law and order integrates the economic and civil relations of a large, heterogeneous population through systems of accounting, the creation of official history, and monopoly of physical force.

However, the underlying connotations of these terms lessen their utility, since, popularly (like Morgan's terms) the one is worse, the other better. Primitive, furthermore, implies that a culture so labeled is rudimentary or lacking (usually in an area in which Western culture excels, e.g., technology). The notion of advanced cultures asserts that others are backward, as if there were some universal, but unvoiced end state by which to measure cultural change. Such undertones do indeed dehumanize people and distort their cultures. The terms are in fact ethnocentric. They take as the measure of civilization Western imperialism, whose ability to dominate cultures with less powerful means of production and of political control naturally engenders the belief that this is the pinnacle of human development toward which all other cultures must tend.

Some anthropologists have tried to eliminate this sort of ethnocentrism by using other terms. No completely adequate set has been found. *Simple* and *complex* are the current terms; they express the meaning of the dichotomy without the value judgment. However, they are slightly off the mark, for while a society may be simple in that it has only two or three basic social units, the operation of these units may be complicated. The number and kind of social groups in a society and their interrelationships may be diverse, but the basis of everyday social relations may be quite simple, e.g., commodity exchange. Furthermore, this dichotomy does not exhaust all possible types of society; there are forms in between the two extremes, which are neither simple nor complex, nor a blend of the two.

THE PARADIGM OF CULTURE

The point is, of course, that typologies and terms are not merely a convenient shorthand. Rather, the choice of one or another set depends on one's purposes, which in turn depend on one's theory —that is, on what one thinks it is important to study. As we have seen, the concept of culture directs us to study certain things; it therefore contains some sort of theoretical orientation. Its theory, however, is scanty; if used alone without additional theory, it can mislead us. There are indeed many other theories in anthropology; here I want to make explicit and evaluate the theory we have used so far.

The concept of culture assumes that cultures can be named, bounded, and isolated for the purposes of study. Thus, we can do an ethnography of the Samoans or the Cheyennes. It proposes that one part of a way of life cannot be understood without reference to all others, so that we must continuously cross-check among all of them. Thirdly, it proposes that all those parts are integrated with each other, yielding a coherent wholeness that we must grasp.

The concept of culture insists on the relevance of all aspects of life and on the integrity of each way of life. This insistence is both accurate and profoundly humane, because it replicates the way life is at any one moment, coincides with our intuitive sense about life at least some of the time, and does not reduce us to any one dimension, such as "economic man" or a Skinner-boxed creature. The theory's directives are so general that they do not restrict our observation to any particular thing. The very minimality of theory makes our research free and flexible, and has functioned as a valid, productive discovery procedure. For example, by not assuming that the provision of goods and services must fit a particular pattern, it has allowed us to discover how economic systems alternative to our own can work. The production of food can be organized by the household heads of family farms or led by village priests, as well as controlled by industrial agriculture; the economic system may be based on the principle that periodically one must give away one's excess goods as well as on the one that tells us to keep everything.

But the openness of the culture concept also has pitfalls. Because it specifies that we study everything, it implies that everything cultural is of equal importance in determining the characteristics of a particular culture. The theory makes no propositions about what makes a culture the way it is. That is, there is a paradigm of sorts in anthropology (though perhaps not explicitly recognized), but it is a paradigm of content rather than one that formally structures how we are to understand and interpret the data it directs us to discover. It comes from an idea of the anthropologist Clark Wissler, "the universal pattern," which sets out the kinds of things all cultures share. We do not phrase this outline precisely as he did in 1923, but most courses in introductory cultural anthropology and most textbooks include the following rubrics which must be described in order to understand a culture: Ecology, Economic Organization, Kinship and Marriage, Social Structure, Political Organization, Religion and Ritual, Myth and Folklore, Art and Creativity, and Socialization and Personality.

In field research, we are supposed to fill in this outline if we want to do a "complete" ethnography and produce a genuinely holistic study. It is, of course, impossible, as I have said, to get everything. Yet for many of us, it is a goal that secretly lies at the back of our minds when we do research. In trying to reach it, anthropologists have often concentrated primarily on simple societies or small peasant villages, whose low population and putative simplicity and stability are thought to guarantee success. This reasoning bares another assumption of the culture concept, that such societies are so homogeneous and stable that a lone fieldworker can learn their culture by living in them for a year or so. Until the 1950s, most anthropologists rejected the study of complex cultures because their heterogeneity, size, and changeability proved too much for this underlying holistic orientation.

Yet these assumptions are misleading: One individual fieldworker cannot grasp the essence of even simple societies, as is amply demonstrated by the volumes of ethnographic description and theoretical disputation about the kinship system of Australian forager cultures. That simple societies are not in fact so homogeneous is revealed by the discovery of significant variation from community to community within them. For example, some of Malinowski's interpretations of the culture of the Trobriand Islanders were invalidated as generalizations for the whole society since he lived with and observed chiefs and their families, who behaved differently from commoners.

But the concept and paradigm of culture provide no basis for understanding variation within a culture, for they, along with cultural relativism, sometimes imply that there is only one way of doing things in each culture. The theory of the culture concept indicates no starting points for understanding a complex society with intracultural variation. Do we begin with the governmental structure or the religious tradition? Do we start off in Detroit, Hollywood, or Little Rock? By remaining silent on this, it is almost as if the concept of culture excluded complex societies from its purview and in so doing produced an unintended result: Primitive and complex societies appear to differ in kind. Our romantic longing for the pristine human culture has almost contradicted our paradigm of the universal pattern. Simple societies appear to possess a wholeness that we lack; they are comprehensible, our culture is not; they are unchanging, we are not. They are the "not-us," we the "not-them."

This distortion is brought about by reification. The concept of culture assumes, for the purposes of study, that a culture, like a thing, has limits or boundaries, and that a culture may be sufficiently described within those limits. Likewise, our paradigm assumes that each category or rubric is discrete. That is, we make certain "as if," or heuristic, assumptions at the outset that may in fact not accord with reality; we treat cultures as objects, and separate parts of them off for study. But, as I said in Chapter I, another step in the analysis must follow: We must return the culture or parts of it to the context from which we have abstracted them. The formulation of the culture concept, however, says nothing about this or about what we might for now call intercultural structures. It ignores the relations between cultures or groups that are said to be cultures.

Now, to pick up a theme from Chapter I, it is all too easy to take our concepts of the world for the world itself, to let words, our symbolic representation of the world, take the place of material reality, and to assume that because two cultures have different names and are geographically separate, they also have no connection, or that any connection they may have is of no account. But meaningful connections exist. It is often hard, except in the case of an island culture, to say where a given culture begins and ends. We can easily see this by taking a detached look at fieldwork itself: The act of studying another culture connects two cultures. The anthropologist studies a primitive society as an individual from a specific culture. The fact that we study other cultures is itself cultural; our culture has institutions that support, finance, and encourage field research. When we study another people, we share an experience with them, and there is therefore a connection between us. This then questions the whole notion of an entity called culture: Are we two separate cultures? According to whom? Who draws a culture's boundaries? If we have established some relationship with another culture, what is it? To whose culture does it belong? Does a culture cross national boundaries? To put it another way, we and the people we study are part of the same structure.

If there is no overt statement that cultures actually lack visible boundaries, it becomes possible to think of each culture as if it were a solid smooth ball, spinning off by itself, eternally the same. Such objectification prevents us from seeing that fieldwork initiates or continues a process in which two ways of life mutually change one another. The culture concept, as constructed, cannot encompass change and has therefore led us to misunderstand primitive societies as well as our own.

In this sense, the concept of culture is not true to the real world of relationships whose character is processual, not static. All cultures change, and as they do, the interrelations of parts of culture show increasing amounts of conflict. Conflict then is as inevitable as change and evolution. The concept of culture, on the basis of its assumptions, cannot make sense of the fact that the many once-autonomous Native American societies that first sparked an interest in ethnography are now dependent parts of a larger structure. Whether we call this structure a culture or a nation or many subcultures is really irrelevant to the main point of process.

There is an intimate connection between this reification of culture and the need to focus on a stable situation. As long as we continue to see each system as separate and as long as its analytic boundaries are taken for the real ones, we can not and need not understand that the real ones shift. But, it seems to me, the source of change in any system is the interaction between it and another system, which implies malleable, if not permeable, boundaries. Thus, a biological organism will change as a result of interaction between its genetic system and the environment it inhabits. Similarly, a society or social system will change according to the various interactions between it and its environment, the psychological systems of individuals, and other cultures.

The conceptual isolation of cultures from one another is another instance of the same kind of thinking that deprives the paradigm of culture of a theory of how its parts are related to one another. The culture concept makes no statement about whether the parts of culture have equal weight in their integration. In turn, because of this, it cannot explain why one culture will resemble a second and differ from a third. More generally, it cannot explain why similarities and differences arise among cultures, and therefore how cultures interact and evolution thereby takes place.

From time to time in this chapter, I have discussed the cultural bases of our ideas; now let me try to analyze this last point in the same way: We take "as if" premises for reality in part because our theory is inadequate and in part because cultural experiences influence our views. We should look further into the matter and ask why we study the cultures we do. Within our own culture, we social scientists have found it easier to study the lower class because the upper class have the power to keep us out; in the same way, it has been easier to study primitive or simple cultures. The question about intercultural structures has now another dimension: We study simple societies as members of a politically and economically dominant nation and culture; the foci of our research are part of a structure of dominance, and our relation to the people we study cannot but be affected by that structure.

At the same time, our study of them has led us back to ourselves, for in pursuing the unrealizable holism, we have found one cause of their structure (and of ours as well) to lie in the relations between us and them. The original theoretical validity of studying simple societies has disappeared, but the anthropological emphasis on the process of integration remains true to life and valid for the theory of our times. It counterpoints imperialism's ideology of one nation/one culture, in which each nation's culture is relativistically sanctioned "on its own terms." As long as each culture is kept separate and bounded in theory, each nation can be likewise seen as separate and ethically accountable to no one but itself. But if one were to see the connections among nations/cultures, this relativistic, "separate but equal" attitude would dissolve.

These ideological blinkers also prevent us from grasping the seemingly elusive wholeness of our own culture. For the wholeness does not lie merely within the physical boundaries of the United States. Our highly developed industry depends on the labor and products of underdeveloped, undeveloped, or developing nations. Our control of these resources stems not from our goodwill or manifest destiny but from concrete relationships with other nations whose financial and political separation is more apparent than real. We do have a way of life. Its integrity may be less romantic or honorable than we would wish, but it exists and it holds promises for future good and honor that we can perhaps yet realize.

III.

Why Is the Sky Blue?

Theories and Explanations

Selective Observation

I once taught a senior seminar in anthropological fieldwork methods, and for the first assignment, I sent the students, a dozen in all, to the college cafeteria. They were to sit at adjacent tables and take notes on all that they observed for half an hour. During the next class, they compared their notes: Some had narrowed in on details like the color and number of tables and chairs; others described only people. Some noticed dress, others did not. While some remarked on the racially and ethnically arranged seating, others neglected it. Most of the former simply classified the groups as black, white, or Latin, and ignored Asians. Some speculated on what motivated the actions of those they observed; others avoided guesses and stuck to uncomplicated numbers, like how many entered, left, and when. Finally, whereas some recorded only what they heard, others also included what they saw.

The students were amazed by the way their perceptions varied, but I would have been surprised only at identical reports. If twelve people watch the same busy scene, they are unlikely to describe it in the same way, even if they are all from the same culture. Even when they share formal training in the same school of thought, their perceptions still vary in details. They probably will not even see the same things. To put it another way, no one person can observe everything in any given situation. Despite the students' familiarity with the cafeteria, they could describe it only partially and selectively, for they recorded not merely different things, but also different kinds of things. They, like the rest of us, see, or do not see, in particular ways.

We are usually unaware of this process of selection and its bases. It would indeed be hard to notice, in the course of living our daily lives, that we choose to see some things and to ignore others. It would be harder still to notice the kinds of things we do not see as well as the kinds we do see. We couldn't get anything done that way, because we would be spending our energy figuring out what we were doing. Broadly speaking, we observe according to what it is we want to do and eliminate anything irrelevant to our goals. For example, if we are hurrying to cross a busy commercial avenue, let us say Fourteenth Street in Manhattan, in order to keep an appointment for which we are late, we notice the color of the stop light and whether there are cars turning into the crosswalk. But we don't simultaneously take note of the fact that we are ignoring the street hawkers of Woolworth's latest type of rug shampoo and the variety of the crowds around us.

For the most part, then, we are not aware that every time we look at the world around us, even with multiple, or diffuse, goals consciously or unconsciously in mind, we activate a set of criteria that structure the environment and relate our behavior to it. Yet this awareness is part of what scholarship is all about. In my seminar, the few students who had thought about this problem froze up in the cafeteria, and could only record concrete details. One student was so self-conscious that he decided just to compile statistics of people, tables, chairs, time, etc.

Because we usually lack this consciousness of how we segment our environment into relevant units, we tend to feel that our perception of reality is identical with the reality itself, and is, therefore, the only perception possible. When the students took notes on the cafeteria, most thought that they were describing reality, but each actually produced a different description. If each student segmented reality according to different criteria, is it then possible to describe the reality of anything? In principle, the answer is no. There are potentially as many realities as there are pairs of eyes.

But if that were the case, then why did the twelve observations not sound like they came from a dozen different places? It makes sense that different reports of the same thing usually coincide, at least a little. But what accounts for this apparently self-evident fact that we can commonly agree, without prior consultation, that some things are the same? These questions are about complex processes, and I can only suggest a sketch of an answer. There are two factors, the view and the reality, between which there is a subtle play. First, people will view reality similarly (and equally selectively) if their realities are similar. In other words, viewers from the same culture or same part of it will share criteria of selection because views are socially constructed; views are partly determined by cultural reality itself.

Since each culture exists in some particular, delimited time and place, each cultured world view or variant part will be similarly limited, or partial, and will diverge from others. Criteria of selection vary, then, not only between cultures, but within them: among regions, political groups, ethnicities, or personality types, from careless everyday life to academic rigor, from less to more rigorous disciplines. Given this, what is the basis for shared criteria among partial views? Here is the second and tricky part: Since reality remains what it is, no matter what we say about it, it constrains some constancy even among the world views of different cultures, or individuals.* The problem is that we do not know how to predict the segments of reality on which any two variant world views will agree.

* Reality may change if we do something about or to it, but that is another matter.

Because of the complexity of these processes, the success of scholarly or scientific thinking depends on making the criteria of selection explicit. My first assignment aimed to make the students aware of the fact of selective observation and of the difference between external events and their ideas of these events. I wanted to show them that selection was not haphazard, but was based on sets of criteria whose systematic relations came from their more or less conscious theories of how the world works. For example, I remember the surprise of one student, an extremely intelligent, politically active white woman of twenty-nine, at her failure to note that most blacks and whites sat separately in the cafeteria. In trying to understand her temporary blindness, she found that she had been following an old code of values: She had learned when she was younger that it was impolite to notice racial variations and, if one noticed them, one didn't mention them. Her unconscious use of these criteria made her not see something in front of her nose.

Such criteria, however, represent more than mere politeness. They represent specific, though unarticulated theories, each implying a different vision of human nature and sociocultural possibilities. The code that led to the student's omission derives from the following set of ideas about social change: If only each and every one of us behaved as if differences in color, race, religion, etc., didn't exist, our problems of racism would disappear; a combination of goodwill, legislation, and hard work would then quickly right painful wrongs. This theory maintains that people can, individually, change society by correct thinking, firm will, and legislation.

We all know by now that this theory doesn't work. It leaves out half the relevant data, which have to do with the economic and political conditions that facilitate the realization of individual desires, common adherence to law, and good thoughts. The theory omits, for example, the fact that most blacks get less remunerative jobs than most whites. It denies the fact that a capitalist economic system depends on the security of the few and the insecurity of the many. The theory ignores the realistic fears of whites that the opening of economic doors to blacks might close off their own livelihoods. Such relations between people and basic resources will perpetuate racism despite all the goodwill, superficial attitudinal change, and legislation we can muster.

But to include such relationships in one's description means to have another set of ideas, another theory, about what it is important to observe. Different theories select different data. A second student, a twenty-five-year-old Puerto Rican male, also an activist, was fascinated by the seating patterns. He made them the subject of his term paper and analyzed them precisely in terms of the relations between people and property. He was aware of his theory and its criteria. The first student was not and only discovered hers after comparing the results of her observation with others. Now, in fact, her conscious theory of social change agreed with his, and the process of criticizing her own observation forced her to confront the contradiction between her conscious theory and her previously unexamined habitual approach to society.

The difference between these two students can perhaps be related to their socio-economic positions. It is likely that the second student could brook less contradiction in his ideas, because, as a working-class member of a dark-skinned ethnic minority, he was daily conscious of the effects of economic inequality on social behavior. The first student, though working-class herself, had "white skin-privilege" and shared the common white habit of averting one's eyes at anything racially unpleasant. This habit enables one to avoid being reminded of one's advantageous position in one of the many American structures of inequality; it permits one's stake in skin-privilege to drop out of awareness, and thereby maintains institutionalized racism.

One may not always be able to uncover such unconscious ideas; the theory behind them may be too obscure or fragmentary. But I believe that they exist. When people describe something, they may do so without thinking, but not without thoughts. To assume the latter is to assume that people are either automatons, acting without will or desire, or dunces, acting without any brains. Most of the time, people (and this includes scholars and scientists) act with semiawareness of what they do; some of their reasoning rises to surface consciousness, some of it does not. This means that in daily life, they can juggle the discrepancies in their views of the world. They do not systematically, relentlessly isolate each perspective, discover its structuring of reality, and then correct it when another view shows that there are data the first doesn't include or account for.

Scientific theories and, therefore, theorizing stem from normal everyday thinking, like figuring out how to cross the street or describing a cafeteria. But although both kinds of thinking have to do with ideas about reality, they are not identical. The semiconsciousness of everyday conceptions of the world contrasts with science's conscious articulation of its principles. Furthermore, the processes of working with, developing, and creating theories differ from ordinary attempts to understand the world while trying to survive in it. One of these processes, for example, is to make the premises of our reasoning conscious so as to ensure their consistency.

Whereas, then, we tolerate many contradictions in ordinary thinking, scientific theorizing ideally requires a continually self-correcting process to eliminate them. Scholarly inquiry does not proceed wholly deductively, by fitting the world into rigid schemes; we do not let the theory we work with be our only frame of vision, but always have additional or alternative ones at the ready to glimpse errant facts. Nor does science construct theories objectively, or simply inductively, from pure data uncontaminated by preconceptions. Rather, there is an interplay between reality and one's ideas of it. After each observation, one stops and examines how one's ideas work, what new data one has discovered, what other theory has revealed them, and how one's old theory must change. Thus, the first student had to stop juggling and to resolve the contradictions in her ideas; she scrapped her original approach in her later study of the cafeteria. Finally, each time one strips down one's ideas and adds new ones, one has to try them out again on the data.

Our daily thinking and scholarly thinking are two opposite poles of a continuum of thought, which are, finally, qualitatively different. The scientific process is based on explicit concepts that state what one wants to explain and how to explain it. These concepts analyze reality into units and postulate connections between the units. These ideas and concepts are made meaningful in relation to one another by principles which are the bases of theories. A theory is a set of concepts systematically linked to one another in the form of propositions, or statements, formulated so as to explain, or make comprehensible, observed events. A theory usually focuses on certain classes of events, things, or acts, selecting some and eliminating others.

STRUCTURAL-FUNCTIONAL THEORY

Any given discipline contains different kinds of theory. Usually all agree on the basic subject matter to be examined, as, for example, biology is concerned with life. But what is relevant for one theory may not be for another. The analytical units of each depend on what the theory aims to explain and on its principles. This chapter presents three major kinds of anthropological theory, which exemplify some of what I have said so far. I want to show the kinds of data it is possible to examine, and to illustrate a few types of anthropological explanation.

Before I do that, however, I want to explain some preliminary assumptions common to all theories. We need data to illustrate this; let us each imagine a cafeteria. Mine is the one that my students studied, and they have given me permission to use some of their data to which I will add my own. Let us narrow our observation to a crucial act, payment for food. From what I have said already, selective observation precludes us from talking about this act "as it is"; as soon as we begin to talk about it, we structure it according to underlying ideas. All ideas are contained in language, which necessarily presents an image of reality. There is no way, then, that I can present fundamentals of theory without transmitting a particular theory.

I can, however, suggest the kind of choice that each theory makes and that confronts each observer. If we consider what to begin with, there are two major possibilities: We can segment the scene into analytical units, or we can take it as a whole. There are five physically bounded units: the cashier, the customer, the food, the money, and the cash register (and other material surroundings). But these physical units may not be analytical units. They may not, in other words, suit the requirements of a given theory. For example, if one's theory concerns the sexual distribution of occupations, then what is relevant is the cashier's sex/gender; one would also want to know the customer's sex and job, and so on.

The second possibility, to take the scene as a whole, means that we are looking not only at units but at relations. *Relations* means what goes on between two units, or the behavior of each toward the other. Our focus on them implies that the physical boundaries of units are less important than the connections among them. The totality of a scene consists of a set of relations that includes also relationships between relations, such that the association of units and their interconnections in the same time and place somehow make sense. For example, the relation between customer and money is that she tangibly possesses the money and can use it at will. The relation between customer and cashier involves the customer's relation not only to money but to the food; if she takes food, she must give money to the cashier, for the cashier is the guardian of the food. The cashier in turn has other relations to the money, and these depend on her relations to those who own the cafeteria. If we take the scene as a whole, then, our analytical units may change from type of person to type of relationship, or even to the whole set of relationships; in the latter case, the significance of the totality lies in its connection to something else (such as the ownership of the cafeteria or the cafeteria's contribution to the gross national product).

The point is that reality confronts the observer simultaneously with a divisible reality and with the connections between the parts in a particular context. In our traditional Western approach, we usually see and speak of units or things first and relations second; but, I think that, like all people, we perceive both things and relations simultaneously so that they mutually define one another. This definition emerges in action, which means that in the study of social behavior, we cannot discover the relationship between units unless we see them in action. For example, we must see the customer pay the cashier, and the cashier ring the register, to know of their relations.

All theories must recognize and deal with this existential simultaneity. Some begin from the ground up by isolating units and their relations and then by building sets of relations. Others start with gross relations, and clarify the units in terms of them. But since the initial bounding and choice of units depends on what one wants to know, and since this depends on how one defines a situation, the overall vision of the situation must come before one can even begin to construct a structure of relations between analytical units.

This very concern with overall context marks anthropological theory and therefore the anthropological definition of situations. As holism implies, no part of a scene or of a society can make sense except in contextual relation to other parts and to the whole; to study each unit separately would be to take it out of context. Now, it might very reasonably be asked, How can you understand the whole unless you understand the parts? Well, obviously, you can't, but neither can you understand the parts unless you understand their interconnections. Their relations constitute the structure of the whole context in which the parts exist, and are as essential to the whole as are the parts themselves (as we have just seen, relations are as important as units in understanding the act of payment).

So, as we analyze the parts, we also cross-check them against the whole as defined by the theory we use. For example, one part of cafeteria life is the act of payment. But what dictates the choice of this part for study, rather than another? One might say that, intuitively, it is more important than the perpetual card game that occupies one corner of the college cafeteria. But intuition is a choice, resting on a prior notion about how the whole thing is put together. Initially, I chose to begin with payment for utilitarian reasons: It is a graphic, immediate, and familiar illustration. But as I began writing, I realized that I must have had some other reasons, because there are, after all, other graphic actions. I had weighted one part of the universal cultural pattern and had chosen an economic relationship because certain theoretical considerations led me to think it more important than others.

Payment seems to me crucial because it contains relations fundamental to the operation of cafeterias as we are familiar with them in a capitalist economic system and because the exchange of money for products is our culture's major social relationship. It is the way we get our food and shelter, and its particular form and consequences depend on and determine the character of our social relations and of our lives. Therefore, and this is the second reason for its importance, exchange provides an entering wedge into the entire social system.

Other starting points imply a different perspective. We might, for example, have begun with someone sitting alone at a table and being completely absorbed in eating a hamburger, french fries, and a Coke. But this seems a poor choice, first, because it is inconsistent with our holistic sense of the workings of a cafeteria. A cafeteria is not merely about eating; it is about paying for, and only then eating, prepared food that is available in a certain style. Secondly, the consumption of food is only the end product of many preceding operations. Finally, to begin with someone eating a hamburger is to focus on an individual. But we, as social scientists, want to know about the actions of groups of individuals in the context of a social structure. If we found some relation between the solitary diner and others, we could then have a more solid basis for beginning with that individual. For example, the fact that some persons regularly eat alone while others regularly eat in groups raises questions about social structure and the relations of individuals to it; it may, therefore, be a valid starting point for certain theories.

Let us now return to the action that I halted a little while ago. The first customer has left, the cashier rings the register, and a new customer comes to pay for food. The act may differ in some respects from the first (the customer is different, the cashier and customer may converse, the amount of money be more or less, etc.), and for other purposes these variations might be of interest. But, the similarity of the act and its continual repetition in the course of a day have their own significance that we can discover by defining the relationships both between part and whole, and also between the act of payment and the other parts. If our notion of the context is explicit, it really doesn't matter which of these we do first, for when we do one, we will always have to look back at the other. I would prefer at the moment to look at the whole context, because it brings up an important issue in anthropology. We have three possible contexts: the cafeteria itself, its institutional setting, or the whole economic system. I have chosen the last for this section.

I would say that there are two kinds of active relationships between part and whole: One has to do with maintenance, the other with change. Another way of saying this is that there are two major questions one can ask about society or culture: How does it continue to exist? How does it change? We know from general experience that both continuity and change are true; the world, and social institutions within it, maintain a semblance of similarity from day to day, year to year, decade to decade, but, and this is an important *but,* they also change both fundamentally and superficially.

One theory that explains how a social structure persists is called structural-functionalism. This theory finds its fullest codification in the work of the British theorist A. Radcliffe-Brown. It goes as follows: If there are acts that are repeated, then it is likely that their consequences have something to do with keeping the structure in which they occur going. They have, in other words, a *function* in relation to the whole. The analogy that provided one of the inspirations for this theory may clarify it: In order to understand a biological organism, we must understand its parts and how they work together to keep the whole organism alive. So, with a society, we analyze its parts and their operation in relation to each other as well as to the whole in order to understand how it keeps going.

What, then, does payment function to maintain, and how does it do it?* Since the chosen context is the economic system, we look to that. Using the theory, then, I propose the following hypothetical scheme of how this works: The economic system of the United States is based on private ownership of property and labor. The owners of property, or land, capital, and money, manage it to make a profit to which they have an acknowledged right. Those who own labor—the workers—can sell their labor for wages to owners of property. Both kinds of activities take place in social institutions called corporations, and these are regulated and financially supported by government, whose laws uphold these basic principles and structures. The legal relations to property mean that one must sell products and labor in order to receive income. Property relations establish relations between people as well, since the owners of property determine the goals and daily organization of work and therefore regulate what owners of labor do with their time. Finally, the United States economic system emphasizes the view that people can increase their happiness the more money they make and thereby motivates them to continue doing so.

Although the system has many other dimensions, these are its fundamentals. Now, paying for food in the college cafeteria does not, in and of itself, keep the entire system going. But it does maintain specific instances, or parts, of it in certain areas. We know this because if the cafeteria ceased to exist, those other parts would cease to exist. In order to understand which parts these are, we must now see what the act of payment connects to in the cafeteria by following out subsequent transactions with the money. As we move through the day, the manager collects the cashiers' take and deposits it in a bank, from which it will later be withdrawn and disbursed among the employees of the cafeteria. At other periods, money will also be given to other people and institutions: the wholesalers who sell food to the

* Structural-functional theory was first developed to analyze simple societies organized by kinship. Structural-functionalism is therefore usually associated with kinship and more properly social, rather than economic phenomena. I will discuss kinship in Chapter IV.

cafeteria, the suppliers of paper plates and plastic tableware, and those who service vending machines, kitchen equipment, and cash registers. Finally, a percentage will go to the college for the rights to the concession and the rest to the owner(s) for their profits.

That account suffices for our purposes: Several groups of people and organizations would suffer were the cafeteria to cease to exist. The cafeteria then, is part of an economic system in which people earn their livelihoods, and payment functions to maintain all this. The cafeteria is not the only institution, nor payment the only act, to perform these functions. Banks and their services are just one other example of what is needed to support this system. Several institutions can serve the same function.

A function differs from a purpose. Usually, when one goes into a restaurant, one does not aim to pay employees' salaries, to furnish the owners with profits, or to keep a network of wholesalers, vending machine companies, and maintenance services in operation. But in effect that is what one does by paying money for prepared food. Thus, when one goes to the cafeteria, one is also an agent of an economic system. The concept of function begins to make sense of the individual's relationship to the system by clarifying one relationship I have already described: Through a circuitous route, the customer pays the salary of the cashier.

However, if one of us stopped buying food at one particular cafeteria, little would happen to all of the associated people, institutions, and technology. The functions would still be served if everyone else continued to eat there. Nor would we accomplish much if, for example, we individually tried to influence the kind of food available. Let us say an individual decided that there was too much fried food and too few fresh vegetables, and stopped eating there. If everyone else continued to buy the fried food, it would still be served. In other words, change in a social system, or part of it, can come only when groups of people change their behavior. In turn, people will not change their behavior unless certain conditions change, particularly those that make it likely that people can realize their desires and put their ideas into action. But the potential for change in either conditions or behavior cannot be actualized unless the location of decision-making power changes.

This brings us to the next point. Like many or all other social acts, payment is multifunctioned. Our obligation to pay for food is also an obligation to maintain the distribution of power. This makes the principles by which money, the most powerful form of property in our economic system, is controlled and disbursed relevant to our understanding of the scene. The person, persons, or institution (e.g., corporation) owning the cafeteria has the right to dispose of its revenue, just as the customer has rights to her money. The cashier's right to take the customer's money and the obligation to turn it over to the owner's representative, the manager, become clear in relation to the owner's right to possess that money absolutely and to the relationship between owner and cashier. Because the owner owns the money that he gives the cashier for wages, he has power over her. The cashier has no decision-making power about either the money or anything else that the money facilitates in the cafeteria.

Similarly, the customer controls neither the allocation of money, nor the type of food, nor the surroundings available for the consumption of food in the cafeteria. The owner has the right and power to make decisions about these as well. Neither cashier nor customer, but only the college, governed by the Board of Higher Education and ultimately by the City (and, soon, the State) of New York, decides who gets the concession. This discussion has thereby added another potential context to the cafeteria, the political system. This means that one of the elements in the structure of the cafeteria is inequality, between cashier and owner, between customer and owner, and possibly between all of them and the political powers that be. Payment of money functions to maintain this inequality.

What does this say about the individual's relationship to a functioning system? It does not say that every time we purchase prepared food we initiate a situation of inequality. That would mean that each of us causes inequality in every act of exchange;

this is not only an intolerable moral burden but a falsefood. I am not talking about causes here. A cause is something that happens before other things and brings them into being.* In this section, I have been talking about functions, not causes. Functions have to do with how something stays the same, causes with how it changes. When one looks at an act as part of an ongoing system, one sees it in all its connections to acts which come both before and after it. The act of payment is preceded by the establishment of the cafeteria itself, by the decisions to provide certain kinds of food, and by the rule that one pays for food in this society. It has consequences as well, but they come as much from these prior conditions as from our act. Causality lies outside any one individual's action, although each individual participates in a stream of causes.

Nevertheless, even though we do not cause a structure of inequality to come into being when we participate in it, our participation helps to keep it going. The same would hold for any individual's act in a structure of equality, which we, by living it, would help to maintain. But no lone individual, or even many separate individuals, can either perpetuate or change society in whole or in part without the proper conditions, like a structure which supports such change.

For, in fact, these social structures are what determine and maintain relations between individuals. They are formed by the principles of the society operating as forces which separate people into social groups. General economic principles create such groups: In the cafeteria, there are not only cashiers but also employees, owners as well as employers, and customers and consumers. These labels do not merely put people in categorical boxes, but imply specific relationships between them and others. For example, we call our cashier an employee, because she depends on her employer for a living and has peer connections with other types of employees. Likewise, the consumer depends on

* The definition of cause is more complicated than this, but let this one suffice for now and I will return to the issue below.

the producer (owner) for needed goods and services. The principles of the system make people in different groups relate to one another in systematic, analyzable ways.

Some of the more familiar groups which economic forces create are classes. As the differential possession of money and power creates different standards and styles of living among those connected within the cafeteria, so it does in the society as a whole. We can see in the microcosm of the cafeteria some of the societal consequences of economic principles. Employers and employees belong to different classes because the former control capital (money and technology), and therefore the productive process, and the latter control only their own labor. Employees in the cafeteria are connected to employees elsewhere by their common limited access to basic resources; this gives them the experience of being employed in common. This does not mean that they know one another or have any immediate interests in common; in fact, they often don't. A relationship may thus involve the actual interaction of two people, like cashier and, let us say, busboy, or it may involve the more abstract or statistical connection of membership in the same social category, as we see here.

This means that although we can label people in the same way, they do not necessarily think or act in the same way. The purpose of recognizing such categories is not to stereotype people, or to reduce them to one dimension, but to locate them in the social structure so as to reveal the cultural forces which make them similar and different. Although two people may be similar because they share group membership, each one also participates in other groups whose principles may conflict with those of the first.

For there are other kinds of groups in the society besides the classes and occupational units we have seen here. Some of these are formed, or influenced, by the economic system alone, others are generated and maintained by other principles or forces as well. I have in mind ethnic and racial groups, political parties, families and other kinship units, and so on. A whole society, then, consists of such overlapping structures. Which of these we begin with depends on our theory, but ultimately our aim is to understand not only each kind of group, but the way the groups interact. By understanding possible conflict among them, we may also find out what makes people act in such a way that their actions either maintain or change society.

Structural-functionalism provides anthropology with a basic common language to describe the world, although actually it constructs reality as much or more than it reflects or describes it. Structural-functional theory creates problems as well. For example, it models society after an organism, but whereas we can define the latter's boundaries and measure the functioning of its parts by the relatively unambiguous standard of its health, we can not do the same for society. When, after all, is a society healthy? Though adherents of this theory might deny any claim to judge a culture's health, yet such evaluation is implicit in the theory.

To go one step further, an organism goes through a normal cycle of birth, growth, and death. But societies or cultures do not, although they do indeed change. Structural-functionalism can deal only with an unchanging, balanced state, with a "moving equilibrium," in the words of the American sociologist Talcott Parsons. The theory knows nothing of change and, in fact, tacitly validates the status quo as normal. These limits to its utility call for additional theories of change and conflict, to which I will return after the next section. Suffice it to say here that even though the organismic analogy breaks down, as all analogies must, the theory's advantages thus far have outweighed its problems, as sociologists and political scientists have also discovered with their versions of this fundamental theoretical approach.

STRUCTURALISM

I would now like to show how a different theoretical perspective, called structuralism, leads us to look at other kinds of data. Whereas structural-functionalism focuses on what it is about part and whole that enables the functional relation to work, structuralist theory zeroes in on the relationship itself to see how it affects parts and whole. Since a relationship is invisible, it is rather difficult to focus on, and we need a way of phrasing it. One idea we can use is the notion of *contrast.*

One general though controversial theory of human perception, to which I subscribe, is that people don't simply perceive things just "as they are," but as they are in terms of or in relation to, something else. We cognize in terms of differences; we say two things are similar because both differ from something else in the same way. In other words, we define things just as much because they are not something else, because they contrast with something else, as because they are what they are. An apple is seen to have particular attributes in contrast to something else, such as an orange, which does not have those attributes and has others. This means that we do not see things merely as opposites, in twos, but in threes: the apple, the orange, and their relationship of difference. Such sets can be expanded: apples and oranges in contrast to, let us say, parakeets. Finally, each thing calls up the other; the term *binary* is often used instead of *contrast* to indicate this inextricable linkage between opposites.

The basis for this kind of perception is thought to be psychobiological. It is assumed that there are innate dual psychic structures in *Homo sapiens* connected to biological bilateral symmetry. They organize not only consciousness, but also unconscious perception. They find expression in, among other things, linguistic structure, ideas, spatial arrangements of people and things, and social institutions. Thus, the widespread cultural opposition of male/female has symbolic parallels in the contrast of right/left, or day/night, and repeats on other levels, for example, in household arrangements where the inside is the women's province and the outside belongs to men, or in the conscious classification of the world into culture/nature, or in the unconscious division of the world into self/other.

Structuralism, in anthropology, tries to account for this repetition of dual patterning. It looks not only at the contrasts, but at the relations between them. It seeks to find what is similar in the relationship of difference as expressed in each level. Thus, one might ask: Is the relationship of male to female the same as the relationship of culture to nature?* Structuralist theory also sees contrasts between levels and finds successive contrast pairs to be transformations of one another; if it finds that, for example, day/night expresses the same contrast as right/left, it seeks also to find the way the first pair differs from the second and how one then gets logically from first to second. Another aim of structuralism, then, is to peel off the layers, to watch the process of transformation from one to the other, and to look through the surface appearance of structures to the deepest latent content. Some structuralist theories give rules for this process of transformation; the linguistic theories of Noam Chomsky come to mind.

Unfortunately, structuralist anthropology, as developed by Claude Lévi-Strauss, the French anthropologist, does not operationalize its concepts. *Operationalism* means that primary theoretical and descriptive concepts are constructed so that the specific acts of observation one performs to apply these concepts to reality are clearly stated. For example, a very strict operational definition of *intelligence* is "the results of the Stanford-Binet IQ test." Structuralism does not say what operations one performs, or what selective criteria one applies to cultural data, to find a structure or to discover the changes that occur in it from level to level. It also does not say how one then proceeds to interpret what one has observed in a structuralist way.

French structuralist anthropology also is vague on the *epistemological status* of its propositions. This means that it does not say how it comes to know what it knows. For example, since people give meaning to what they see on the basis of binary relations, structuralism invites us to think about the meanings that situations and acts have for people. But Lévi-Straussian structuralism does not state whether the meanings are consciously

* The American symbolic structuralist Sherry B. Ortner emphatically answers, "Not quite." I discuss male/female issues, as well as theories of psychic structures, in Chapter V.

recognized by those who are observed by anthropologists, whether the observer only infers the meanings (and, if so, from what data), or whether the observer thinks the inferred meanings are conscious or unconscious, among other questions.

In fact, in the final analysis all its interpretations represent unconscious structures. In other words, structuralist analysis presumes that all behavior, institutions, and ideology are continuously shifting externals of deep, binary psychic structures as old as the species; they will change only if the species changes. In this sense, structuralism posits a determinism by innate human mentality. Thus, it becomes annoyingly vague and abstract; it loses its specificity, that is, the connection of the structures to the actual culture in which they are located.

Despite this problem, to which I will return, let us see how one might interpret the act of payment structurally. We have discussed what it is, but now we have to talk about its opposite, about what it is not. First, it is certainly not about receiving food without paying for it. What does this mean? Of course, in this society, all food is ultimately paid for, but in our experience, there are times when we aren't immediately aware of the payment. The most familiar of these is when, as infants, we received food from adults, usually parents, without having to do anything to get it. They gave it out of love and parental obligations, but we incurred no immediate return obligations. Food was thus shared in the context of a diffuse relationship with others, to whom we were connected in multiple, emotionally deep ways.

Buying food in a cafeteria or a store is none of that. For all of us, its first meaning is its difference from our early experience. It means nonsharing and, therefore, a separation of interests between the parties to the exchange. When we pay the cashier, we engage in a precisely defined, one-dimensional relationship; the transaction is limited by time, by the objects transacted, and by the surroundings. Both parties to it calculate: We match cost against hunger and other needs; the cashier measures our money against what we have taken, looks to see whether we have stolen anything, and may also count the number of hours left to the working day. The act of payment thus lies in the shadow of the whole economy, with its hierarchy, inequality, and power differences.

According to structuralism, the relationship between the parts (between giving/receiving and paying/receiving) affects each part. When we look for meaning, we are not just asking how one thing differs from another, but also how the differences affect our understanding of each. We play back the relationship on the parts. The significance of paying for food is a summation of both what it is and what it is not. Reciprocally, once we have had to pay for food, the receipt of food "for free," as from a friend at dinner, takes on new and added meaning, for it lacks those one-dimensional characteristics of capitalist exchange. Thus, we see, structuralist theory does not deal with functions, but with the processes by which interactions between parts of a social or cultural system reverberate to create a shared universe of meaning for its members.

People can share the meaning because of their common experience. Let us see how this might work by narrowing the cafeteria's context from the economic system as a whole to the college that it serves. Aside from its manifest, or intended, function of providing food for the college population of 10,000, the cafeteria's latent, or socially unintended, function is as a student reaction area. Although others—faculty, administration and staff—also use it, most people in it are students, and anyone who sits at a table for longer than an hour is probably a student.

The meaning of the cafeteria comes from its contrasts with other facets of student life. A major one is that of college routine versus cafeteria. To students, the cafeteria is a place of relaxation. It is the scene not only of eating, but also of socializing, gossiping, cardplaying, horsing around, meeting pickups, and so forth—everything that the students do not do or are not supposed to do in the college classroom. The cafeteria is a place, and represents a time, with no authority figures or schedule. In contrast to the grades, ranks, and major subjects that divide students in college, everyone sitting at the tables is the same and, in a sense, equal. The difference between the college routine and the cafeteria is the difference, for the students, between work and play. The meaning of the cafeteria has also to do with the contrast work/play.

At this point, we might consider the problems in structuralism's ambiguous stance on meaning. Partly because different social forces give each individual a different position in society, each person may have a different understanding of the same thing. When interviewed by members of my seminar, most students mentioned socializing as one of their main reasons for coming to the cafeteria instead of going to another restaurant or bringing their own lunch and eating it alone somewhere. Some did say, however, that it was just a convenient place to get a quick bite between classes. Not all shared this sense of play about the cafeteria.

Does this invalidate the structuralist interpretation? It would, if we insisted that each individual fully share all meanings with all others in her/his culture. But human beings characteristically attribute multiple meanings to what they do, and it is possible for them to tolerate even contradictory ones, as emerged in my seminar. Furthermore, as social scientists, we are interested in the social or cultural meaningfulness of things, as well as in its connection to individual consciousness. Meanings are shared in each culture or part of it, and as members of a culture, we can comprehend them, even though we may not personally agree with them. Those shared meanings are the elements of a cultural world view. I would guess that most people in this culture would understand and agree with my view of the payment/nonpayment contrast.

However, there is also a problem of how conscious these meanings are. Almost all people would be willing, I think, to agree with the work/play contrast I have drawn, even though no one is likely to be constantly aware of it. But, as I have indicated, structuralist theory also suggests meanings of which we may be wholly unaware while living our daily lives. For example, let us infer another dimension of the work/play contrast: The happy egalitarian play of the students takes place in conjunction with the workaday marketplace world, within a hierarchical institution run according to endless calculations aimed at providing someone with a profit. Though the students did not voice this distinction, there is nevertheless evidence for it in the cafeteria's physical structure and in the students' behavior: To get and pay for food, one leaves the seating area, which occupies two-thirds of the cafeteria, and enters another area marked off by turnstiles. There, instead of pushing past and bumping into people as one does to get to a table, one keeps one's private space and lines up behind others. One does not have the extended rambling discussions that one has with dining companions, but exchanges a few brief, directed words about the choice of food and the amount of payment. For a moment, then, the student has entered the world of private ownership and one-dimensional relationships.

But as soon as the food is paid for, the student returns to a world where eating takes on the aspect of a shared experience. One holds tables and space in common, and participates in those complex, diffuse, equal relationships called friendships. The extent of the mutual exclusion of eating and paying, of play and work, appears in the nonbehavior of the students toward the workers; most do not even notice when a busboy comes to clear the tables, and most in fact feel that the cafeteria "belongs to the students" and has no owner.

To return to a major theme of this book, let us see how one's relationship to these contrasts affects one's vision of their meaning. For the cashier, the act of payment, or of receiving payment, is not a significant contrast. This is because, to the workers, the cafeteria is the workplace whose owner, their employer, is in charge. They punch in and out at specified times and have specified things to do when they are there. Whereas for the students being in the cafeteria is its own reward, the workers' reward is in their paychecks. The workers' play lies outside the cafeteria in the leisure time that is part of the rest of their lives, is more valued for itself than is their work, and is therefore more real.

We have, then, a second contrast: worker/student. Furthermore, the fact that most workers are old enough to be the parents of college-age students reveals a third contrast, adult/child, in which childhood means freedom from the social responsibility for oneself characteristic of adulthood. This does not mean that every student is an irresponsible child, but it does, I think, go some way toward illuminating the attitude of the three eighteen-year-old workers who uniformly thought the students "dumb." Their denigration of the students probably comes from the conflict between their poverty-enforced adult social position and the ability of their own age-peers to remain in a child's world. In contrast, the older workers thought the students were "nice kids, except for the crazies," indulging them as adults do children. The workers, then, were conscious of some contrasts of which the students were unaware.

So far, we have been working with dualities, but as I said earlier, structuralism really works in threes. Thus, in looking at a contrast such as work/play, we have a third term: their relationship. The differences (between working for a living and not, and between old and young) bring us to the meanings of the college itself. College is not play, since it involves hard work; but it is not work either, for going to college brings in no money. The people who attend college are not children, for they can vote and fight in the armed services, but traditionally, they are not adults either because they are not yet expected to take on adult obligations. College is also supposed to be its own reward, but at the same time it is expected that a college education will get one something once one graduates.

College, however, is not merely a blend of the contrasts we have seen, but something whole and unique in itself. It differs from both parts of the cafeteria, for it has a patterned organization of people and things, i.e., a particular institutional structure, and performs a manifest function, the training of critical thinking through the transmission of knowledge. But its latent function makes its meaning ambiguous: It is a place and time of transmission between childhood and adulthood, between social recruit and productive member of society. It is the third term of our contrasts, or dualities, of play/work, child/adult, student/worker.

I can summarize what I have said so far in diagrams:

Why Is the Sky Blue?

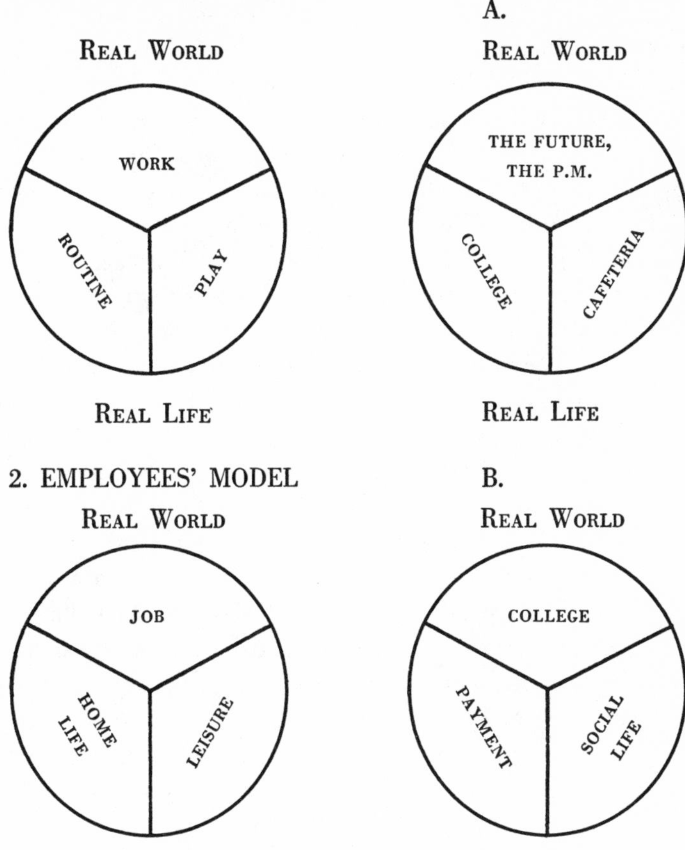

These diagrams illustrate the way general levels of meaning can be shared despite differences in the position of individuals, for all that needs to be shared, according to the American anthropologist A. F. C. Wallace's view of cultural communication, are the lines of contrast. Circle 1 represents the general cultural model for all of us. Each of the other circles represents the round of living for each of our social groups at any one moment. For most of our lives, we dichotomize work (Real World) and the life that really matters to us (Real Life).

As in Circle 2, everything outside our job is important. The major dimension of contrast between them is control; Real Life is all we can control, since most of us must sell our labor and since our work life, in capitalist society, lies in the control of the owners of productive forces. In principle, we alone control our Home Life and our Leisure. Real Life does contain Routine, or obligatory elements, but they, unlike our work, are not controlled by an impersonal authority. Translated into Circle 2, Routine consists of Home Life, cooking dinner or making beds, changing the oil or cutting the grass, elements that are necessary to the maintenance of our own health and well-being; since we personally decide on how and when they are done, they are unlike our Jobs. The rest of our Real Life is our Play or Leisure, in which what we do is for pleasure and emerges spontaneously from personal desires.*

Circle 1 also shows in what way we have not a dual but a triadic structure. It is as if we begin with a dichotomy, Real World/Real Life, but then the tension in their relationship undergoes development. This development is of a transition to get from the first to the second term. The dichotomy of Real World/Real Life becomes internally divided, so that the Real Life segment contains two terms, and Routine becomes, as it were, a transition between Work and Play.

The other two circles are transformations of the general cultural model; in other words, each circle maintains the triadic structure, or the same relations between the segments, but they change the segments' content. In Circle 3A, for students who work, College and Cafeteria fit into Real Life as Routine and Play respectively and contrast with the Real World of a Job. For those students who don't work or who do not perceive the workaday dimension of the cafeteria, the first part of the dichotomy, Work, becomes transformed: In Circle 3B, since paid Work lies in the future, it disappears. College then takes the structural place of Work; it is treated like and feels like work, even though it yields no money and its tangible rewards are in the future. Since Play (Social Life) can only take place in contrast to

* At least, this is our ideal. But even leisure has come to be "colonized" by industry and mass culture, as Stanley Aronowitz describes.

hierarchy and authority, Payment in Circle 3B takes the place that College has in Circle 3A; Payment is the student's version of Routine.

Structuralist analysis of particulars takes us very quickly to a consideration of general themes. As distinct from structural-functionalism, which keeps our focus on the particular part and whole, structuralism's emphasis on relationships yields structures that are fundamental not only to our society but to all culture and humanity. From the point of view of our own culture as a whole, it shows three triadic stages:

CULTURAL CATEGORIES

LIFE PATH TRIADS	MAJOR ACTIVITY	SOCIAL GROUP	SOCIAL AGE
FIRST	Play	Children	Child
SECOND	Learning	Students	Teenager/ Young Adult
THIRD	Work	Workers	Adult

Whereas the diagrams are cyclical, each Life Path Triad is part of a linear sequence of states of being: The progress through life goes from first to second to third Triad, or state of being; each state of being has the different Cultural Categories of Activity, Group (and name), and Age. Though each Triad contains these same categories, as do the student and worker circles, their relationships as well as their content are transformed. For example, the transition from one Activity, social Group, or Age to another increasingly distances play from what one spends most of one's time doing: First embedded in school and college, play later drops out into nonworking time. To be an adult, one must cease to play; play is childish, adulthood is ridden with care and work. Along with play, adults lose egalitarian relations, the enjoyment of non-goal-directed fooling around, the re-creation of diffuse relations reminiscent of family sharing, and the spontaneous creativity that sparks the whims of play.

The transformed structure and content of the sequential states thus signal the changes individuals go through in their lifetimes.

This structuralist interpretation of the child/adult change both accurately describes a major configuration of our society and reflects a moral recommendation of our culture. What we see, then, are continual transformations of the relations between the same elements in different dimensions of the same society, from particular situations to universal ones, as in the child/adult contrast; from one life-style to another (students and workers); between levels of analysis (from social category to general cultural model).

The potential of structuralism for the development of general anthropological theory lies in its multiple applications: It works for meaning, for individual consciousness, and for the unconscious; it applies to language and to social structure. Its broad compass reflects connections which perhaps run through all human phenomena. It may even provide a theoretical link between two levels of reality that no one has so far successfully put together in one theory, culture and the individual.

But it needs critical work. The theoretical problems raised earlier are connected to other ones of ontology. In other words, where do these structures actually come from? Do they exist only in the observer's mind? Are they unconsciously in the people observed? Do they ever rise to consciousness? Can observer and observed share the creation or recognition of them? Are dyadic and triadic structures innate? Immutable? The only possibilities? If they are, how can individuals and cultures change? Does a structuralist view of culture assume that "the more things change, the more they are the same," even if they look different?

These questions have theoretical import. Though unconscious structures and processes without doubt help to form culture, people still relate to one another, their culture, and their history through conscious interpretation of self and other, of nature and culture. Consciousness mediates, or translates, between the individual unconscious and the cultural ideology, between the source of the universal, eternal structures and their varying material and institutional expressions. Structuralism, coupled with a theory of conscious meaning, would re-introduce the individual, or subjectivity, into the picture, and so lead back to the specific culture being analyzed, instead of to an ever-receding human unconscious.

The school of symbolic analysis tries to effect such a joining of structuralism and a theory of subjective meaning, though it does not answer all the questions I have raised. One relevant characteristic of human thought processes of which symbolic structuralism makes use is the push toward synthesis, toward making order out of chaos. As much as human consciousness perceives by contrasting, it also seeks to unify what it discriminates at higher and higher levels of integration. *Symbols,* as analyzed by the American anthropologist Clifford Geertz and others, are words or things or acts that represent both this joining and the discrimination. Symbolic structuralism, as seen in the work of Sir Edmund Leach and Victor Turner, as well as of Geertz, takes this cultural and ideological attempt to unify opposites as one of its premises and proceeds from there to show how specific cultures carry out this universal process. This process is important for our understanding not only of culture, but of the relations between individual and culture, for it can link conscious meaning to both unconscious structures and concrete cultural circumstances. I shall discuss this theory and these issues more in Chapter V.

MARXISM

Though no one knows for sure either where they are going or where they have come from, culture and society are perpetually changing. But social change is difficult to understand and theories about it inevitably cause dispute. First of all, since change, like relationships, is invisible, and we can infer it only after it has happened, our theories leave a great deal of room for error, doubt, and therefore, argument. Secondly, people don't like to change and so don't like to think about it, despite its ubiquity. Since social theory has the property of simultaneously describing and prescribing for social reality, theories of social change comment on the viability of one's own society and are therefore apt to provoke anxiety and anger.

The most solidly grounded theories of social change are Marxian. They derive from writings of Karl Marx and Frederick Engels in the nineteenth century and of their followers since then. Many people avoid these theories because of their avowed political association with communism. But no social theory is value-free, nor does any theory lack opinions about human action. Structural-functionalism, for example, favors the staus quo, or no action; structuralism stymies action, since it confusingly states that human nature remains essentially the same eternally, but that its appearance is ever-shifting. Marxism is premised on the unity of theory and practice, and enjoins action aimed at eliminating all class and hierarchical distinctions and at equalizing economic and political power.

Like anthropology, Marxist theory is holistic. Everything cultural is relevant and interconnected. But unlike the meta-theory behind the universal pattern, Marxism weights parts of culture. The material facts of life and the social form they take are primary determinants of the rest, in the long run. This is the meaning of its theory of *historical materialism.* To analyze the operation of a culture at any one moment, one must understand the distribution of control over basic resources among social groups, which is also what one must change if one wishes to change society. Unequal distribution of wealth and power are the result of contradictions, or opposing principles. An example of a contradiction in our culture is that people are ascribed unequal social positions because of unchangeable characteristics like race, yet told that there is "equal opportunity" for all to climb to the top. Another contradiction, in capitalism, is that property is privately owned, but work is socially carried out; the results of work, or products, are produced by groups, but are eventually appropriated by individuals. Contradictions engender conflicts, and these generate social change. The individual's consciousness of self and society grows out of her/his relation to these conflicts, and leads to the action that brings about change. Therefore, *ideology,* part of which is the cultural expression of consciousness, also depends on particular historical or cultural conditions.

Historical materialism thus leads inevitably to considerations of social change, evolution, and revolution. This means that it focuses not only on a momentary socio-economic formation, but also on what came before and after it, and on what other cultures it interacts with. This theory, in other words, roots the objects of its study in specific times and specific places. The time and place on which it focuses are delimited, in turn, by the presence of specific conflicts.

These conflicts, according to Marxism, are generated by the process of the production of goods and services, because this activity is the heart of the re-production, or creation, of the life of a culture. Conflict within the production processes comes from the relations between its two constituents, the material forces of production and the social relations of production.* The material forces, i.e., the tools, labor, resources, and knowledge used by a culture to produce needed goods and services, develop independently of the relations, in the long run, though this self-propulsion is not yet well established by historical materialism. In any event, in human history, the changes in these forces have typically preceded the slower-changing social relations. These consist of the forms in which production is carried out, the rules by which products are distributed, and the ideology which justifies and motivates the concrete social interaction of cultural life. The distribution over the means and results of productions sets the character for the relations of production. These relations are identical to the relations between those who control the results of production and those who produce; for example, if the producers and controllers are different people, then the relations between them, the relations of production, are *class* relations.

Contradiction and conflict thus have two sources in this view: The relations of production may hinder the development of the material forces. And/or the interests of different groups may become so opposed as to make the relations between the groups unbearable. These contradictions generate strains in the rest of the culture, in the institutional structure, and in ideology. The strains appear, for example, as friction between social groups and as discontinuities within systems of ideas or moralities. This

* These concepts are discussed and defined more fully in Chapter VI.

means that there is a lag between the origin of conflict and individual or cultural recognition of it. People are thought to become conscious of, and to fight out, these conflicts through ideology. Their growing awareness of the contradictions makes them take actions to change the unbearable social conditions.

But why, one may ask, are people not always aware of the contradictions? What accounts for their being unconscious of conflict as it is forming? These questions reflect a more pervasive problem of Marxist theory, the nature of the relations between socio-economic structure and ideology, or, in other words, between material base and superstructure. Marxism calls the ideology which ignores these conflicts false consciousness, but gives no satisfactory explanation for it. Marxism holds that even though the conflicts in production generate contradictions in ideology, ideology is not merely determined by economic forces. If it were, how could historical materialism have come into being? If it is not, then what are its sources? How do consciousness and ideology produce actions that undo the very conditions that breed and nourish them? How, in other words, does the dialectical process occur in which people's consciousness is produced by, and is also constitutive of, their culture, place, and time?

All these questions are good ones, and they at present have no satisfactory answers. Although Marxism proffers the theory of dialectical materialism to treat these problems in parallel with historical materialism, it provides essentially no more solutions than I have summarized here. Historical materialism still needs a developed theory of consciousness, such as the sociologists Peter Berger and Thomas Luckmann, or the Critical Theorists like Max Horkheimer or Herbert Marcuse, have tried to construct; perhaps one can eventually be evolved through a link with symbolic structuralism. For the relations between individual and culture, ideology and society, consciousness and history, are all aspects of the same issue.

Anthropologists have criticized Marxism, not only for its cloudy position on the individual-culture relation, but also for its ethnocentrism, in that its premises and concepts were developed to explain nineteenth-century European industrial culture, and are not cross-culturally applicable. For example, it lacks an adequate theory of the integration of single societies, since it knows nothing of the importance and operation of kinship or of domestic arrangements for production. Like any system of ideas, Marxism reflects the social conditions in which it grew. But this does not preclude its modification by new ideas, as feminists are now doing, to attempt to explain the universal disparity in rights, privileges, and statuses of female and males.

Here, what is more important is the general point of Marxism's indisputable utility for analyzing change. Marxism locates the processes of change in social conflict. Conflict does not refer so much to disputes that arise in a given situation and are then resolved, but to inequalities integral to the fundamental character of social relations. A general contradiction in the life conditions and interests between groups of people underlies particular instances of conflict, such as labor disputes; these cannot be eliminated and finally resolved until the basic relations themselves are transformed or disappear. Since such processes of transformation occur over time, and since we don't know the future, we must seek time depth in the past, when we know for certain not only that change has occurred, but also what has changed.

Until anthropologists began to study societies with written histories, their data did not confront them with the problems of time and change. In fact, Radcliffe-Brown frowned on any attempts to reconstruct the pasts of preliterate peoples as "conjectural" or "pseudo" history. As long, then, as there was no way to recover the past, anthropologists and other students of primitive society focused on the present; this also led to their acceptance of structural-functional theory, including its bias toward the status quo. But theories of change and of the past as incubating the present become vital as our sights shift more to the present, as primitive societies coalesce into complex Third-World nation-states, and as contemporary cultures spin with change before our very eyes.

Facing change presents anthropologists with not only the need to learn to study history, but also the need to revise anthropology's own view of the world. As long as change is happening, cultures and their parts cannot have total internal consistency. The paradigm of culture falsely assumes that they can and do, as I explained in Chapter II. But we see that all parts of culture are in perpetual motion, and like the material forces and social relations of production, they are usually unsynchronized. It is true that as one part changes so do the others because they are functionally connected. Yet different parts may change at different rates, and the rate of change in one part may depend on the rate in another, as sometimes occurs in biological organisms. The anthropologist's problem is to create a theory that figures out these complex interactive sequences and takes account of their history without losing anthropology's key ideas of culture and holism. Historical materialism may help to do this.

Let me take a risk and give an example here of a current change that will illustrate both this dynamism and the relationship between conflicts and change. We have seen, in the cafeteria, that most students voluntarily sit in racially and ethnically segregated areas. The seating pattern reflects the politico-economic forces that shape the whole culture. The United States has always contained many diverse ethnic and racial groups, but not until recently have these and others like them developed a consciousness of themselves as subcultures whose values and lifestyles are valid and meaningful. In the past, their inferior politico-economic position made them devalue their ways of life.

What conflicts, or contradictions, is this emergent phenomenon related to, and where is it going? The first place where Marxism looks for conflict is between classes, at their unequal control of resources and power. This inequality makes for a perpetual undercurrent of conflict and antagonism between the few in our society who own the means of production and dominate the places of power and the many who do not. Although wealth and power do not correlate absolutely, and there are degrees of wealth and political strength, nevertheless, over time, wealth brings power, and power wealth. This general conflict spawns those politico-economic forces that in turn create the subgroups and their accompanying ideologies.

These forces generate the contradiction we saw earlier. They assign people and groups to unequal social positions on the basis of immutable characteristics like race, culture or origin, or inherited wealth. In the United States, they also create an ideology that insists that individuals, and therefore whole groups, can change their lot if they are personally endowed or if they try hard enough. In other words, the myth of a classless society, envisioned in the slogan of "equal opportunity," masks the division of power that propels the nation's growth. If all are equal and all have equal opportunity, so the ideology goes, all can succeed and have only their individual selves to praise or blame for failing. This, then, is the dynamism of the conflict.

Lines of conflict are maintained, and power retained, not merely by brute force, but also by social and ideological means. Classes contain or are in-marrying, in-socializing groups that have a particular way of living, or life-style, and an ideology that justifies it. Part of this life-style is "high (elite) culture," or the appreciation of art, music, literature, and so on, which grows from and builds on the Western aesthetic tradition. Though in fact contingent on the politico-economic prerogatives of the upper class, until recently the liberal ideology of democratic capitalism saw it as the culture of the American nation-state, equal to all other cultures and accessible to all. If all its population did not live this life-style, it was because many of them (such as immigrants) did not know any better. The ideology (like much applied social theory, the formal version of ideology) therefore prescribed education, more and more of it, as a route not only to upward economic mobility but to the learning of American culture through the acquisition of "high culture."

In other words, the knowledge of traditionally revered art, literature, and philosophy, and the skills of writing and talking about them, had made up one common system of communication for one class. This system comprises one major kind of knowledge customarily provided by institutions of higher education. They thus taught shared use of space and time, as in attendance at concerts, the purchase of paintings, or the enjoyment of gourmet food and wine. "Elite culture" provided the social glue for the ruling class when they weren't working in their interlocked positions of power.

In Marx's terms, "the ideology of the ruling class" became "the ruling ideology" of the culture. Liberal arts education, like other socializing institutions elsewhere, functions in the United States to reproduce the society, particularly the class structure, by re-creating and reinforcing social and ideological structures. One component of this ideology has been "high culture." "High culture" functioned as a symbolic means to instill and validate a particular subcultural style of life, that of the ruling class. It ethnocentrically presented this style not only as one way of life, but as the best one, the one that would confer not merely honor, but also power on its bearers. It performed this function even when taught in public, land-grant colleges that were set up to educate the poor and the middle class.

The twentieth century saw the expansion of higher education, and therefore appreciation of "elite culture," to the children of European immigrants, and at the beginning of the second half of the century, to blacks and Latinos. This last expansion of the 1960s came on the tail end of the post–World War Two economic boom. It inflated hopes that indeed all could make it up and out of the working class. But as more people began this new emigration, more saw that although they might acquire the trappings of the upper class in a liberal arts college, its monetary or political power was not available. For college provides neither access to basic resources nor vocational training for salaried jobs. It never has, for the function of a liberal arts education is training not in parochial specialized skills, but in generalized learning, in the ability to create new questions and knowledge, and in an understanding of the masterpieces of one part of one cultural tradition.

At a particular historical point, then, some expressions of the basic contradiction emerged quite clearly, and this emergence took the form of an explosion of subcultures. The expansion provided room for the fissures within the underclass to widen and fragment into separate subcultural groups. The ideologies of the many groups crystallized, and in contrast, the upper-class culture emerged as merely another subculture, whose life-style was an alternative to those of people of color, white ethnics, gays, feminists, and geometrically increasing numbers of other groups. With the subsequent economic recession, upward mobility has lessened and the lines of mobility have become more tightly drawn. There is one cohesive upper class, and the differences within the underclass may seem disabling as each subgroup separately coalesces.

But as such circumstances change, so does the significance of already existing structures, institutions, and values. Their meaning, in other words, is historically contingent. The differences within the underclass may paradoxically be a source of power. The social bonds through which politico-economic power is activated are being created within each group on the basis of previously binding residential segregation and/or their developing ideologies, which also provide a way for the members of each group to discover themselves as individuals. The assertions and demands of the variegated subcultures, in eroding the uncritical reverence for the upper-class way of life and ideology, create competing models of living that function as guides for individuals. By demystifying "high culture," these models erode its intimidating symbolic value and pave the way for the discovery of its real value.

This is, in turn, transmitted by enculturation, particularly by college. Enculturation is supposed to make individuals accept their culture; free public college education, now only a memory in New York City, was a major way to enable immigrants to acculturate, or to learn their new culture. But in new circumstances, educational institutions may lay the basis for the creation of alternatives. The process is dialectical: As much, for example, as college departments ("ethnic studies"), or even government agencies based on the new subgroups may coopt the process of the creation of a lower-class power base, they also foster it. Its formation is facilitated by what high school and college teach. The skills of reading and writing make possible not just school learning, but the communication needed to hold political groups together. The theories and values of equality and intellectual liberation are not just objects of appreciation, but become aspirations that draw and direct action. The social skills of getting along with strangers and banding together with equals against authority become useful not just for manipulating authority in working life, as in school, but for fighting the persons and institutions in power. I think it is just this sort of process that partly accounts for the informal ethnic and racial segregation in the cafeteria.

Social change thus involves a subtle kind of cause, one with many dimensions. We usually think of a cause mechanically, as something (an origin) that occurs before a second thing and makes the second thing happen. But multifaceted cultural change and the multiple connections among parts of culture show that this idea is not adequate to the complexity of social reality. The causes of social phenomena do indeed precede them, but neither distinct events, nor things in themselves, can bring about changes from one to another social form. Events like war (really a series of events and processes) may precipitate social change, but they would be ineffective without the social system that made them and their effects possible.

This means that the system itself and its internal processes must be explained. To do this by going back in time to the causes of the capitalist system, for example, beyond that to the causes of the feudal system, and so on until the beginning of time, is ridiculous and unsatisfactory. There are no absolute points in time or space for the origin of cultures or of their parts. We tend to think there are only because we usually see the world in static and bounded units (as structural-functionalist theory does). We forget that our idea of a culture, or an institution, is merely an "as if," or heuristic, device, which allows us to analyze only some aspects of our world.

The explanation for social change lies in its unchanging processes. Change is ambiguous because each succeeding social forms descends from an earlier one, but its descent is brought about by conflicts that continually pull on it. The contradictions in ideology come in part from prior ideological systems and in part from social and economic conflict. The contradictions in institutional structure come in part from earlier form and in part from conflict. Socio-economic conflict comes in part from the contradictions among the principles of the re-production of culture of economy and social relations, and in part from conflicts between different economic systems; together, internal and external conflict force the economic system to change.

For example, although, in the long run, the system of production and its conflicts create the form and content of ideology, in the short run, production and ideology mutually influence one another. Thus, the belief of generations of immigrants and internally colonized people that education would give them power made them demand the general education that a developing economy was gradually beginning to require of its specialists. The present ubiquitous claims for practical, vocational training may be similarly successful. But like the earlier demands, they may not bring us what we want either, for they may limit us to what the class structure requires. Practical training is by definition narrow; to take control of one's life demands general knowledge. Our narrow expectation that parochial training will assure us this control comes from our position in the class conflict. But the contrast between our expectations and the reality, between the promises of the culturally shared ideology and what we actually got, also works its way into our consciousness and may eventually trigger fundamental changes not only in college education but in the society.

Theory and Fact

The theory one uses determines what one will see and therefore one's understanding of what one sees. Here I have discussed three alternatives. Perhaps a glance at their use of time and space can best summarize their variations: Structural-functionalism stays with a moment in time, structuralism to any and all time, or to eternity, and Marxism to a stretch of time delimited by the presence of a particular conflict. The first works with a fixed, particular context; the second slides easily among society, social group, individual, and back around again in no fixed order;

and the context of the third is defined by a particular type of relationship. Each of these theories is as natural and true as the other in the following way: A cafeteria does exist in a bounded place and when we are in it, we are there for a slice of time. The meanings it has for us are simultaneously particular, contrastive, and universal. And its institutional setting has a specific history and is connected to its past, present, and future by pervasive, inescapable processes. Each theory, as we have seen, has different implications for politics, individual action, and morality.

Overall, this presentation indicates that there is no dividing line between theory and fact. What is fact depends on how we think; class conflict is a fact for one theory, but not for another. Everyday wisdom has it that the validity of theories, their ability to tell the truth, depends on how well they predict or at least fit the facts. But it is clear that the canons of truth depend on what one wants to know, which in turn depends on one's theory, which, in its turn, depends on one's culture or position in it. An example of the influence of social position on understanding appeared in the final seminar reports on the cafeteria. Although each student used a different theory, nearly all their reports focused on the students. The only paper that studied the workers, as much as the students, did so because it took off from the Marxist theory of production. And neither I nor the seminar students noticed our unconscious bias until two years later when I first wrote this chapter. Our oversight reflected our positions in the academic structure, and illustrates the hidden difficulties in studying one's own culture.

However different their methodologies and explanatory power, these theories do share certain meta-theoretical premises that are essential if there is to be any social theory at all. All assume, first of all, that human behavior and cultural form are not random, but can be explained by general principles that we can infer from knowable data. If we cannot formulate such principles, it is not because they are nonexistent or forever hidden; it is because our methods and/or ideas are weak. A second premise is that all cultures can be explained by similar naturalistic principles that not only operate uniformly in the present, but also hold for the past and the future. Thus, when we attempt to explain past cultures or cultures other than our own, we do not seek a different set of principles for each. A corollary of this premise is the cornerstone of Western science, that "like cause" produces "like effect"; the processes of change are universal.

Finally, about the only other thing different schools of thought agree on is that one can't make anything up. One has to tell the truth as one sees it, but one must also say how one sees it. This brings up a final aspect of the problem of human truth. Unlike those of physical science, the subjects of social science can talk back and have their own view of society. Very often, people's views of their lives differ drastically from the observer's view. Indeed many readers of this chapter may have disagreed with everything I have said about their culture.

The American theorist, Marvin Harris, has drawn a formal and fundamental distinction between these two views. He calls the viewpoints of those who are observed the *emic* view, and that of the observer the *etic* view. Harris's distinction resembles the Marxist position that one should not necessarily trust people's views of themselves. In fact, structural-functionalism and structuralism also mistrust self-explanation by the observed, but they do not say this so clearly. Given my seminar's oversight, there is more than a shadow of a doubt about the reliability of the emic view.

In any event, Marxism is theoretically explicit on the subject: Since ideology is culturally conditioned, it is a datum and requires explanation. It does not suffice as an explanation of itself. Historical materialism proposes that explanation must come from elsewhere. And here is the problem: From where can it come? By its own premises, historical materialism is a product of its time and place. How is it to say that it is any more true than the false consciousness it seeks to explain?

Harris's position is vulnerable to the same criticism (although it does not label as false the consciousness of the observed). It is also vulnerable in that it cannot account for the origins and operation of consciousness and ideology. It holds that just as one cannot penetrate to the unconscious on which structuralism bases its theories, so one cannot know the consciousness, or subjectivity, of another person. Harris's concern, rather, is to develop an intersubjectively valid theory of, and method to describe, observable—i.e., visible and tangible—behavior. Etic anthropology (like Harris's determinist, Marxist, but nondialectical theory of cultural materialism) presumes that the observer describes culture using primary analytical units that are operationalized, such as the relation of people to objects in their environment. This procedure enables two different observers (subjectivities) to know what each other is talking about, and to produce comparable, intersubjectively understandable research on the same topics in different places. Although not all anthropologists follow Harris's method or agree with his theories, most now use his distinction, for it introduces order into a very confusing mass of data. Generally, when one presents ideas about a particular society, one distinguishes the etic ones from the emic ones. Thus, these concepts have entered the anthropological conceptual lexicon on a par with the concepts of structure and function.

Because of this disparity between emics and etics, and because of the influence of theory on fact, I decided not to focus on some exotic culture in this chapter. For, if I had chosen an institution like the Kula Ring of the Trobriand Islands, which includes in it economic exchange, power plays, sexual prohibitions, and religious beliefs, I would have had to describe it. In so doing, I would have had to choose one of its aspects to begin with and would thereby already have chosen, unbeknownst to the reader, a particular perspective from which to do so. Instead, I took something intuitively familiar, a cafeteria, which needs little description.

A friend of mine, when he was about eight years old, once asked his father why the sky was blue. His father replied with a question: "Do you want the short answer or the long one?" Through youth and inexperience my friend unfortunately asked for the long one, which lasted more than two hours. Culture, like the sky, requires the long explanation, for the short ones are neither complete nor satisfactory, even for children. It will make sense, then, if I say that this chapter just barely begins to approach the problems of cultural theory. The next three chapters will, in a sense, expand on this one; in them, I will not only examine the more explicit subject matter of anthropology, but also evaluate different ways of understanding it.

IV.

Separations and Connections: Kinship, Marriage, and Households

From Micro to Macro

This chapter is about the stuff of which soap operas and gossip are made—the niggling little bits of life in which women are said to be particularly interested and which secretly fascinate men. Centered in the traditional province of women, the household, these bits are bound up with the most mundane, yet most exciting events, customs, and institutions of any culture or life—the passage from birth to death; marriage and the family; sex and morality; friends, lovers, and kinfolk. Perhaps because these daily facts of life are the roots of our personal and social past, present, and future, and are, therefore, too intimate to discuss, they receive little scholarly attention outside of anthropology.

Now, academicians and intellectuals (and men) usually regard soap operas and what they portray as trivial. Some anthropologists share this cultural judgment. This is curious, for soaps present the kind of daily scene in which we anthropologists find ourselves in the course of doing our field research. Indeed, because we live with the people we study, we see, at first hand, how individuals grow, learn their culture, and live out their adult lives only in and through what Malinowski called "the imponderabilia of actual life" which he urged us to study. I use soap operas as one example in this chapter for much of what we observe happens in and near the household, partly because we often live with a family, as my husband and I did in Greece, and partly because many important events occur in the households of other cultures.

What I sometimes find tiresome about soap operas is not this prosaic material, but its repetition. Yet repetition of the same old themes reveals the nature of the subject matter: Soap operas are true to domestic life because the housewife's work never ends but constantly repeats itself; her world is often boring. Soap operas highlight the more interesting constants (love affairs instead of laundry), on the basis of which they create long drawn-out problems that enthrall us because real-life problems never end. In contrast, anthropology tries to bare these constants so as to understand what underlies them in turn. Soaps delight us by presenting a continual mystery; social science delights us by unraveling one.

What is the mystery? I said in Chapter I that to be human is to live with others. Simple enough, yet not so simple, because each individual spends a life with many different others, singly and in groups. The importance of different others waxes and wanes as people mature, change jobs, marry, or divorce. The frequency with which one's social affiliations change varies with the cultural forces or principles operating on one's life. But the mystery is how separate individuals manage to live together in one-to-one relations and in groups, how connected individuals manage to separate, and how these separations and connections pivot on the multiple dimensions each of us has as a social person. How, in other words, do two orders of phenomena, the individual and the social, integrate?

This returns us to a consideration of structural-functional theory: Since we can belong to different groups at the same time, our lives are shaped by overlapping principles that sometimes mesh and sometimes clash. The variegated relationships in which we participate create the many aspects of our social personalities. For example, "Somerset," a soap opera that I used to keep up with, told a story about Sam and his wife, Lahoma, who were in their late twenties and had an infant daughter. Sam was both a lawyer and president of Delaney Brands, a canning company that dominated the midwestern city of Somerset. Thus, he belonged to three groups: He was an *employee* of a company, a *member* of the bar (which made him a *professional*), and a *husband* in a family. Each of these aspects of his, or anyone's, social personality is called a status; technically, a *status* is a position in a social structure that defines one's rights and obligations, desires and expectations, in relation to other statuses in the structure. Each dimension of a status is connected to a corresponding dimension in someone else. Sam had a secretary, Crystal, because his status responsibilities as president required someone to type, answer the phone, etc.

Statuses may come into conflict between persons and within them. Although things ran quite smoothly for Sam and Crystal, they were more complicated for him and Lahoma, because he had multiple statuses in relation to her. In meeting the expectation that a *husband* earn the bread, Sam the *president* often worked late, making Sam the *husband* miss Lahoma's dinners; she, of course, got angry at his absences and he was annoyed at her anger. His statuses of *president* and *husband* were out of synchronization, straining his relationship with Lahoma. Furthermore, since the rights and obligations between two corresponding statuses like *husband* and *wife* interlock, Lahoma experienced stress as *wife*.

The acting out of a status is called a *role*, a concept borrowed from the theater. One behaves differently in the same status depending on the statuses of the others with whom one interacts. Lahoma, for example, had role conflicts as *wife:* She did very well as *housewife* (and *mother*), but since she was not overly bright, she failed dismally as a *corporate wife* in entertaining her upwardly mobile husband's colleagues. Sam already felt that she was unsympathetic to the needs of his work and unappreciative of his fulfillment of the breadwinner role, and her ignorance of urbane conversation aggravated his now guilty anger. Her despair deepened her sense of inferiority, particularly in the presence of Crystal, a sophisticated New Yorker. The result was inevitable: Crystal, secretly working for the Syndicate which wanted to take over Delaney Brands, had already begun to seduce Sam, and now had her chance to succeed. He, in turn, had ready excuses for his now more frequent absences; his role conflicts, of course, also intensified.

Such harmonious and acrimonious reciprocal relations between statuses form the framework of the social structure, on the basis of which we live out our hopes and disappointments. Sometimes, conflicts among relationships produce action that reduces or eliminates discord and realigns the statuses. In Somerset, Crystal's duplicity was eventually discovered. Lahoma then left Sam to return to their hometown. Sam next quit his job to follow and win her back. With the problem resolved, that story ended, and a new one, already begun, assumed the main dramatic focus.

Soap operas rarely depict relationships with unresolved conflicts, and this is where they are not true to life; in this sense, soaps reveal themselves for what they are, a part of our cultural ideology that portrays our wishes and not our real lives. An ethnographer studying this culture would see that most people live in relationships that contain built-in discord. For example, Sam's company employed many blue-collar workers, but none of them appeared on the screen. We may guess, however, that they and the owners of the company (and therefore the management who represent the owners) disagreed about certain things. For example, as in any company, both employer and employees would want to make a living. Employees frequently feel that they are not getting paid enough and usually they aren't. Their interests conflict with those of the employer and management, including Sam, who want to keep costs down so as to keep profits high. On the one hand, then, both want the whole enterprise to continue; on the other, both want to get more in a situation in which only one can get more. All this then would hum along as love affairs rose and fell and the laundry got done every week.

Separations and Connections

Status and role provide a microlevel view of social relations in contrast to the macroview of structure taken in the last chapter. Instead of starting from the top down, as in analyzing a cafeteria, college, or economic system, we look from the bottom up, as we would if we were to analyze relations between employer and employee, or among students. We then build on *dyadic relations,* i.e., those between two statuses, to describe the framework of the larger structures, or institutions, within which statuses exist and roles are acted out.

In other words, dyadic analysis is a way of beginning with the part rather than the whole. Dyadic analysis also is more personal, for its data are like our everyday experience, which is the kind of intimate experience anthropologists have in the field. Firsthand interaction with others' daily lives provides the evidence to test our theories and the data from which we construct our understanding of higher-level institutions like the family, corporations, and class structure, in the context of which everyday lives are lived.

Let us move on (or back) to some of these higher-level structures. Institutions vary in the degree to which their organization is explicit. A corporation, for example, has a physical plant, written rules, a chart of organization detailing specialized tasks, and manifest functions that are quite specific. In social-scientific terms, it is a *formal institution,* although it also has its informal aspect, as proverbially appears around the water cooler. The family, in contrast, while not exactly an informal organization, has no written set of rules or publicly codified apportionment of jobs; it has multiple functions and its relationships are diffusely emotional. Truly *informal institutions* are groups such as bowling leagues or bridge clubs, whose existence depends on the continual and relatively voluntary leisure-time participation of their members.

Family, school, corporations, bowling leagues, and the other institutions coexist, their relationships determined by the organizing principles of the society. Let us look, for example, at the connections between families and bowling leagues (or bridge clubs). Our families are small, based on a sexually exclusive tie of monogamy between an adult male and female, and on obligations to feed, clothe, house, and educate children. Implicitly, this *nuclear* family is also expected to provide adults with all the social interaction and emotional gratification they need. Its absolute inability to do so is a deeply buried fact that burdens family members who are supposed to pretend to themselves and others that they don't know it.

The problem then is how adults can find contact with outsiders without destroying the precarious psychosocial balance of their familial ties. One of the status obligations of family members is to maintain the family itself. Fragile, it provides few links for external adult relationships and is particularly vulnerable to intense dyadic connections. Highly charged single-sex friendships, just as much as heterosexual ones, threaten the tightly interdependent nuclear family, not so much because they suggest tabooed homosexuality (an idea usually not even imagined) as because they bare people's need for contact with others. Children, in contrast, can have many friends, for their lives are those of play, not like the serious adult routine of running a household.

One solution is the weekly night out with "the boys" or "the girls." An informally organized group puts neither marital nor parental fidelity into question. Its manifest functions, like bowling or bridge, cover its latent functions of escape and companionship. Bowling leagues and bridge clubs also have built-in limits: Since everyone has to go home at the end of the evening, the intensity of the ties they create is limited in time and space, and thus the diffuse intensity of the family is protected.

But when leagues and clubs take on a life of their own, as they tend to do, they are taken more seriously as threats. The principles of family togetherness and team loyalties compete; the conflicting needs for heterosexual and monosexual companionship strain both institutions. Family and informal club clash when the night out lasts until 3 A.M., or spills over into weekend bridge marathons, and when the nuclear family rules out an extra beer after the game or an international match-point tournament. The members of each regard one another with mutual hostility, as the person they share suffers conflicting loyalties. In order to carry out marital and familial obligations, the person will quit the extracurricular activities, and play a role of denying the importance of the bowling league, in order to affirm that of the family.

The preeminent value that our culture places on the nuclear family reveals a major principle of social connectedness and separation, the economic and therefore social independence of the nuclear family. The family's inward pull is a force that separates people in similar statuses and social groups from one another. As we saw in Chapter III, just because people are employees, they (quite reasonably) do not necessarily owe primary loyalties to one another: Since one's employer hires and fires according to his own needs and desires, and since all employees are subject to this same unreliable dependency, one's co-workers can never be one's last resort. One's bridge companions are likewise not reliable; they are employees or married to employees, and they too are insecure, relying only on their primary or family relationships.

Of course, no nuclear family is really independent, since each depends on being employed by someone else; this dependence, however, is not accompanied by any security. In contrast, in cultures where survival is not left to the needs of an employer, obligations tend to be spread more widely. Each person or family relies on a larger group of people, and the domestic scene consequently includes more people. Although individual loyalties there grow, like ours, from shared statuses and group memberships, the principles or forces that govern their connections and separations are different from ours. We will examine some of them in this chapter.

Relationships among institutions, such as I have just discussed, form the structure of a society. A society, then, does not consist just of "a group of people who are interdependent," but of particular organizations of people in groups or institutions that are themselves organized with respect to one another in determine ways. A society is thus defined by the relations among its institutions, and among the statuses within them. A society may contain structural diversity; it is not necessarily a homogeneous entity, nor are its institutions continuously uniform. Family form, for example, may differ from region to region, or ethnic group to ethnic group. But the principles that link groups, institutions, and regions together into a functioning structure enable us to talk about this or that society.

Admittedly, this is a qualitative definition, and it leaves room for dispute about when we know that we have found *a* society. Some theorists prefer harder definitions. For example, one might begin by calculating the statistical frequency of interaction among people, locating the boundaries of a society at the point where the number of interactions reaches some low point. But without interpretation, statistics are only numbers, just as a computer is nothing without the human intelligence to use it. To conclude, for example, that Alaska and Wyoming are not part of the same society because their inhabitants don't meet would be to ignore concrete connections like the Alaska oil pipeline, which has created both great distress and many jobs and which is itself a product of more abstract connections, like the economic principles that govern both states. Furthermore, if the boundaries of cultures may be transnational, may not also those of a society? The pipeline, after all, runs through Canada. Jet-setters and managers of multinational corporations spend much more time with foreign nationals than with members of the working class of their own society. I suppose that to push things this far is to risk emptying our concepts of meaning, yet I think we must take the risk, in order to prevent our being blinded to a reality which is ever-changing. For example, do the pipeline and jet transport presage the emergence of a world society?

IN AND OUT OF FAMILY AND SOCIETY

If one watches soap operas long enough, one will see unlimited permutations of the same old fascinating problems. In the melodramatic view, such problems come from troubled individuals who mysteriously, almost randomly, appear on the scene. But in the social-scientific view, the problems come from social structure; each of us, in one culture, encounters similar problems not because people never change, but because the conditions in which we live are similar. The structures of our social lives constitute one set of such conditions. Structure has an essential characteristic well captured by soap opera's repetitiveness: It will continue to exist despite the passage of individuals through it. Separate and different from the individuals who occupy its statuses, it is not, of course, a Platonic form, floating above us; it needs people to keep it going. For example, the structure of a college remains the same, even as a whole new group of people (freshmen) enters every year, and a whole other group (the senior class) leaves, as faculty, staff, and administrators are hired and fired. The same principle holds for the nuclear family: Even as members grow up, move away, and die, the institution of the nuclear family continues to exist; barring any major change in society at large, other people will form new groups with the same status and role relations. And even if we have never belonged to a bowling league or a bridge club, even if some disappear every day, a club is a club.

Particular families do, of course, fade away and die. One of my former professors tells of the student who wrote in an exam essay that the nuclear family is the sole institution that is created only to disappear.* In our society, the nuclear family begins to break up as children grow up and move out. This is expected, encouraged behavior. Indeed, one reason that the adult taboo on external dyadic ties does not apply to children is that their friendships are a major bridge by which people can leave the *family of orientation* into which they are born and set up their own *family of procreation,* or, at least, their own independent household. Nevertheless, the process can induce tension. Even though the changes through which each family goes on its way to dissolution are prefigured in its structure, they often produce explosions.

For example, parents' inability to accept the prerequisite changes in their children formed the theme of another Somerset story. Rex and Laura, a middle-aged couple, had an only son, Tony, about twenty-one, who loved and married Ginger. Laura, a very possessive, psychotic mother, kept insisting that Tony and

* The professor gave the student an *A* on the strength of that insight and didn't finish reading the exam.

Ginger come to live with her and Rex. In fact, she hated Ginger, and was continually nasty to her, never having been able to adjust to Tony's adulthood. When Ginger became pregnant, Laura accused her of having had an affair with Virgil, who was an employee of both Delaney Brands and the Syndicate. He had assaulted Ginger once, but she managed to escape rape and the child was indeed Tony's. Following Tony's independent refusal to believe her accusations, Laura killed herself. Somerset has also shown the reverse, as when Heather, a wild teenager, could not accept the decision of Eve, her widowed mother, to re-wed, and spread rumors which ruined Eve's engagement to a wealthy older man.

With each such change, as the birth of a child or the death of a spouse, the rights and obligations of each status change. New relationships may be added (Laura gained a hated daughter-in-law) and old ones take on new content (Eve had to go to work to support Heather when her husband died). The original nuclear family disappears when its remaining members have died, or become unable to care for themselves. They became incorporated into another institution, such as a child's own family, or a nursing home. These changes, which happen in every kind of family, are called "the domestic (or developmental) cycle." Like the transitions from child to adult which I discussed in Chapter III, these alterations in status relations are repetitive, not innovative. They are anticipated by socializing admonitions like, "I hope that someday you'll have children so they'll make you suffer like you're making me suffer." The cycle is subject to the principles of the society in which it occurs. For example, the departure of children from the North American nuclear family (Tony's setting up his own home) is consistent with the family's independence, the ideals of individualism, and the definition of adulthood in terms of separation from one's parents.

Children, of course, don't always become adults when they marry, but they are supposed to. The ideologies of social institutions often consist of moral systems that state what people "ought" to do. The contradictions between such ideals and how social institutions actually operate are usually crucial points of strain in the society, and people are very threatened when they are pointed out. Soaps, in fact, play on this tension. The distinction between ideal and real culture or structure, one anthropological view of this discrepancy, is too superficial. In the first place, *ideal* culture has different facets. The nuclear family, for example, appears in advertisements as two healthy, fun-loving parents on a carefree picnic with their attractive son and daughter. Soap operas wipe out that saccharine harmony, but they also implicitly support another widely shared ideal of family structure: Marital relations include sexual fidelity, love, companionship, a division of labor, benevolently protective male domination, and grudgingly nurturant female submission. Parents give children love, care, education, and authority; children give back love, obedience, intelligence, companionship, and care for parents when those parents are aged and enfeebled. Ideals about the sibling relationship are less precise, but include at least loyal friendship and jealous rivalry.

Yet such factors as class, ethnicity, and religion, for example, influence how these relations actually work and therefore what ideals people have. For example, although the dominant ideal of the marital division of labor is for the husband to bring home the bacon and the wife to cook it, it is often the woman who works and cooks, when the man can't or won't. Or, perhaps, both must work in order to make ends meet, or both want to work in order to maintain self-esteem. Even where they follow the ideal, some people might prefer that the husband give his wife a portion of his paycheck as her household allowance; others might think it best for him to give her the whole thing and for her to give him an allowance; and still others might pool their money completely.

When we move on to *real* culture, or structure, our first question is, According to whom? The ethnographer? The husband? The wife? We have returned to the methodological problem of emics and etics, which is also one of insiders and outsiders, and of the sociology of knowledge. For example, the preceding description of the nuclear family, as I, a member of the culture, see it, assumed that the family stays together until the founding spouses die. But an outside observer might take this description not as truth but as ideology and might look beyond it and find that the North American nuclear family goes another route: One in three marriages ends in divorce. Even though most divorces are followed by remarriage, a generous proportion of households will consist, at any given time, of one spouse and the children, and of spouses living alone. Because of the high divorce rate, the outsider might expect the insiders to include divorce as an alternative developmental phase of the family. But since, before marriage, most of us do not expect to divorce or be divorced, and since our ideology denigrates divorce, the outsider also will question this discrepancy between our behavior and our conscious expectations.

Like most ideologies, our own takes its underlying principles and our behavior for granted; it frames our view of ourselves as eyes frame vision. This is why outside observers might very often, though not always, see some things more clearly than members of the culture, who can be befuddled by ideology into taking the ideal for the real. On the other hand, insiders have greater intuitive knowledge about how their social structure actually works, even if they can't say why. If their view of marriage, for example, is that it is supposed to last forever, this implies that there might be economic and social supports for the ideology, if not for the institution, and that the observer should seek them out. Emic data help, then, because their hunches about what's going on come from a lifelong intimacy with a culture, not all of which is formalized by social-scientific knowledge.

In this sense, everyone in every culture is an anthropologist or sociologist. Given that everyone therefore has a theory about society that more or less works, it might seem superfluous to have specialists make up more theories. There is, however, a difference between everyday observers and specialists, and it is precisely that between insiders and outsiders. The former assume the underlying principles, the latter make them explicit and perforce question them. Insiders, immersed in the structure, do not always see or question either its bases or its contradictions. The outsider is a professional skeptic. She/he knows that there are other principles that inform societies elsewhere, that societies may rest on contradictory or at least heterogeneous principles, and that societies must change, and so she/he wonders why societies are the way they are.

The interplay between theories and data thus appears once again. My analysis of our own culture, for example, rests on a combination of (1) what I observe with my own outsider's training (i.e., etics), (1) what I experience as an insider (emics), and (3) what others have observed and think about it (etic and emic). Is all this, I try to keep the ideal and the real separate. Our reports of other cultures try to do the same, and likewise depend on an interplay between etics and emics.

Of course, each of us is also an outsider; at times, we all feel distant from our culture. This is why soap operas work: By portraying people who are totally absorbed in their domestic lives, they replicate our cultural immersion. By letting us observe their absorption, they replicate our occasional skeptical detachment. The disciplines of social science bring out and refine the potential for this detachment, so that they almost constitute a specialist's way of life, just as athletic training hones natural and learned skills of coordination. Perhaps, then, the difference between social scientist and social person is also the difference between professional athlete and weekend ball player, bowler, or bridge player.

KINSHIP IS NOT BIOLOGICAL

Like people of all cultures, we are most deeply immersed in our family lives. Like people in soap operas, we don't go much beyond the domestic scene (although soaps, like our lives, are most interesting when they do). But because the domestic scene is so familiar and commonsensical to everyone, it also seems pompous to invent special terms, or jargon, to talk about it. In anthropology, we have a few technical terms, but for the most part, we use ordinary English. Because of this, people often infer, incorrectly, that the ideas that the words convey are the familiar ones, when in fact they are not.

For example, let us take one of the major principles of social organization and family life, *kinship*. To us, in our language and culture, kinship means relationships by "blood"; our kin are those to whom we are connected by biology and procreation, by sexual intercourse and the exchange and transformation of genetic material. A mother and her biological child exemplify an elementary and universal kinship relationship. But, in fact, even in our own culture, kinship includes more: If a man and woman adopt a child, they behave as if it were their own "flesh and blood"; they are not its biological parents, but are its "parents" nonetheless. We have "aunts" and "uncles" who are not connected to us through genes, like the spouses of our biological aunts and uncles, or close friends of our parents.

Kinship, then, may have nothing whatever to do with biology, just as, we shall shortly see, marriage may have nothing to do with love. Kinship is a universal way of connecting and separating people, based on a biological ground plan that it does not necessarily follow very closely. It is a way to reckon relationships based on a combination of considerations: biology, marriage, and other bonds culturally (emically) considered to be like these first two. Kinship systems vary considerably and sometimes take forms for which we have no conventional terms. We therefore have not only to invent new terms, but also to redefine old ones, as I have just done for *kinship*.

Like all principles of social structure, kinship functions simultaneously on several levels: It links individuals to each other in specific statuses and roles; it forms groups and institutions; and, by contrasting one kind of social person with another, it explains how and why people do what they do. In our culture, kinship is nearly identical with the domestic scene, or family, which themselves imply several different things: the monogamous nuclear family; a nuclear family with a coresident grandparent or two; "blood" (or consanguineal) relatives as against all others; consanguines and in-laws (or affines) as opposed to all nonfamily. However, in other cultures, kinship includes and goes beyond these domestic groups to form the basis for the organization of economic, political, and religious institutions as well.

Let us look at the kinship system of an African people, the Nuer of the Sudan, who were studied by E. E. Evans-Pritchard, a British social anthropologist, during 1930–37. Although the information dates from those years, and the Nuer have changed since then, I shall use the present tense, following the anthropological custom of "the ethnographic present." Nuer reckon kinship by *patrilineal descent. Descent* refers to the connection across generations; its prototype is the biological relation between parent and child: The child is descended from the parent. *Patrilineal* means the counting of descent through males only.*

From the point of view of any individual Nuer, then, one's kin are all those people, male or female, to whom one can trace a connection through males. One is related to one's siblings because they are descended from the same male—one's father. One then moves on to one's father's father so as to include all of his descendants, i.e., his sons (one's father's brothers) and his daughters (one's father's sisters). One can continue to one's father's father's father, and so on. From the top down, it appears that relatives are all those who have descended through males from a common male ancestor; they are members of the same *patriline.* Those to whom one is connected through female relatives constitute a different sort of person. One's mother is a relative, but her father, mother, siblings, etc., who are connected to one by a woman, are not the same kind of relative as are one's father's father and father's brother. One's father's sister is related to one through a male, through one's father, and is therefore a female patrilineal relative. But although she belongs to one's patriline, her children do not; they belong to the patriline of her husband (i.e., of their father), as will the children of one's own sister.

Kinship forms social structure by assigning people to groups and aligning groups with functions. For example, among the Nuer, patrilineal descent creates the groups, or *patrilineages,* in which people live and work. Such a group might contain, for example, a man and wife, two sons and their spouses, and the sons' own married sons and unmarried daughters. This lineage is the functional equivalent of our nuclear family, but it is also more. It

* *Matrilineal* is the counting of descent through females only, as the people of the Trobriand Islands do; I discuss this below and in Chapters V and VI.

forms a separate hamlet within a village, with each constituent nuclear family having its own house, and it is *corporate:* The individual members hold property in common and cannot dispose of it without group consensus. Usually, the eldest male manages property and interlineage relations on behalf of the group. The group behaves toward the outside and is treated by others as if it were an individual, just as a modern corporation is, by legal fiction, a person. When the eldest male dies, his position of trustee will be succeeded to by his eldest son—unless the latter is too young, in which case the deceased's eldest male relative will temporarily take over. In either case, the corporation will go on.

Nuer kinship can also structure larger residential units: A local community or village may consist entirely of one patrilineage, but usually it contains one main lineage to which other lineages are attached by marriage. For example, let us say that one of the married sons in a corporate patrilineage has quarreled with his father and brother and does not wish to live with them any longer. He may then give up his property and take his wife and children to the village of a married sister. She will get him accepted as a member of her community, whose core members are the patrilineal kinsfolk of her husband. Her brother is now living with his affines, and both siblings' children live amongst *cognatic* relatives, i.e., those to whom they can trace both consanguineal and affinal links. Cognatic relationships thus are potential means to form a community.

So far, we see that Nuer kinship forms domestic, economic, and residential units, recruits people to separate groups, and thereby distinguishes them from one another. Kinship can also function to organize social behavior between people in the same society who neither live together nor know one another. Lineages can expand to include large numbers of people by going further back in time; one has only to add to the ancestors from whom one traces descent, e.g., from one's grandfather to great-grandfather and so on, to include more people. A Nuer lineage with a depth of four or five generations is a *minimal* lineage, and is included within a *minor* lineage of greater generation-depth; minor lineages are segments of *maximal* lineages, which are parts of *major* lineages.

Once one goes beyond four or five generations, the forebears are, of course, no longer living. Since one must count ten to twenty generations back to get to the common ancestor of the most inclusive (major and maximal) lineages, names are often forgotten and exact links are obscured. At a certain point, actual relations between kinfolk are forgotten; people still asert, or stipulate that they are kin, but cannot demonstrate the genealogical links. Such a group, which is formally identical with a lineage, is called a *clan.* Although some Nuer clans are themselves thought to descend from an even more shadowy common male ancestor, there is no more encompassing structure beyond the clan level.

This very ambiguity permits lineality to connect people who don't know one another. The 200,000 Nuer are divided into well over a dozen tribes sharing a common language and identity as Nuer. The Nuer also identify with their tribe itself, which morally obliges its members to unite for warfare and feuds. Each tribe, with its own name and territory, contains one dominant clan and lesser lineages within it. A tribe can also contain, however, members of more than one clan and, therefore, more than one lineage, so that tribes can share lineages. This comes about because, as we have just seen, corporate lineages sometimes split up. Quarrrels and other events may, over the years, have scattered patrilineal kin all over the 30,000 square miles of Nuerland. At birth, then, each individual joins a group of actual or presumed patrilineal kin (*patrikin*), some of whom coreside and some of whom compose a network of kin dispersed within a large population. When people travel, or migrate seasonally as the Nuer do, they usually set up temporary camps with members of this network. Kinship thus unites Nuer from different tribes, and therefore all Nuer, on a personal basis, for it is both an abstract principle and a part of an individual's personal identity. Nuer patrilineality establishes the way two individuals are to behave with one another; the rights and duties between two people with the status of patrikin means that they must offer each other their homes, hearths, and food. Thus, in Nuer society, people who don't know each other but have a similar status do, in fact, share interests and a common basis for interaction. This contrasts with our society, where we can trust only our immediate family and must work to build relationships with strangers. Nuer society contains no strangers, in our sense of people with whom no given basis for interaction exists and with whom we therefore, awkwardly, don't know how to behave.

Kinship also serves political functions. In conjunction with the principle of territory, it provides each tribe, and therefore all Nuer, with a source of cohesion for the concerted efforts of larger groups. Nuer communities are organized into geographical districts, or *sections* of increasingly inclusive size. The smallest are tertiary sections; these are combined into secondary ones, which in turn compose primary ones, which, finally, form a tribe. Each of these sections bears the name of its dominant lineage and has a sentiment of identity and its own territory, which is included within the territory of the next higher section. The smaller the section, the stronger one's sense of identification and loyalty; one's allegiance to the tribe becomes crucial only in time of war. The tribe thus consists of patrikin who are geographically organized on intertwined kinship and territorial principles.

The tribe is a political unit: It controls territory and therefore the relations between territorially organized sections, as well as between it and other tribes. The tribe adjudicates disputes through the institution of the *leopard-skin chief*, an office that men of certain lineages inherit. This man arbitrates when, for example, someone from one section has killed a member of a second and has refused to pay the required blood-money of cattle to the victim's family. But this ritual chief has no enforcing power; he can only coax, cajole, and, if disobeyed, level curses on the recalcitrants. His authority comes from the fact that he is a sacred person, not from the power of wealth or physical force, for neither he nor his lineage is better off or necessarily stronger than any others. Politics, then, does not necessarily involve intratribal power. The Nuer recognize leaders only in war. The tribe and its sections therefore have no formal governmental structure.

Daily law and order are achieved by structural checks and balances: Kinship and territory divide and balance loyalties, and thereby maintain daily continuity in tribal and Nuer-wide relations. They do this by a metaphor: Territorial groups are seen as descent groups. Although the territorial units to which the individual Nuer owes primary loyalty are based only partly on a core patrilineage, the Nuer often speak of communities as if all villagers belonged to one patrilineage. Their ideology thus both mirrors and distorts the material reality. Though all Nuer know that territorial units actually contain cognatic kin, they phrase the relationships within sections and tribes in terms of kinship. Thus, when two adjacent communities have a dispute, each individual sides with his or her section, rationalizing the choice on the basis of kinship loyalty. But the two local communities rarely come to blows, because, in reality, residents of one may have kin in the other. The system automatically limits intercommunity fighting, because those elders with kin in both camps will vociferously argue against any actual violence.

Kinship ideology temporarily submerges the territorial principle only when fighting breaks out between tribes or between the Nuer and other peoples. In the latter case, one simply identifies with the dominant lineage of one's primary section and follows representatives of minimal through maximal lineages; in other words, one goes into battle as a member of one's tribe on the basis of ever more inclusive kinship segments. Since all Nuer tribes are thought of as being patrilineally related, the kinship metaphor provides an unambiguous way of uniting thousands of people. All the Nuer can be called up to fight in an instant, because the order of loyalties and of battle is clear.

An ideology of patrilineal descent can even make Nuer out of non-Nuer. The cultural environment of the Nuer includes other African peoples, as well as the British colonists who permitted Evans-Pritchard's study. Evens-Pritchard estimates that at least half the population of most Nuer tribes are descended from one of these peoples, the Dinka. Their territory encircles one-half of Nuerland, and the Dinka's traditions, economy, and language resemble the Nuer's. Both recognize this fact. However, they also are traditional enemies, raiding each other's cattle every year or so. When they engage in warfare, the Nuer win consistently, because the Dinka's social structure lacks the organizational efficiency of the Nuer's all-encompassing lineage-territorial system.

After winning, the Nuer absorb the Dinka by marrying them and/or by revising kinship history. At first, the conquered Dinka have a lower rank, but in most tribes their children become equal to other Nuer and assimilate by marrying in. Sometimes Dinka can establish independent lineages that over the generations come to be thought of as Nuer, as follows: Either Nuer and Dinka jointly invent a myth linking the male ancestor of the Dinka lineage to the male ancestor of a Nuer clan, or, if a Dinka man marries a Nuer woman, they temporarily suspend the patrilineal rules. The descendants name her as their founder and her patrikin will agree to accept them as members of the patrilineage, even though the linking relative is only a female. Kinship thus functions to incorporate even biologically unrelated members of one culture into another and, in so doing, provides a remarkably simple way of managing conquered people and territory. The boundaries of biological kinship are as easily crossed as are those of societies or cultures.

Marriage Is Not About Love

Structurally, though not necessarily in terms of personal feelings, patrilineal descent creates a closed group of people, distinct from other similarly organized, but separate groups in the society. Patrilineal descent can do this because it reckons through only one sex or *line*. It is one variety of *unilineal* descent. The other variety is *matrilineal* descent, which reckons through females only.

Unilineal descent not only places people in actual groups, but also, like other systems of relationship, communicates something about them: In saying that all those within one lineage are the same kind of person, its ideology simultaneously states that they differ from others. One dimension of its meaning has to do, for example, with shared residence, inheritance, and so on. Another has to do with marriage. Unilineages usually do not permit their members to marry one another; they practice *exogamy*, or marriage out of the group. Descent and marriage are, then, opposite sides of the kinship coin. Exogamic prescriptions create additional relationships between descent groups.

Like descent ties, marriages are important connecting links in any kinship system. For example, in Nuer villages, they forge the social framework and enforce the public order by creating the cognatic ties that both populate communities with a mixture of kin and constitute the basis for the solution of intervillage or sectional disputes. As in most cultures, marriage connects separate groups within one generation, in contrast to descent, which connects people across generations. But, in so doing, marriage also maintains the lineal descent groups. The continuation of the descent group requires procreation, which usually is legitimized ceremonially: A wedding announces publicly that two people are eligible to form a new unit within the society.

Like descent, marriage is multifunctioned. Among the Yanomamö, who live deep in the Amazon tropical forest in Brazil and Venezuela, marriage actually serves the political and organizational functions that are served by descent among the Nuer. According to N. Chagnon, the American anthropologist who has been studying the Yanomamö since 1963, Yanomamö villages contain two or three separate patrilineages linked to each other by marriage. The patrilineages are organized into nuclear families, each having its own food supply and territory within the village's territory. For as yet unexplained reasons, these villages are continually at war with each other, and subject to constant and unexpected raids. Survival requires intervillage alliances. But, unlike the case of the Nuer, patrikin in different villages rarely join together for any enterprise. Instead, males, who carry out warfare, must create alliances with men of other lineages in different villages by arranging marriages for them. Thus unrelated men can become allied by providing each other with wives.

Marriage, then, is a political institution, and the negotiations for it, coupled with its repercussions, make up the basis for the currents of daily Yanomamö life. Brittle descent ties, particularly between brothers, constitute the structural reason that men must seek support outside their lineage. This fragility is reinforced by warfare-produced patterns of socialization which teach males to compete pugnaciously for prestige and, since prestige depends on controlling women, for women. A man demonstrates his power by arranging the marriages of his sisters and daughters; he and his brothers, and their father, compete for the right to dispose of these women. A man also gets power by marrying several women himself; the Yanomamö practice *polygyny*, the marriage of one man to more than one woman.* Since he must marry outside his lineage, and since there aren't all that many neighboring marriageable women available,** he and his brothers become rivals for potential wives. This generates mistrust and weakens the sibling relationship.

In contrast, the relationship between men of different lineages is potentially amicable, because, as the Yanomamö see it, they don't directly compete for the same women. In fact, they see themselves as cooperating, since they often agree to provide one another with wives. Each finds one for the other among his own sisters, daughters, or other female patrilineal relatives. This *brother-sister exchange* establishes a personal bond between the two men, which, by extension, also links their nuclear families and, less strongly, their fellow villagers. The marriage tie obliges the parties to aid each other in war. If one village is routed by an enemy, the allied village is supposed to give them shelter and garden plots until they can set up a new village. The relationship, however, is tense, because only the actual brothers-in-law are

* The reverse, the marriage of one woman to more than one man, is called *polyandry; polygamy* simply means plural marriages of any type.

** This shortage is due to polygyny, with older men having more wives than younger men, and to female infanticide, the selective killing of unwanted infant females.

allied. The political bond is less immediately compelling for the other men in the host village, who will have contracted their own marriage ties with still other patrilineages and villages to whom their own loyalties go.

Marriage continues to play a political role over time. To solidify their shaky alliances, the original brothers-in-law encourage their children to marry each other, practicing what is called a *positive* marriage rule. That is, in addition to the *negative* exogamic rule not to marry within the lineage, the Yanomamö also want to marry particular kinds of people; they prefer that the children of a brother and a sister marry. A man can give his daughter to the son of his sister and brother-in-law, and find a wife for his own son from among their daughters, or from among other women whom his brother-in-law controls. If this practice continues over three or four generations, it promotes many marriages and therefore a tighter alliance between the two lineages.

Fraternal rivalry, brother-in-law solidarity, and multiple marriages create a structure of alliance that eventually weakens the original lineal relationship between brothers. The descent tie, in other words, begins to fall apart, and disintegrates when the brothers' natal village must split up. This happens because continual warfare and, perhaps, relatively limited food production (the Yanomamö raise a few tropical crops and hunt game) force villages to move from time to time. When they do so, they frequently fission along descent lines; each brother joins his brother-in-law to form a new village, which will again consist of two or three affinally linked lineages. The original lineages of the first village will then be dispersed.

What, however, if there is an accident of biology, and a man has no sisters to swap, or a woman no brothers to swap her? Does the whole structure of kinship and marriage collapse? No, because, as we saw in the previous section, kinship is only partly biology. It is also social structure and, of more importance here, metaphor. It is language as well as action and is therefore expressed in words that classify people into groups and relationships. The Yanomamö system of kinship terminology provides men with "sisters" and sisters with "brothers" even if they lack biological siblings of the opposite sex.

Let us begin with the Yanomamö's kinship terms for the people of one's parents' generation, for then we can see the logic of their terminological system. One refers both to one's biological father and to one's father's brother by the same term. Likewise, one's mother and her sister receive the same term. Thus, whereas we, in our culture and language, think that only one person can fit the category of "father," the Yanomamö include at least two, father and father's brother. It is the same with the category mother.

Such *classificatory* kinship terms do not mean that the Yanomamö do not know who their biological fathers and mothers are. They do, just as most of us, and most people in all cultures, do. The application of the same kinship terms to two different people communicates not that they are not individuals (like everyone everywhere, each Yanomamö has a personal name), but that they are the same kind of social person and that one relates similarly to both. Presumably, this is what we say by classifying two different people, e.g., father's sister and mother's sister, as "aunt" or mother's brother and father's brother as "uncle." Among the Yanomamö, if one calls two women "mother," then one treats both like a mother, and both of them treat one like a daughter or son.

People are classified together not only because of their status-role similarities, but also because of their shared differences from others. The terms reflect the nature of human perceptions, which I discussed in Chapter III; we perceive by contrast, and classify things as similar if they differ from something else in the same way. Among the Yanomamö, one's mother and mother's sister, for example, are a different kind of social person from one's father's sister; though all three are similar because they are females of the same generation, the first two differ in the same way from the father's sister, who contrasts with them because she belongs to a different lineage. Likewise, father and father's brother belong to one lineage, the mother's brother to another.

Kinship terms thus signify group membership as well as one-to-one relations.

The kinship terms create both additional siblings and additional spouses. It follows from the logic of terminological principles that the children of one's "fathers" (father's brothers) and "mothers" ("mother's sisters) will be one's "brothers" and "sisters." Indeed, one has even more siblings, for the Yanomamö apply these kinship categories to everyone in their lineages: All the women of one's own generation in one's lineage are one's classificatory "sisters," all the men one's "brothers." (And in the same way, one's parents have more of their own same-sex "siblings," providing one with even more siblings.) Thus, the Yanomamö male has more women to control, although, by the same token, he has more "brothers" to compete with.

But, by the same token, he has more potential wives and brothers-in-law. For Yanomamö terms classify the children of one's mother's brother and of one's father's sister as either potential spouses or potential siblings-in-law. They are marriageable because their lineages differ from one's own, since their fathers are in different lineages from one's own father. But not only are they eligible, they are preferred spouses. For, in marrying the child of one's father's sister or one's mother's brother, one continues the alliance that one's (fore)father(s) began, for one is marrying into the lineage to which one's father gave women (his "sisters") and from which he took his wife or wives (one's "mothers"), i.e., into the lineages of one's father's sister's husband and one's mother's brother. And, just as the sibling relationship is extended to all age-appropriate members of one's own lineage, so is the potential and preferred spouse and sibling-in-law relationship extended to all age-appropriate members of the lineages of the actual father's sister's husband and mother's brother.

Although, in kinship-based societies, such categories and the principles behind them regulate marriage, still there is choice within the categories which, after all, contain a number of people. Occasionally, the Yanomamö, like people of all cultures, do make forbidden matches (e.g., within the lineage, as between a man and a woman whose fathers are brothers and who are therefore "brother" and "sister"); but most choose within the appropriate groups. Among the Yanomamö, the right of choice, like all decision-making power, belongs to the male, and his decision is influenced by political and structural forces. Although he wishes to create a new alliance for himself, he also prefers to marry the daughter of an actual mother's brother or father's sister, because then he does not have to obey two bothersome rules: The first is that mother-in-law and son-in-law must not speak or make eye contact unless they are already related consanguineally. This "mother-in-law avoidance" symbolizes the ambiguously hostile yet possibly friendly tie between two kin groups or villages, the potential and tabooed sexuality between a younger man and his wife's mother, and the reluctant transfer of power over the wife from her family to her husband. Since, on marriage, the couple lives *patrilocally*, or *virilocally* (with the husband's parents or family), mother-in-law avoidance might seem to be a minor issue.

But the second rule makes it major: When a man marries a woman of another village, he must, before he takes her home, live with and work for her father and brothers for three or four years. This *bride-service* is a kind of compensation to the bride's family for giving her up and is one way her brothers solidify their tie with her husband. It is obviously difficult for a man to live in a small village of about a hundred people and have to avoid his wife's mother, especially since the whole village lives in one open house, each nuclear family having its own section in it. He is also uncomfortably under the control of his wife's brothers and fathers, who may prolong the bride-service by refusing to let him take her home. If, however, his in-laws are also his geneological relatives, none of these problems arise, for then he and they are likely to be living in the same village.

Females lose out among the Yanomamö; anthropologists often point to their plight as evidence for the extremes to which male dominance can go. And, indeed, no satisfactory explanation, ideological or politico-economic, has yet appeared to account for the severity of their position. The female is as subject to the political decisions of her father and adult brothers as she is to the beatings and bodily mutilations that her husband often inflicts upon her. Recognizing her importance, she prefers to marry close to home, literally and figuratively. She is more secure if she marries the son of a biological father's sister or mother's brother, because, since her husband and parents-in-law are also her consanguineal kin, they are more likely to treat her well. Furthermore, if she marries within her village, she will then be nearer to her biological father and brothers who are supposed to protect her. But if political needs demand a distant marriage, then she is out of luck, for she must live virilocally.

Yanomamö marriage clearly has nothing to do with love. Nor is it merely a matter of procreation or domesticity. Rather, it is political and, in fact, forms the only metaphor and structure on the basis of which Yanomamö can speak of and build a frame to hold their lives together. When Yanomamö men exchange women, they are dealing in prestige and power over one another, their control of which is always very tenuous. Ultimately, might makes right here, which is why a man wants his son-in-law around. Though their relationship also contains elements of moral obligation, in the end the morality rests on force. As long as the wife-receiver has not paid back with a woman, he is indebted to the giver, and liable to be attacked if he does not return the gift. And it may take time to even the balance, because he can't always lay his hands on one. For example, though he can promise his "sister" to his in-laws, he cannot deliver until she is old enough (above puberty). Until then, the customs of marriage bind him to them and so regulate the daily lives of all concerned.

Let us now contrast Nuer marriage, so as to get a sense of how the principles of descent and marriage fit together to form a social system. Because power among the Nuer comes from the corporate economic base and the overarching kinship/territorial structure of the tribe, marriage exchange does not alter the position of Nuer men or descent groups. Intermarrying lineages are initially separate and equal, and remain that way. Their system of marriage exchange symbolizes this position of balanced distinctness by means of the institution of *bride-wealth:* To get a wife, a man or, more properly, his lineage, must give to the bride's lineage valuables consisting of cattle, tools, and more recently money. The lineage elders negotiate the amount, which the bride's lineage eventually uses to secure wives for its own young men. Bride-wealth, like bride-service, transfers rights over the woman's labor power, sexuality, and reproductive ability from her lineage to her husband's.

The transfer is sequential and conditional: Some goods are given at the betrothal, some when and if the wedding comes off, and a final payment at the birth of the first child. This caution guarantees the rights of the kinship groups and the spouses. If the woman is barren, the groom's family may demand a replacement or a second, polygynous wife to live beside her. But if she is treated badly, her lineage may demand her return, with or without having to return the bride-wealth. And, if the final payment is not made to her family after she bears a child, her lineage will take her back and legitimize the child as her own.

In contrast to the merging of the affinally linked Yanomamö lineages, the Nuer lineages remain separate at the close of this finite exchange. This allows each lineage to contract new ties with new lineages, which each prefers to do so as to expand its kin network. Whereas Yanomamö marriage connects potentially ephemeral lineages or hostile villages, Nuer marriage links equal corporate groups whose internal solidarity and perpetual existence guarantee the solidity of the marriage and the good treatment of the wife. The only guarantors of the Yanomamö bride's well-being are her father and brothers. Nuer institutional structure—the strength of community opinion, the power of corporate lineages, and the ritual authority of the leopard-skin chief—support the wife's rights as well as the rules of exchange.

The structure of Nuer society is held together by the secure integration of the principles of descent, marriage, and territory. Marriage functions to establish domestic groups, descent and territory serve to regulate power. Each principle is, in a sense, specialized. Since each serves only one major function, it does not conflict with the other principles. Thus, Nuer groups can remain closely but separately linked. In contrast, Yanomamö groups seem ready to fly apart at any moment. Yanomamö principles of descent and marriage clash because they overlap in function. Yanomamö marriage establishes both domestic groups and power bases. But Yanomamö descent also underlies power: A man's control of his daughters yields control over unrelated men, and brothers, though rivalrous, fight alongside each other and their fathers until their village must split up. Marriage ties split lineal ties, and even when two affinal lineages set up a new village, their relationship can disintegrate when a new and stronger lineage appears. Disloyalty is almost built into the structure of Yanomamö society. In contrast, the loyalties of the Nuer are caught up by a structure that takes them beyond themselves and their immediate families to connect them to several higher levels of organization. And yet the Nuer are a relatively "simple" society.

Domesticity and Politics

If we were to write a soap opera about the Yanomamö or the Nuer, we would have to include conflicts and characters that differ from those in American soaps—the decisions of lineage elders instead of the wills of rich uncles; breakaway nuclear families instead of runaway children; a priest's curse for unpaid bride-wealth instead of social snubs; jealousy not of the new woman in town but of a co-wife; hatchet wounds inflicted by jealous Yanomamö males instead of emotional ones by neurotic Western spouses. The domestic scene would still be our focus, but it would be embedded in larger, more permanent units of people. The neighborhood would consist of consanguineal and affinal kinship, and there would be no non-kin. The ongoing economic and political affairs of life would still form the background, but both domestic foreground and public background would be couched in the same metaphors, i.e., those of multifunctioned kinship.

Even if kinship is not about biology, and marriage is an

affair of politics rather than of love, kinship and marriage do, nevertheless, everywhere intersect to create social groups within which procreation takes place and love can develop. Kinship and marriage do for most other cultures what they do for ours: They organize people spatially and socially into households that perform maintenance functions, providing shelter and rest, a reliable and regular source of food, a place where people of different generations care for and learn from each other, and, often, "space" for psychological self-renewal. In most cultures, one domestic unit carries out all these functions, and each person in it has not one role but several. This is so in our own also, where long lists have been made, in fatuous praise, wry despair, or militant anger, of the many jobs of suburban American housewives: angel in the kitchen, harlot in the bedroom, solicitous hostess, loving mother, child psychologist, chauffeur, nurse, etc.

Cultural differences between domestic groups come from the way these multiple functions and tasks are carried out. Whereas in our small nuclear family, we are socially and emotionally burdened with them all, the Nuer's *extended* family parcels them out. The coresidence of their corporate lineages makes at least three generations live together—a husband and wife, one or more married sons, and these sons' wives and children. Tasks are allocated according to the principles of sex, age, and marital ties. The men care for the cattle, cultivate a few crops, and take over the education of boys when they reach puberty and can begin to herd. The women raise children and cook, aided by growing daughters. In monogamous marriages, each woman cooks and raises her children separately; if there are cowives, they may work together even if they live in separate huts, and their mother-in-law may also sometimes baby-sit for their infants. Women share play as well, for co-wives and mothers-in-law and daughters-in-law provide companionship for one another.

One of the reasons, then, why love between two individuals is a minor criterion for marriage in these societies is that spouses have to get along with other people besides each other; in fact, the Nuer woman may spend more time with her co-wives and mother-in-law than with her husband, who may work more with his father and brothers than with her. The Euro-American emphasis on romantic love is a consequence of different arrangements of people in spatial and social relationships. Our domestic scene does not incorporate the married couple into ongoing kinship and/or territorial units; it isolates them in accordance with our dominant cultural principles.

In the Euro-American system of kinship, marriage is the only principle to establish domestic groups, because our descent rules do not distinguish concrete groups from one another. Although we inherit our surnames from our fathers, we consider ourselves to be equally related to both sides of our family. This system of *bilateral* descent tracks relationships through both sexes, or on both the mother's side and the father's side, without limit. Along with marriage, it creates only two cognatic descent groups. One is the *kindred.* This group consists of all kin traced on both mother's and father's sides through both males and females; the distance one traces varies, usually ending at second cousins (the children of one's parents' first cousins), that is, all those with great-grandparents in common. Another way is to conceive of this group as all those people whom one would invite to one's wedding if one were on equally good terms with both sides of one's family.

The second descent group is the nuclear family, whose core is created by the conjugal couple's usual establishment after marriage of its own *neolocal* residence. Since the nuclear family is equally related to the families of both spouses, it is part of neither. We signal its separateness by our kinship terms, in which it is an island of uniqueness in a sea of classificatory kin: All those outside the two-generation nuclear family and the two generations immediately above and below it receive classificatory terms. Thus, both father's brother and mother's brothers are *uncle;* we do not have separate terms for each separate uncle. Or, to put it another way, where the Yanomamö make distinctions, we do not: Their classificatory "brothers" and "sisters" are only one part of the group we call first cousins, within which group we also include people whom the Yanomamö call spouse and sibling-in-law. The only people to whom we apply special, *descriptive* terms are our parents, siblings, children, grandparents, and grandchildren.

The linguistic symbolization of the nuclear family's closure reinforces its structural isolation and its culturally preferred economic independence. The only built-in regulations that force it outward are incest prohibitions, which, in our culture, stipulate that one may not have sexual relations with primary kin, grandparents, and grandchildren. All cultures share an incest taboo on the nuclear family, but from then on, nothing is sacred. What we judge to be rather incestuous, such as marriage to a first cousin, the Yanomamö only prefer (though they prohibit marriage to parallel cousins, i.e., to those cousins who are classificatory siblings, and prefer marriage to the other first cousins, called cross cousins, to whom the term of "spouse" is applied). Marriages which we permit, such as to a distant relative linked through males to one's father, the Yanomamö outlaw. But unlike the Yanomamö, we have no explicit positive marriage rules; emically, there are no particular kinship groups or individuals whom we are supposed to marry.*

Structurally, this means that the nuclear family household lacks defined relationships to any other continuing group. Such stable connections, which elsewhere are prescribed by the kinship system and guarantee economic aid and companionship, must instead be carved out of the rest of social life by each generation. The only institutionalized ties for the older generation of the nuclear family are the affinal links created by their children's marriages; but even these are voluntary and not often maintained. As we saw, people seek other connections from informal groups, but friends provide little security. Kin are the only reliable source of ties in the sense that one's relationship to them is in some sense given. But even between them, the means of communication are flimsy; as "Somerset" showed, parents and married children have a hard time relating to one another.

Yet such links are often forged. For example, although a married couple will live neolocally, they very frequently will

* Unless one counts races, ethnicities, and so on as kinship groups, which in a sense they are, as I suggest at the end of this chapter.

choose a house near the bride's family (on "Mary Hartman, Mary Hartman," Mary lived next door to her mother). This is like *matrilocal* residence in which spouses live with the bride's matrilineal group (her mother and father, her mother's sister and their husbands and children, and her own sisters and their husbands and children). It differs because the rule of descent differs. Nevertheless, it is similar in that it results in mutual aid between consanguineally related women. By living near her mother, a woman reduces the loneliness and workload of keeping house and caring for children. After the birth of children, for example, closer relations tend to develop between the two households as she calls on her mother for advice and baby-sitting services; the latter may permit her to take a full-time job to bring in additional income or pin money.

But the kinship network, etically considered, is extremely important for the poor and the rich. Those who do not have, and/or cannot get, permanent, adequate employment depend for their economic survival on a group of kin—paternal, maternal, or both. *Matrifocal* households, held together by a line of mothers and daughters, represent one type of extended family that appears among the poor in nineteenth-century European industrial cities as well as contemporary North American ones. Kin also may live separately and yet help one another out, as Elliot Liebow describes for black working-class people in Washington, D.C. and as Michael Young and Peter Willmott do for the London working class. Indeed, on "All in the Family," Gloria and Mike moved in with Archie and Edith, her parents, when they got married; but even when they moved out after the birth of their son, they only moved next door, and continued to request and to get baby-sitting services and meals.

The extended family thus appears in another guise, not as a concrete household or a corporate group, but as a network of mutual aid relations that may expand and include more than just mother and daughter. Our ideology does not really acknowledge this network; instead, it idealizes the middle-class nuclear family as it idealizes the individual who makes it on her/his own, and this emic view is what soap operas portray.

Paradoxically, the wealthy also use the extended kin group for financial security; but they do it to live even better, not merely to stay alive. Family lines with large holdings of stock, for example, can dominate major corporations. The Rockefeller family has much of its wealth, though separately owned by each individual, jointly managed by corporations, trust funds, and foundations. And people in such families manage their nationally and internationally vital businesses to their mutual advantage.

The wealthy also use marriage, another kinship principle, to retain their position. In a system of bilateral descent, marriage extends inheritance claims to an unlimited number of people. But if marriages are kept within a small circle of friends, the goods will also remain within that circle. And so they are; the newspaper society page shows that the wealthy very often marry the wealthy. They practice the opposite of exogamy, *endogamy*, or marriage within a group. Other societies, too, have preferential endogamy, even within lineages, as a means to consolidate wealth. By these principles, of course, endogamy is not to the financial advantage of the underclasses, although it may reinforce or create a sense of subcultural solidarity and thereby enhance political leverage.

In our culture, endogamy happens without our willing it. Although our ideal marriage preference is to "fall in love," the lives of different classes of people are socially structured so that people are bound to fall "helplessly" in love with someone not only of their own class, but also of their own religion, race, ethnic group, and even geographical area. For example, religion, race, and ethnicity form the social bases of neighborhoods, which are common meeting grounds for lovers. Clubs perform the same match-making function, and their membership rules, often restricted on religious or racial grounds, in effect keep their young from meeting the "wrong" people. Like some colleges, clubs may charge very high membership fees, which also effectively limit their patrons to one class.

The rule of endogamy becomes conscious when someone breaks it: In Somerset, when Andrea, heiress to Delaney Brands, fell in love with David, a fledgling middle-class lawyer, her mother did her best to break up the relationship. But the engagement finally ended only when Andrea gave David a car for his birthday. Since he was poorer than Andrea, he couldn't accept it—it made him seem less of a man. And even if such values don't break up the engagements, marriages can always be arranged, bending the rules a little to allow first cousins to marry, a traditional technique of European royalty to conserve their power.

It has long been thought that the principles of descent and marriage no longer integrate the social system in industrial, complex societies. Perhaps they have declined in emic importance for all of us, and in etic importance for the middle-class nuclear family household, to its misfortune. But the wealthy and the poor use extended kinship to their advantage; the wealthy manipulate marriage to maintain their power; and many of us try to better ourselves by marrying up and out of our class. The few who achieve upwardly mobile marriages are quickly assimilated by the upper class. They acquire its trappings of behavior, values, and relationships, and drop their old ones. David couldn't do this and so he didn't make it. Kinship, of course, does not structure our social lives all by itself. Whereas the Nuer and the Yanomamö separate people by rules of descent and marriage, we do so by rules of wealth and power as well. The fact that those who do marry up soon cut their ties to their poorer kin reinforces the internal socio-economic uniformity within each class and the differences between classes.

The Comparative Method

It is now time to sum up in a way that soap operas never do, and perhaps don't have to. The principles of society structure the lives of people in particular ways and give them limits within which they create their lives. The particular form a society takes depends on the relationship of the principles to one another, as well as on the principles themselves. The Yanomamö are organized by descent and marriage. The Nuer add the principle of territory. We add the principle of economic control. These principles may overlap in the domains they cover, which, in effect, increases the chaos of the society, as in the Yanomamö case. Or they may be more specialized, like those of Nuer society, and thus promote social integration.

Or they may be so specialized that it is hard to see how they connect, as in our society, where marriage seems to have no other function than to connect individuals and to establish a household, but actually supports the class structure by connecting families within classes. The result is that all people in our society are interdependent strangers. Each of us hides out in the nuclear family, desperately trying to make contact with others. Our social isolation underlies the obsessive concern of soap opera with love, sex, and marriage, which we hope will connect us solidly to others, but which are really very fragile supports to bear such burdens.

In some ways, then, all these cultures are the same; in others, they sharply contrast. Their similarities and differences have emerged through the anthropological technique of analysis called the comparative method. I have described selected parts of three cultures to see how they are similar and how they are different. For example, I took the function of domestic maintenance as a constant and examined how the structures which carried it out varied. We saw that, in all three cultures, households perform this function, but that their structures and principles of formation differ.* One universal the households do share is the mutual aid among women for routine maintenance tasks, but the ties among the women vary, from affinal among the Nuer to bilateral or patrilineal among the Yanomamö to some version of *matrilateral* among Euro-Americans.

Let us compare one more dimension of social structure to make this method clear. We and the Nuer both have nonkin groups. Also called "voluntary" associations because they are not in the metaphor of kinship, they actually are socially obligatory. Ours and those of the Nuer differ not only in content, but in their unifying or divisive functions. The Nuer have age-sets. Every year, all puberty-age (14–16) Nuer boys in a single tribe undergo an initiation ritual which makes them socially recognized adults.

* In our culture, other institutions also perform domestic functions, e.g., orphanages, hospitals, jails, the military.

All those initiated together become lifelong friends and have a group name. Different tribes coordinate their rites, so that all Nuer of the same age are linked. Typically, the Nuer apply the kinship metaphor to age-sets. All members of one age-set are "brothers," and their sisters are "sisters" to all (though they don't share their wives). Anyone in one's father's age-set is a "father," and any man in a senior age-set who is not in one's father's age-set is a potential "father-in-law." Furthermore, one must respect and defer to all those in senior age-sets. This nonkin system thus helps to set up marriages and eases social relationships among nonkin.

We do something similar. Within our classes, religions, and other groups, we have voluntary associations like bridge clubs, bowling leagues, fraternal orders, country clubs, and so on. Immigrants have formed nationally and locally based burial and mutual-aid societies. Although most of these are truly voluntary, social pressures sometimes make us join them even if we don't want to. Unions are less voluntary. Union membership, though not obligatory or even available in some cases, is in other cases necessary not only to get good treatment in a job, but even to get work at all.

In pinpointing these similarities and differences, the comparative method allows us to question them. For example, although, like the Nuer, we apply the metaphor of kinship to nonkin associations (Elks are "brothers"), we differ in the functions that these associations serve. The Nuer associations, by adding the principle of age, integrate the society by crosscutting tribes, lineages, and sections. Ours add principles like sex, religion, national origin, class, and race, which are based on interests of only parts of the population and so may further divide the society. But why should this be? Why do different societies have different principles and, therefore, different structures? Why do the same structures carry out different functions? Conversely, why are governmental and political activities carried out by descent among the Nuer and by marriage among the Yanomamö? Why does our society have yet other political mechanisms?

One theoretical issue here is the relationship between functions and the form in which they are carried out. For example, every society needs to apportion territory and to deal with other societies and must have some institution to do so. Since the need is constant, however, it cannot explain the variable forms its satisfaction takes. As universals do not explain particulars, so functions do not explain the structures that perform them. Structural-functional theory can only explain how an institution is put together and how it works. It can reveal its internal dynamism and coherence, but cannot itself explain their presence. Explanations for the specificity of structure must come from the operation of other parts of culture. The next chapter examines one such part, systems of values and meanings, and begins to search in the rather indirect relationship between ideology and structure for their mutual and dialectical shaping of one another.

V.

Symbols and Sensibility, or "You'd Better Go See a Doctor"

MIND, MATTER, AND COMMON SENSE

On December 24, 1967, in a Greek village in which I was doing ethnographic research, I suddenly came down with a fever of 105°F. My husband and I were living with an extended family, renting one room of their two-room house. It was very cold, since the prohibitive cost of wood restricted their use of the wood-burning stoves, the only source of heat, to the evening. Feeling quite weak, I spent the day in bed covered by several blankets. I was dosed with aspirin by my husband and fed chicken soup by the ladies of the household.

Everyone thought I just had a cold, but when my fever didn't abate by the next day, the members of the household became rather concerned. Twenty-five-year-old Aliki took the first step to heal illness and tried to exorcise the evil eye from me. With her husband and his younger brother watching, she poured some water into a glass, and some holy oil into her left palm. She dipped her right forefinger in the oil and made the sign of the cross three times over my face. Then she let some oil drip from her right pinky into the water and crossed the mouth of the glass three times; she repeated the whole procedure twice more.

Aliki carefully watched the oil droplets merge into one small and three large blobs, and then said: "You're only a little bit sick. You were given the evil eye by the neighbors. They saw you writing at the movies the other night [I had been taking notes] and became suspicious of you. They envied you too; you look too young to be married." After the diagnosis, she told me to take three sips of water; her husband and brother-in-law watched eagerly to make sure I didn't drink too much. Finally, she daubed my forehead and hair with oil from her right index finger, and the exorcism was over.

But my fever remained high, so Aliki's mother-in-law, Maria, gave me a slightly different treatment in the evening. First she made the sign of the cross over my head three times. Next, she filled a glass with water, into which she dropped three live coals, crossing the mouth of the glass with each one and listening to the sizzle as each hit the water. I then drank a little from the glass. Next Maria dipped her right forefinger into the water and dabbed me successively on the forehead, left cheek, right cheek, chin, left palm, and right palm. All the while, she mumbled prayers which I could not understand. Next she peered at the floating coals. Finally, she said, "You're very sick, and you'd better go see a doctor."

And so on December 26, my husband and I left Maria's household for the nearest city. By this time, my husband had a fever too, but he had refused a proffered exorcism. We checked into a hotel and called a doctor, who prescribed an antibiotic. In a couple of days, I had recovered completely, but my husband continued ill. In another week, we found out that he had hepatitis; he was sick for the next three months.

This story shows the universal way an ongoing ideological system can incorporate opposites like magic and religion, religion and science, belief and knowledge, mind and body. It shows how individuals distinguish themselves from their public culture by their private attempts to reconcile its conflicting premises and to control uncertainty. Finally, the story has a message about meaning and communication, particularly between anthropologist and "native." The story and this chapter are about the intangible dimension within which our more observable, concrete activities occur and in the context of which our social institutions function. Culture contains this dimension because of the nature of the human beast: Both thinking and feeling, part rational and part emotional, we remember and, unlike the elephant, remember to forget; and, in us, each of these contradictory processes takes place simultaneously.

These processes receive cultural form through systems of morality, codifications of knowledge, and conventionalized symbols of communication, but still they slip from our grasp. Concrete representations of them in such acts as ceremonies and in such artifacts as amulets mean nothing outside the processes that generate them. The only way the outside observer can learn about them is by trying to see the world as the insider sees it, as Malinowski urged all field-researchers to do. Yet it is hard enough to discover how a next-door neighbor views the world, let alone glimpse the world view of someone from another culture who speaks another language and believes in different demons.

For example, the Greek villagers both "believed" in the evil eye and "knew" that I had been affected by it and that they might be able to do something about it. I could not share their world view, nor am I entirely sure I understood it, not only because it includes a supernatural power in which I do not believe, but also because it confounds belief and knowledge. For them, the eye is real; for me, it is a construction, because, for me, knowing and believing are different. Yet a detached look at the distance between our views finds that beliefs and knowledge are really somehow connected. They have the same relationship as theory and fact. We humans cannot perceive or "know" (find facts about) the world without having some idea (theory or belief) about it. Nor can we think without there being something to think about, i.e., a world to stimulate our thought processes.

Belief usually implies religion, but to say that a world view, or belief system, is *religious* means specifically that it is premised on the existence of supernatural forces and beings, i.e., things not of the everyday world, and that this premise makes certain actions appropriate and/or necessary.* However, a world view may also require some belief without being religious, as does a cultural creed like free enterprise, or a political philosophy like Marxism. According to this definition, then, not all cultures have religions. Indeed, A. F. C. Wallace suggests that religion may disappear in the course of evolution. His suggestion undermines two beliefs cherished by many in our own culture. One is that the only "true" religions are Judaeo-Christian monotheisms and world religions like Islam, Buddhism, Hinduism, and Confucianism. The second is that these belief-systems represent the highest level of human development so far achieved. The possibility that a belief-system or world view that excludes supernaturals may be as valid as a "true" religion is a touchy one for many of us. One dominant theme in our world view is that a culture cannot be "civilized" and people cannot be truly "human" if they don't "have" a religion. And when their beliefs take forms unacceptable to us, we call them superstitions or magic.

Yet magic, like science, can coexist with religion. The Greek women were quite certain that Greek Orthodoxy was the true religion, and attended church services at least once a week. But they could also comfortably practice a form of magic. In Greece, as well as in other Christian and Islamic nations of the Mediterranean, people believe that the evil eye constantly threatens one's well-being. For protection, mothers pin amulets on their infants' clothing; some Greek priests, as well as the laity, have a small blue bead sewn into their garments. The *evil eye* refers simultaneously to a power, to the effect of this power, and to the name of the affliction. Almost anyone can possess and give the eye, but some people have stronger powers than others. The eye can cause accidents and both physical and mental illness. It can be

* The definitions of religion, magic, supernatural, and so on in this chapter are anthropological definitions. Members of or believers in particular religions may have different definitions, which those given here do not deny or dispute. I make this point because, for reasons which we shall see below, people sometimes object to the attempts of social science to specify what they do.

either unintentional, as when it follows upon a friend's compliments, or deliberate, as when witches (usually female) cast spells on others.

The power of the eye both resembles and differs from the *mana* of the Pacific cultures: *Mana* is a force analogous to electricity; people believe it to exist independently in nature and to be able to flow through people and things. Whereas the evil eye always harms, *mana* can also bring good if one knows how to handle it; in this way, it is like "Luck." In Polynesian kingdoms, chiefs can handle much *mana,* commoners little. Since *mana* can flow through its carriers into the ground, and from the ground into others, chiefs rarely walk; any ground they touch is *tapu,* or taboo, hence forbidden to commoners. Like the chief with *mana,* the carrier of the evil eye is not affected by it and does not necessarily control it at will. In other words, since one can not predict its behavior, one must take precautions against it. Unlike *mana,* the eye is not connected with any social differentiation; like luck, the eye is egalitarian.

Although we, like the Greeks, view our religion, or world view, as all of a piece, yet it may contain coexisting but separate belief systems with different premises. If, with Wallace, we define "the religion of a society" as a "loosely related" set of "cult institutions" and other loosely organized beliefs and rituals,* we can see Greek Orthodoxy and magic as part of one larger religious system (and, with science, as part of an even wider ideology). Just as, in Wallace's view, American culture may contain four coexisting religious cults—the denominational (e.g., Christian sects), the political (organized around the idea of nationhood, Thanksgiving a major ritual), the superstitious (for which Valentine's Day is one ritual), and the children's cult (including the celebration of Halloween), so there are at least two cults in Greece, or in any other culture or country. Thus, even though the evil eye is not formally part of Greek Orthodoxy, the Greeks believe in both.

* Rituals, including ceremonies, refer to a stereotyped sequence of acts, which are based on a belief system and which use certain symbolically meaningful objects; they are discussed more fully below.

But the two systems differ. The exorcism is magic because it attempts to control or direct supernatural forces, in contrast to religious ceremonies which try to propitiate them; through magic, one attempts to realize one's own will, not to submit to that of the supernatural as in religion. Magical acts rely heavily on the correct performance of gestures and recitations, and emphasize belief less than do formal religious cults. For instance, the Greek women wouldn't explain their sacred incantations when I asked, lest the phrases lose their power. What was important was not for me to believe or understand, but to do as I was told.

Beliefs and rituals of any sort perform social functions. For the Greeks, magic meets unpredictable forces (perhaps those of evil) on their own ground, in the profane, mundane world of the household, in contrast to the holy ground of the church. It is in this everyday world that unpredictable things happen; in church, people are on their best orderly behavior. Magic thus tries to control the uncontrollable, a task that the Judaeo-Christian church has abandoned. By recognizing the rampant uncertainty of life, magic allows individuals to express anxiety and thereby to discharge tension. Magic thus becomes a means of individual action for which the church provides no scope.

The Orthodox religion and magic express the contradictions inherent in any society, like the tension between individual and social group, or, what is another dimension of the same thing, between private and public. In the Greek case, the church is public, magic private. The formal religion contains a social structure and hierarchy that are tied to and reflect the community structure. It is this public character of formal religion that requires its internal consistency. It brings diverse people together in a public expression of their joint membership in a community through open sharing of beliefs and ritual; in order to provide a basis for communion, it must give them something in common or reflect what they share. Since its consistency communicates and symbolizes unity, the religion can function to maintain the social order.

Another universal contrast that these supernatural institutions bring into play, besides public/private and social/individual, is sacred/profane. E. Durkheim and his students, Marcel Mauss and Henri Hubert, used this distinction to refer to a classification of people, things, and acts with respect to their holiness and to their mundane characteristics, respectively. In this view, what was holy and therefore sacred was that which represented or celebrated society, for Durkheim thought that religious feeling came from a "collective consciousness" or "collective conscience" of social being. The profane was all that was individual, non- or anti-social, and in the realm of ordinary experience.

In Greece, as in most societies, the male/female contrast parallels the sacred/profane, and profane females are at the bottom of the social order. Like women in Spain, Italy, and elsewhere, Greek women go to church more often than men. They may need to, for, in the view of the formal Greek religion, they are dangerously contaminating. Being profane, they are the logical ones to traffic in the darker areas of life and to be able to inflict and to remove the evil eye. Women also symbolize those things that threaten community solidarity—differences between people, the private sphere, and the desire to be free from social control. In Greece, as in our culture, it is usually only in private, at home, that one allows one's individual idiosyncracies and asocial tendencies to appear. Appropriately, then, women carry out their magic rituals privately, in their own domain of the household, and they keep their knowledge secretly to themselves. Greek magical practices may function as safety valves, as a means to express the asocial, perhaps the amoral, and the conventionally unmentionable, to control the unpredictable. In other cultures, the formal religion, or a nonreligious belief system, may perform these same functions. Here, magic, through its power to heal both individual and society, may even permit women to become sacred.

Magic has, however, another aspect, for in so far as it aims to control, it resembles science. Both magic and science include theories or ideas about the physical and social worlds, on the basis of which certain practices are carried out and certain effects expected. The main difference appears to be that the one relies on faith and invisible forces, the other on hard facts and proof. This difference is significant, even though scientists can't always see what they talk about (e.g., nuclear particles) and disagree about explanations (e.g., wave theory versus particle theory). For the application of scientific theories to technology has resulted in degrees and kinds of control that magical ideas have not. We can see this clearly in the course of cultural evolution, particularly in our ways of dealing with the physical environment, in our food quest, and in the construction of means of transport and shelter.

It is less clear that science has advanced beyond magic or religion in dealing with the social environment, either with individual human beings or with groups of them: It has made possible progress in the pursuit of war but not in the construction of peace. It allows us to understand social catastrophes by hindsight, but not to prevent them by prediction. It has permitted the cure of some diseases or the alleviation of some pains, but sometimes we don't really know what makes people well, any more than I knew what had caused my illness or my recovery in Greece.

Western science explains some things, but obviously not all. Its deficiency may be due to the Western cultural world view, which keeps it from looking in the right places. Why, for example, did my husband get hepatitis and not I? It is entirely likely that I had once been exposed to the disease and had developed antibodies. But, if so, why did I fall ill at all? And, once ill, how did I recover so quickly? I might raise the possibility that the exorcism cured me, since that was the only difference in the treatment we received. I am considering here not so much the effect of some supernatural power as the interaction of psychological and somatic processes, such that the interpersonal experience of trust and friendship between me and the women may have enabled me to recover; my husband did not have this experience and so he succumbed. In our everyday thinking and to a lesser extent in our scientific thinking, we have tended to see this in either/or terms: We are sick either in body or in mind; either technology created through science or belief validated in religion cures us.

Or, if we fall physically ill because of emotional distress, we dismiss it contemptuously as "psychosomatic." Again, like our religion and our beliefs, our system of knowledge is usually uncomfortable with contradictions. It must smooth them over or ignore them. The old Greek woman, Maria, knew better. Her commonsense view of the situation was that my illness had developed to such a degree that it was qualitatively out of her domain, and therefore I had to go to the doctor. But she accepted that two different kinds of cure were possible, and that two different kinds of illness, though connected, could exist in one body.

SYMBOLS AND THE UNITY OF OPPOSITES

I have suggested that culturally organized systems of ideation that we ordinarily think of as different, such as a political philosophy and a religion, may function similarly in different societies. More generally, anthropology postulates that every culture has some system of ideas, an *ideology,* which enables its members to do several different but connected things: to make some sense of the world, to say what is good and bad in it, and to justify the actions people take. Ideology is vital. It is public and therefore shared, but it is also contained in and expressed by individuals. Ideology, then, has two faces: It represents and often comes to symbolize its culture, and at the same time it becomes a means for the individual to comprehend her/himself.

Perhaps most importantly, it is the means by which adult individuals are rationally and emotionally persuaded to participate in their culture, and by which individuals connect themselves to each other and to the culture as a whole. According to C. Geertz, each culture has in its ideology an ethos or esthetics, which is connected to preferences in style. Each culture also has a world view, or a vision of order, a way of making sense of chaos. The work of belief and ritual is to bring them together, to render the ethos intellectually reasonable, and the world view emotionally convincing.

I have said too that everything we do has an ideological dimension. Marriage, for example, consists of a ceremony, a set of rights and obligations, and an enveloping ideology that includes values, or social attitudes (e.g., "It is better to marry than to burn"), and meanings (e.g., social adulthood). Ideology accompanies everything we know and do, because one of our means of survival is to think abstractly, to create new ideas (or new connections between old ideas), and regularly to communicate our abstractions. By *abstraction,* I mean the intangible (ideas like "love" or "time"), the invisible (a black hole in space, the unconscious), and the never-before-imagined (the reader may fill in this blank).

Evolutionary theorists concur that human society and culture could not have evolved without this particular mental ability or without the human ability to produce a communication system that both shapes and expresses abstract thought. It may be that animals also think abstractly and create new ideas; but, so far as we can tell, these abstractions are not communicated very frequently, nor have they led to the social or material creativity of which humans are capable.

Another way of putting this is to say that we not only act, but also think about our acts before, during, and after them. We reflect on these acts and on ourselves; we can distance ourselves from ourselves and observe ourselves. Some psychoanalysts say that one can split oneself into two parts, one which experiences and one which observes, and still remain whole and healthy. Indeed, sanity depends on this ability, as does human evolution. By means of this splitting, one can find out whether or not one is doing what one intended to do, and how to correct one's behavior according to internal or external demands. This splitting, in other words, enables one to heed the needs of others, as well as one's own needs; it is therefore fundamental to culture. It may also be what permits the process of change, for just as one is partly separate from culture and from oneself, so one may look with a cool eye on one's way of living and decide that it needs to be refashioned.

The core of the process (itself an act of a sort) of thinking about, reflecting on, and evaluating our acts is giving meaning to them. Meaning is the human way of understanding the relationship between the self and everything else. Since we are driven not only to do this, but to communicate it, meaning and communication go together. The ability to communicate abstractions is called the ability "to symbol." "Symboling" is a complex process. One form it takes is speech, in which we make a connection simultaneously (1) between something we perceive and its meaning, (2) between a meaning and a group of sounds (a word), and (3) between the sounds and the perception; we then communicate the sounds, and therefore the meaning and the perception, to another person: We speak. The word represents something more than its sounds; it symbolizes something else. Human beings symbol also by means of gestures (e.g., with the hands), objects (e.g., clothing), and other devices.

So, of course, do all animals. What is special about this human way of communicating is that we can create new symbols. The communication systems of nonhuman animals are almost wholly genetically inherited and stable. But we humans inherit only the bare ability to perceive, think, and communicate; we must learn how to do each in the particular language and culture we grow up with, in every situation we encounter. This leaves room for mistakes and ambiguity, but also for the creation of new content.

Such creation comes partly from our thoughts, images, and feelings. We usually consider these to be private, individual experiences, but they actually have a public dimension. This is so not only because learning to think and to feel takes place socially. It is also true because we carry and transmit our thoughts and feelings primarily through our social currency, words. In order to be understood, the meaning of words must be agreed upon (tacitly, of course; none of us sits down with another to agree on what words will mean, except for, say, passwords on the battlefield). But we use words to share our individual, unique experience, which may sometimes be unheard-of even among family and friends. As we try to bring together a thought-image-feeling experience and a word, we alter the latter to fit the former, and vice versa. Thus, the word shapes our inner experience, while, conversely, our experience can also change the meaning of words, though only more gradually.

Words, then, come to symbolize both private and public meanings, both individual and social experience. For example, to us the word *religion* is more than its definition; it also connotes values (the Ten Commandments), customs (weekly church attendance), social structure (Jews and Christians, Baptists and Episcopalians), and political relations ("godless" communists). For each of us, the idea of religion will have personal meanings as well, such as a particular place of worship or a conversion experience. However varied the individual experience, the ideas, images, and emotions it calls up are systematically, culturally interrelated to one another. They constitute, in Geertz's phrasing, "a model of and for reality."

Geertz applies this phrase also to objects that he calls "sacred symbols." Such an object, like the word, may stand for one or usually several other things, including actions, structures, words, and ideas. Like the ideational system it represents, a sacred symbol both describes and prescribes reality; it says simultaneously what the world is and how one ought to behave in it. But it is a concrete model of and for reality. Religions, for example, have symbols like the Cross; the Greeks' magical system has the blue bead. Sacred symbols are also associated with nonreligious world views. The American flag stands for a nation, a history/mythology, and a set of values and ideas about "Americanism"; the Red Star of the People's Republic of China symbolizes the same kind of things about another nation, tradition, and ideology.

Symbols correspond more to our dreams, or our waking images, than to our speech. Like dream images, they can condense many meanings and therefore be very powerful. They carry a high emotional charge through which people can identify themselves with them and because of which people respond to threats to symbols as if they themselves were in danger. Symbols can thus validate a whole way of being. By virtue of this they are called sacred.

Symbols validate by means of another universal, the "ideology of ideology." Underlying each ideology is a subtle, rarely verbalized set of ideas about the rightness of the system itself. Just as, in other words, we have an ideology about marrying, making money, or going to church, so we have a way of seeing, understanding, and evaluating our ways of seeing, understanding, and evaluating. The outcome of the evaluation is never in doubt: Behind each ideology lies a conception of the world of which the ideology is made to seem the only correct representation and explanation. This is the cultural basis for ethnocentrism, which, as I said in Chapter II, has been inevitably universal (perhaps until now).

But ideology is neither consistent nor satisfactorily explanatory. Much as religions consists of loosely connected cults, so ideology may encompass different systems (religion, science, esthetics, magic). Indeed, it must be able to contain diversity because of the conflicting elements with which it must cope, like ideas and beliefs, thoughts and feelings, words and acts, and the cultural contradictions it reflects and attempts to resolve. Whichever specific ideological systems a culture contains, together they express or recognize these conflicts. Geertz, in fact, suggests that each culture requires its conflicts to be reconciled either by active elimination of some of them or in ideation. Ideology reconciles conflicts by simultaneously describing, explaining, and in the course of all that, justifying them. Thus, ideology serves as a theory that selects and orders the facts. And, conversely, the facts then substantiate the underlying view of the world which explains the facts.*

To look at it another way, ideology resolves each contradiction by recognizing both sides of it and then by making each side meaningful in the other's terms. Through symbols, ideology creates a unity of opposites. Because symbolic structuralism treats of the synthesizing, or mediating function of ideology, it goes beyond the Lévi-Straussian structuralist arrangements of continually transformed dualities. We have seen, for example, that the Greek Orthodox church ceremonies synthesize individual diversity into public communion, the exorcism fuses the social problem of the unpredictable with personal attempts to control it. They do so through symbols as well as acts: The blue bead is a symbol

* It is this circularity that Western science, including social science, attempts to avoid; I am by no means sure that it succeeds.

whose socially accepted use by both priest and laity overrides the hierarchy separating them, by pointing up their common vulnerability to human misfortune. The sign or symbol of the cross, as an integral part of the exorcism, validates the ritual in the church's terms, and the church in those of the exorcism; with it, the women both sanctify the profane ritual and return to the church its true power over them and their acts.

Symbolic structuralism also differs from Lévi-Straussian structuralism in that it takes account of the social actor's subjectivity, or the meaningfulness of things to individuals, which the German sociologist Max Weber said was essential to sociological analysis. Geertz thinks that ideology fills a universal need to link the subjective and the objective by reconciling them. *Subjectivity* means our perception of the world in terms of our individual selfhood, experience, and background; its meaningfulness is personal. *Objectivity* means the understanding shared by people as members of the same social group or society; its validity, in contrast to that of subjectivity, is not to be disputed and does not vary from person to person. Objectivity serves as a fundamental means for continued connections between people, subjectivity as a way for individuals to remain separate, integrated beings. Each is essential. Since, however, social systems and individual systems differ in content and needs, subjectivity and objectivity may conflict. They must therefore be reconciled.

Ideology universalizes individual experience until this experience seems to typify not merely the society, but humanity; it does this through, for example, myths of great individuals or culture heroes (e.g., the self-educated Abraham Lincoln reading by firelight). On the other hand, ideology makes society meaningful in terms of direct individual experience. It metaphorically transforms society into an individual either by homology (the head of state makes the society into a national person), by analogy (the fatherland makes the nation into a parent and the individual into a child), or by symbols: The flag comes to represent individual experience because it carries an emotional charge, and emotions are felt by individuals.

Sacred symbols and ideologies thereby bridge intrapsychic

divides between feelings and thinking, emotions and reason, irrationality and rationality. Individuals can therefore use the symbols of the group to explain or justify their own mental processes. Symbols may, in other words, reconcile contradictions on several levels at once, within individuals, between individual and society, and within society and between societies. Through symbols, the value-laden ethos appears to be rational and adapted to an actual state of affairs; the orderly world view pictures an actual state of affairs especially arranged to accommodate a chosen way of life. It comes to seem eminently commonsensical and self-evident to accept the ethos, to be devoted to the world view, and to live one's culture. One identifies parts of oneself with each, and one's understanding of oneself with the ideology of the ideology.

The power of symbols is frightening, for their satisfying synthesis can affect us in ways we neither understand nor control at the moment of their occurrence. They are deep in us; we learn about and use them early and/or at highly unstable moments such as puberty rites or marriages. Our notion of self comes to be tightly bound up with them before we have a choice. They therefore tend toward stability and have an inherent conservative quality. But they do not have to dominate us: They are but vehicles or carriers of meaning, and the meaning is given them by human beings. It is in the nature of human beings to create meaning and symbols, and to use them to reproduce or transform their lives.

RITUAL AND COMMUNICATION

In some ways, if we look at the Greek curing ritual from a structuralist point of view, it appears to turn the mundane routine upside down: Women, excluded from the church and public power, control the exorcism; instead of calling a male priest or doctor, housewives treat me themselves. Private individuals cure social evil; a disease contracted in a public place can be cured in the private household. The individual subordinated to social hierarchy regains her uniqueness; Aliki and Maria each carry out a different version of the exorcism. A profane hierarchy counterbalances the sacred one; people who can't control their evil eye harm, and therefore control, obedient churchgoers. Finally, then, this ritual resolves contradictions: It makes the ordinary—envy, hostility, perennial evil—seem unusual, by treating or recognizing it in the context of something extraordinary. The ritual defines dangerous feelings or things as nonnormal, and so makes everyday life safe once again and therefore valid.

In short, ritual communicates. Properly defined, *ritual* means a stereotyped sequence of acts and events based on some system of beliefs and employing concrete symbols. Its acts and symbols communicate not only beliefs but other ideas as well, of which its participants may not be aware. In addition to the recognized meanings of the Cross, sizzling coals, or mumbled incantations, the exorcism contains tacit messages about itself and its world. One of these, for example, is about the existence of eternal oppositions and their interdependence—male and female, society and individual, public and private. In thus manipulating received forms, the exorcism, like all rituals and their attendant ideologies, attempts to transform chaotic reality into an image of a simple, orderly world.

Methodologically, this view of ritual asserts that overt emic views coexist with levels of meaning of which observers are aware, but the believers are not. This does not mean necessarily that either is wrong; each may see only part of the truth. But the outsider can assume that, like all acts, ritual communicates both intentionally and unintentionally. Since "actions speak louder than words," the observer is entitled to infer meaning from them. Indeed, like our primate kin, we speak with facial expressions, gestures of our limbs, and our whole body posture. Each culture assigns meaning to such body movements, and individuals also use extrasomatic means (e.g., adornment, symbols) to tell the world and ourselves what we are doing and, by implication, who we are.

However, we face an epistemological problem here. Despite the beauty and utility of unspoken language, it is inherently ambiguous. People use it when they can't or won't be clear, and they don't have to own up to what they say with it. They can make contradictions and get away with them. They can intentionally say or communicate forbidden things, and pretend that they didn't know they were doing so. Although we want to make rational sense of what we observe, if we try to make ritual or its symbols either totally rational or totally emotional, we strip them of their very meaning. We therefore remain in perpetual uncertainty about the truth of our own inferences.

Now, sometimes we must infer meaning from other ambiguities, like tones of voice or words in odd contexts, but in these cases, the speakers can provide us with socially agreed-upon, objective meanings on the basis of which to begin our inferences. A psychoanalytic investigation would be another way to judge the correctness of such inferences. The nature of ritual experience is such that true believers don't think about it. They do not examine the meanings of ritual action with the commonsense reasoning of their own culture, for to do so might be to destroy its power by showing that contradictions are reconciled only in ideology, not in actual fact.* For example, the exorcism symbolically reverses women's low status and makes the evil eye seem unusual. But, actually, women still are subordinate to men and people wish their neighbors ill every day. I think that the ritual communicates this synthesis to the participants and reinforces socially acquired tendencies to accept things the way they are.

Finally, rituals performed by one person or group for another send messages between performers and observers about hidden attitudes and about their relationship. In our everyday communication, ritualized forms of greeting behavior convey not only greeting, but also feelings and connections: Where people routinely kiss each other hello, not to do so implies either distance

* This may be why people often get extremely angry at any attempts to analyze their beliefs, and why social science is potentially explosive when applied to its own culture. It appears there as part of a profane ideology that approaches what its culture sets apart as the inviolate and sacred mysteries, i.e., those political or religious ideologies that smooth out living contradictions.

or extreme closeness. If handshaking indicates equality, its absence communicates hierarchy. In the case of the exorcism, I think that Aliki and Maria were telling me that they were concerned for me; they were communicating friendly feelings, and I know that I felt cared for. They were also conveying trust and acceptance, for they knew that urban foreigners might have denigrated this magic; for this too I was grateful.

But whereas they were (as far as I could tell) wholly immersed in the ritual, I was only partly involved. For me, the ritual was also data: When I first realized what Aliki was about to do, I excitedly grabbed my notebook despite my fever, for I realized that something exotic was about to happen to me, even if I wasn't doing my field research among the fierce Yanomamö. Although I later felt guilty for my socially inappropriate feeling, all that was anthropological in me was very unguilty and very well, not ill at all.

This distance between us could not have gone unnoticed. I think that, unconsciously, the women used the ritual, to tell me that they were aware of my mixed motives, and that they were a little tired of my constant observation of them even though they liked me. I infer this from their diagnoses: First, their statement, that the people at the movies were upset at my taking notes, said, too, that the members of the household felt my detachment to be inconsistent with our overt interactions; I was not really behaving like a loyal member of the household, but manifested an inappropriate and perhaps disruptive awareness.

Secondly, their inference of the others' envy revealed their own. And it is no wonder. As another woman in another village said: "Oh, that's why this girl can sit on her ass for a year; she has American dollars." For all that they liked me, they must have been angry at the capricious injustice that provided me with enough money for a year to have supported three or four families like theirs for the same period of time. And my government (through the National Institutes of Mental Health) had the wealth to support me in part because it exploited nations like theirs. I think that our positions in this structure of politico-economic power were simultaneously too abstract and too close to the bone to be stated openly, and I think that the exorcism was how they dealt with the inequality.

And, after all, my husband and I were in the way: They had two rooms, of which we rented one. This forced a seventy-two-year-old widow, her thirty-three-year-old son and his thirty-year-old wife and infant, her unmarried daughter of thirty-five, and her unmarried son of twenty-five, to sleep in the one other room. They had uses for our rent, but in the end they were too inconvenienced to make our staying worthwhile for them. When we returned to visit them the following Easter, we were not asked to stay, though we were enthusiastically invited to share Easter dinner (and we did).

I realized none of this while we were there. We left their home and village only because illness forced us to. If we had not, perhaps they would have told us more directly that they wanted us to leave. It is only recently, as I have put some distance between myself and the fieldwork experience, that I have been able to put the events in their social context and see how the relations between our two cultures subtly appeared in a ritual of exorcism. At one level, we were the evil being exorcised from their lives. Perhaps at another level, the women were trying to banish the inequities not only in their own lives but in the relations which connected us.

In addition to such occasional and emergency rituals as the exorcism, each culture has a regular sequence of ceremonies that publicly celebrate major moments, or "life crises," in the so-called life cycle of the individual. Birth, puberty, and death are the three biological moments by which cultures universally segment the individual's life path. The ceremonies need not coincide with the actual event; for example, baptism in Greek and other Eastern Orthodox churches does not take place until forty days after birth. These ceremonies are collectively called rites of passage, implying a movement from one social place to another (as if along some pathway with a beginning and end, which is why the term *cycle* is misleading). The path is the sequence of social statuses the individual succeeds to with growth and maturity, as from child to adult, or single to married, or child to parent. Universally, the path is triply divided into the social ages of childhood, adulthood, and old age. The category of the dead is less common, but becomes a major one in, for example, religions of ancestor worship (e.g., the family religions of at least pre-Communist China). Some cultures have many more divisions; we, for example, celebrate annual birthdays, and in Greece men (though not women) celebrate the day of the saint whose name they bear.

The rites, then, celebrate the cultural interpretations of biological changes. Another way to say this is that humans don't accept their physical selves merely as they are, but transform them into something meaningful. In rites of passage, human beings communicate not just that biological changes have occurred, but that the culture has, in two senses, managed them. First, the celebration takes them out of their nonhuman "savage" domain of "nature" and makes them part of "civil" society, or "culture." Secondly, in "civilizing" them, culture makes them what they are: Since maturation is not only a biological but a psychosocial process, the culture has also created the social means to handle the biological raw material. Ritual asserts human control in the world and celebrates the facticity of culture. Ritual re-creates the human creation of culture, in so-called "pure culture," i.e., without the material constraints of everyday life. It is "as-if." It is a representation of being human.

Life-crisis ceremonies signal and segment the seamless transformation of a human animal into a social person. Their social significance appears most plainly when they are absent. In Greece, for example, women achieve adulthood only upon marriage; Maria's unmarried thirty-five-year-old daughter still referred to herself as a girl and spent her free time with teenage girls. But, since rites of passage occur regularly and since most people go through the same stages and therefore the same rituals, the ceremonies often promote social cohesion, as we saw for the Nuer age-sets. They accomplish this solidarity through a combination of techniques. Puberty rituals, for example, are the most common markers of male adulthood, and often involved quite severe psychological, physiological, and social deprivation. An extreme example comes from the Arunta of Australia, who are famous in anthropological lore for not only circumcising the eight-to-fifteen-year-old male initiates, but also subincising them by slitting the underside of the penis to the depth of the urethra, from the glans to the base. Apart from its mysterious psychosocial symbolic content, the ritual's severity is enough to make it comprehensible only to those who have undergone it. By defying retelling, it creates an impenetrable solidarity among the initiates and an unbridgeable divide between them and all others (women and children, and people of other tribes and cultures). Therefore, rites of passage create insiders and outsiders, usually along lines of hierarchy.

In our own culture, formal initiation rites are less striking and less important, and we are generally more cynical about them, possibly because we have less control over them. In our everyday language, *ritual* connotes emptiness and meaninglessness, something which people hypocritically go through "for form's sake." Yet in clinging to forms, it seems to me that people are nevertheless holding on to something real, because as we saw in the exorcism, form itself has meaning. For example, a college graduation ceremony is a rite of passage. It often seems foolish to the graduates; in their view, their diploma, just "a piece of paper," signifies only that they have acquired a certain number of credits, not that they have learned anything. In so far as the ritual purports to be about something which has not occurred, it is, of course, empty of meaning.

The ritual is, however, not only for the graduates, the supposed center of attention, but also for the watchers on the periphery. For some, if not all, parents, administrators, and teachers, it has meaning: It ends a long, drawn-out task and validates the time and effort they have spent on it. It is as if one set of guardians, the college staff, gives a report to another, the parents. In speeches, processionals, and handing over of diplomas, they tell the parents that their hard work of raising a child and saving money was worth it, and that this is, after all, the only reasonable way to rear a child. It promotes social cohesion by gathering different groups of people in a common place, thus permitting communication among them. They can share each other's relief which this, one of our earliest definitive rituals of adulthood, provides them.

The graduation ceremony also communicates to them the ideology of ideology, and so momentarily affirms their way of living and justifies their ethos and world view. It has a formal meaning for parents, whose self-definitions are closely linked with what it is about and what its symbols represent. The ritual of commencement is really about child rearing and the "sheepskin" a mark of adequate parenthood (which, like as not, the parents, rather than the graduates, take and clutch to their breasts). It asserts that at the commencement of their child's adulthood, parenthood has not ended; it reaffirms that the parents have not lost their power over or meaningfulness to their children. All in the same moment, the old adult-child hierarchy and the new equality between parent-adult and graduate-adult are equally true descriptions of and prescriptions for reality.

Still, the commencement does say something to the graduates as well, for like other rites of passage, it is part of the continuing socialization process begun in the family. In describing what is, they tell the initiate how to be and what to do. The graduate feels alien from the ceremony, celebrants, and institution. The distance emerges from the fact that neither the graduates nor their parents have any control in organizing the proceedings or in communicating to the assembled crowd, or indeed, in running all that came before. And the fact that the graduates feel this loss of control is significant and signals the next life stage, or state of being. It characterizes other rituals and institutions in which the graduate will now make a life (if he/she can get a job) and which likewise will be controlled by others. It is significant that it is usually only the students who experience any disenchantment. The others in attendance have long ago learned their lesson, and now is their time to act as if they could forget it. As I said, one aspect of ritual is "as-if."

SEX AND SENSIBILITY

The socializing function of rites of passage raises the question of the psychic nature of the raw material on which it operates, and brings us to anthropological, psychological, and psychoanalytic theories about human sensibility. When we begin, commonsensically, to think about human psychology, we quite soon face the issue of sex. This is not merely ethnocentrism. Just as all cultures assume some inborn human nature (Western culture speaks in the biological metaphor of "instincts"), so do most make assumptions about the natures of males and females.

We face two problems here: (1) We must first question the existence of a universal human psyche, and/or one for males and one for females. (2) We next have to ask the cultural meaning or function of an ideology that proposes that such innate characteristics exist. The first problem, in a sense, stays within the premises of our own culture and accepts the culture's concern about whether there is some innate biopsychological human and sexual character. The second goes outside these particular premises and skeptically treats the issues as data; it thus stays within the premises of social science, in particular, of the sociology of knowledge.*

Let us take the first problem first, and, before going any further, define *psyche*. This is another intuitively meaningful concept, like life or culture, which is so encompassing and so elemental as nearly to defy definition. I mean something like the source in the individual of all action, rational and irrational; an "animating principle"; a sensibility; but I do not mean disembodied spirit. Psyche refers to the unconscious and conscious processes in the individual that permit the individual's survival by interacting with social and other environmental processes outside the individual, on the one hand, and with physiological and

* Perhaps really to go outside the premises of our culture, one would paradoxically have to accept them, since they include among them the assumption that one will question them. Or is this merely an exercise in demonstrating that one can't transcend one's culture?

other somatic processes inside the individual, on the other. Psyche is to personality (defined below) what culture at the first level of abstraction is to culture at the second.

In all likelihood, the characteristics of these psychic processes are universally shared. Chapter I has established that, in the Western world view, we are talking about one biological species, all of whose members can reproduce fertile offspring with one another and whose nature is a social one. Chapter II established that despite physical variation called race, all people have the same kind of mental abilities. This does not imply, as did the nineteenth-century concept of psychic unity, that all peoples share the same ideas and values. These vary culturally. For example, our ideas about procreation contrast with those of the culture of the Trobriand Islands in the Pacific; people there think that a woman becomes pregnant when her womb is entered by a spirit child for whom sexual intercourse merely widens the passageway.

In our culture, when we speak of mental ability, we usually mean intelligence, or cognitive capacity, which is one part of the psyche. Each culture contains a range of intellectual abilities in its population. Each population has a statistically "normal" distribution of intelligence such that a large number of people will share roughly similar capabilities, while a few will have a great deal more and a few a great deal less. Not only do all populations share this pattern, but the degree of ability is constant from population to population, or culture to culture.

Now, it is true that intellectual ability, as measured by, say, performance on intelligence tests, may vary culturally, depending on the culturally learned expectations of tests, as well as on prior education. If the attitudes about tests are favorable and preparation good, then the conditions favor the test-taker's chances to do well. In situations in which an upper class, or subculture, both administers the tests and controls the educational experience of an underclass, the conditions make it likely that the latter will do poorly.

The problem in discovering intellectual potential is that tests, like theories, contain views of the world that find what they are looking for. They reflect the ideology of their makers' culture or subculture and are as partial as any ideology. Thus, one could assert, but not demonstrate, that geniuses emerge in all cultures. The problem, of course, is that genius is relative; what is genius in one culture is of no importance in another. Furthermore, the concept of genius, of standing out from the crowd and the desirability of doing so, also is culturally relative, and perhaps bound only to our own culture. Finally, no test can strip down the individual's mind to the nitty-gritty of intelligence. I believe that there is some kind of nitty-gritty, but I would not expect to find it, for it would have no meaning outside a sociocultural context, and no existence outside of its association with specific affects, or feelings, and other psychological factors.

The question of human psychology, therefore, involves that of personality or character. Following Robert A. LeVine, *personality* may be defined as dispositions toward behavior in the individual that function to organize those processes which "intervene between environmental conditions and behavioral response." These processes, distinctively organized in each person, include cognition and perception, learning and memory, and the use and control of emotional reactions. They are the individual's means to cope with the world. They are the functional equivalents of the specific instinctive patterns which other animals have and humans lack.

The relationship between personality and culture is not clearcut. The American "Culture and Personality" studies, like those by Ruth Benedict and other followers of Boas, have established that personality varies culturally (though Benedict erroneously saw personality as culture writ small, and culture as a blowup of personality). On the other hand, later studies have also shown that intracultural variation in personality traits can be greater than intercultural variation.

Furthermore, recent evidence suggests that personality is a more autonomous system than had previously been thought. Some psychologists think that certain individual dispositions may be inborn, despite the seventeenth-century English philosopher John Locke's vision of the human mind as a "blank slate" until filled by experience, on which much social science and cultural relativism has been premised. I think that the best formulation of the relation between personality and culture is of two interacting systems, with personality having perhaps two phases: Formed in early and late childhood by the culture, it continues to develop in adulthood when it reciprocally helps to form the culture.

Let us then return to what may be universal in the human psyche. But note that our only way to see what is universal is, again, through a cultural lens. In this case, the lens is provided by psychoanalytic theory, both Freudian and more recently developed. This grandly comprehensive theory, created and codified in the late nineteenth century and early twentieth century by the Austrian physician, Sigmund Freud, claims to apply to all humanity (and so resembles the totalizing theories of Marx, Darwin, and others of the time). Not all people accept this claim, arguing that psychoanalysis universalizes that which is actually culturally specific. This valid criticism, to which I will return, applies only to the presumed content of the psyche. What is panhuman is not the content, but rather the structure and processes of human psychology, which, as we saw in Chapter III, structuralism too assumes.

This psychology is a joint product of the human neurological system and of the exigencies of evolutionary conditions to which all humans must adapt. Able to respond to the surrounding world with both intellect and feelings, simultaneously or independently, the individual can distinguish between self and others, subject and object, human and nonhuman. In so doing, she/he is aware of, and comments on, self, others, and her/his cultural and natural world. The commentary is codified as part of ideology and then becomes a part of the world which itself merits comment and about which people have more or less intense feelings. Such self-awareness, as I suggested in Chapter I, makes scientific theorizing, and any other idea system possible.

This awareness is called consciousness. It means that individuals can take their selves as objects, and can also be detached ("objective") about their society, culture, and values. However, a contradictory process of forgetting accompanies consciousness: Each of us has ideas, memories, feelings, attitudes, and nameless fears that exist outside our awareness. At one time, we were aware of them, but, as wishes were denied and dreams betrayed, they became too painful to bear and were consequently conscientiously forgotten. They lie dormant or unconscious in our minds; some are more solidly out of our awareness than others. This repression begins at birth and acts on our experiences even before we can express them. But consciousness begins to develop at the same time. Some cultures may inflict more denial and betrayal and therefore require more repression, than others. Similarly, it may be that in some cultures repression does not last a lifetime; one may remember in adulthood what one forgot as a child. In our culture, we usually come to recognize and transform our repressions only by psychoanalysis or other forms of psychotherapy.

The tug-of-war, however, between forgetting and knowing is probably universal, and through it children learn their cultures. Enculturation of any sort works with actively malleable, receptively creative individuals. Children do not develop without enculturation, but neither do they limply fill the molds of personality and culture. They receive them actively, though we know little yet about how they are able to transform them. Learning, however, of facts and theories, or of school-type work and social rules, or of cognitive and affective behavior, occurs unconsciously, without prompting. One can stop children, for example, from developing abstract thinking only by cruel and inhuman treatment such as we sometimes see in the savage environments of our large cities.

This creation of encultured adults from the young human animals is based on another contradictory but universal pair of strivings or tendencies. Their varied names reflect their multiple dimensions: sexuality and aggression, sociality and hostility, the life and death instincts, merging and separating, creativity and destruction. These pushes and pulls interact dynamically within and between individuals. They also underlie the social structural connections and separations examined in Chapter IV. Their several dimensions—social, psychological, biological—reflect the way these forces wind through the several systems that together constitute and are constituted by the individual organism. These systems interact in cultural forms, as in the exorcism (a spiritual cure for a physical symptom), and in enculturation. For example, the family or any other unit that socializes infants and children, brings together biological, psychological, and social systems in the transmission of culture to children, and in the children's learning of culture. Here is where the culturally formulated, adult techniques of controlling the raw biopsychological material are handed on and learned, the sexual/aggressive strivings molded, and individual personalities formed. Here humans become social persons, the occupants of statuses and the actors of roles.

One mold that these flowing passions are made to fit is a sexual one. Part of becoming a social person is learning how to have sex and with whom one can have it. All human beings learn not only that the opposite sex is culturally preferred, but that sex with one's parents and siblings is culturally prohibited. Now, if human biology and psychology are universal, and if the experience of the learning of sexual taboos is likewise universal, then shouldn't a universal human personality or psyche develop? Such reasoning, I think, led to the much criticized psychoanalytic assumption that psychic events common to Western people such as the Oedipus complex were common to all humans. The problem with this reasoning is its omission of the effect on personality of cultural variations, such as in the learning of the incest taboo and its assumption that the handling of sexuality dominates personality development.

Let us begin with the biology of the incest prohibition. Western ideology ascribes to it biological goals. Physically deformed or mentally deficient offspring appear when both parents have the recessive genes responsible for some given syndrome (like hemophilia or sickle-cell anemia), and parents are likely to share the genes if they are biological kin. One reason for the universality of the taboo, then, is its adaptive, or survival value; a population that prohibited inbreeding might be more likely to reproduce and therefore to survive. This does not require some prehistoric population to have consciously created a theory of the genetic transmission of disease; other factors, like the desire or need for allies, might have brought the rule into existence, and it might then have persisted because it favored survival.*

The individual's experience of the incest prohibition can vary in part because the specifics of the taboo vary. Inbreeding sometimes is socially required. As we have seen, the Yanomamö regularly prefer marriages, and therefore sex, between first cousins. In such cases, the absence of genetic catastrophes every generation may be due to the possibility that in a small, homogeneous population that has been inbreeding for a long time, the load of harmful and lethal genes has been reduced through the deaths, prior to reproduction, of those born with the congenital defects. Of course, such births may be more frequent than we know; in simple societies, women usually kill or expose any grossly deformed infants (whom, in any case, such societies cannot medically care for or economically support). In large, heterogeneous societies, in contrast, the lethal genes are preserved, not eliminated; the routine practice of exogamy and medical care allow their reproduction, so that inbreeding is more likely to result in genetic disasters.

But the incest prohibition sometimes is suspended in complex societies for select people for the sake of political and symbolic exigencies. In ancient Hawaii or Egypt, the only people whose "blood" was pure enough for royalty were other royalty; so Hawaiian and Pharaonic Egyptian sovereigns married their siblings. On the one hand, such royal in-marriages keep wealth and the rights to coercive territorial control out of commoners' hands. On the other, they also consolidate symbolic power: Just as monarchs have more politico-economic power than ordinary mortals, just as Polynesian chiefs can handle more mana, so they can also tolerate the dangers of normally tabooed sexuality. This is quite an effective ideological means to maintain power.

One would, then, not expect the cross-culturally variable incest prohibition to create a cross-culturally constant personality structure, were it not for the fact that all cultures do share the parent-

* This process is part of adaptation and evolution, both of which I will discuss in Chapters VI and VII.

child taboo. Can this not create a core, or nuclear, psychic experience among all humanity? Let us explore the question. Briefly, according to psychoanalytic theory, the conscious learning of the incest taboo brings on the "Oedipus complex" in the developing male child. The complex is a cluster of feelings and perceptions about the fear of castration. It emerges about age three, is repressed by age five, and unconsciously flares up and dies down at puberty. It involves the beginnings of gender-identity and sex-role assumption through the boy's recognition that his father has an exclusive claim to the mother's sexuality. The boy is frustrated in his erotic desires for her and tortured by ambivalent love-hate feelings toward him. Castration appears to the boy as an appropriate punishment for the murderous anger he feels toward his father, who, he believes, has the power to effect this truncation of the boy's virility and thereby preserve his own sexual rights. Turning his rage on himself, the boy represses the murder and fantasizes that his father will in fact castrate him. In a secondary repression, he forgets the fantasied castration, though he unconsciously continues to fear it; later in life, he develops other symtoms, like fear of women.

In developing this theory, Freud took for granted the familial and cultural milieu of his own time and place. But it is likely that the family context in which the taboo is learned, as well as the total social structure in which the family is situated, make a difference in the way the taboo is transmitted and received, and therefore in the development of personality. The most famous attempt to deny the universality of the Oedipus complex was Malinowski's interesting, though not well-documented, discussion of the Trobriand Islanders.

He suggested that in Trobriand culture, a matrilineal complex forms, but that it takes a different shape, at a later age, around a different set of people, with a different force, because sociocultural conditions differ. As in other matrilineal societies, Trobriand males control the agricultural land and resources of their own matrilineage and hold public power. Around eight years of age, a boy leaves his parent's nuclear family household to live with his mother's "brother," i.e., with some male of his matrilineage who will have economic and political power over him. Succession to lineage leadership follows this avuncular relationship and passes from "mother's brother" to "sister's son." Furthermore, childhood sexual feelings are not repressed; parents permit children to explore their sexuality with any other children except siblings. The Trobrianders, in fact, emphasize the taboo on brother-sister incest much more than the one on parent-child sexuality. This prohibition is so strong that a man cannot even discuss the marriage of real or classificatory sisters. He can control only the marriage of his daughter, who is not even in his lineage.

This arrangement contrasts strongly with the middle-class European culture of Freud and his patients. Their society is based on industrial capitalism, private property, and the nuclear family. Males control public politics, the business world, and domestic affairs, and women and children are to defer to these patriarchal household heads. Sexuality is repressed. Women are commonly thought to be nonsexual creatures, fit only for home, child care, and pedestals. Men procreate inside the home and find their erotic pleasure elsewhere. Each man thus monopolizes power over his wife and children and remains entirely out of their control. The nuclear family binds the explosively conflicting forces tightly within itself.

In the Trobriands, the structural separation of political and domestic power defuses their disruptive effect on the nuclear family and therefore their emotional charge on parent-child sexuality. Since a man's father has no public power over him, but only private household power, they may show each other affection. In contrast, a man's relations with his mother's brother are distant, for the latter controls not only his economic-political inheritance and therefore future, but also his preferred wife: The most appropriate marriage he can make is with the daughter of his mother's brother (his matrilateral cross-cousin). Sexual desire, then, becomes problematic for the Trobriand male only at or after puberty, when the issue of marriage and adult sexuality becomes important. Since the mother's brother controls its satisfaction, he, not the boy's biological father, is the most likely object of the boy's anger.

The Oedipal crisis, then, is not everywhere inevitable, and a universal theory of human development and psyche has yet to be formulated. This is especially so because Freud's and Malinowski's theories and suggestions apply to only one-half of humanity, to males. The "Electra complex," the so-called mirror-image of the Oedipal for females, does not really work. An Electra complex would be plausible only if heterosexuality were inborn. In a real mirror-image, females would begin by learning to give up their fathers and later their mothers. But they, like males, actually must also learn first to give up their mothers and later their fathers. The rules for females thus parallel, but do not mirror, those for males. Yet since their sexual futures are different, their experience also is different. The history of this experience has not yet been investigated, much less written. Feminist-oriented anthropologists have only begun to develop theories that will make research possible.

Women's early experience and the nature of human sexuality pose a puzzle whose origins lie in the fact that psychoanalytic theories or, for that matter, anthropological and sociological ones, have not sufficiently questioned their own premises. For example, even Freud wrote that we are all initially bisexual, but the implications of this idea have been generally ignored, because social values prescribe heterosexuality, proscribe homosexuality, and are extremely uncomfortable with the ambiguity of bisexuality. Theory and sometimes clinical practice thus reflect social preferences. This is a case of theory becoming, or not separating from, the cultural ideology from which it grew and which it tries to explain.

Ideology and Structure

The family, though sometimes replaced by other specialized institutions such as schools, everywhere initiates the process of reproducing social relations anew each generation. The universally primary relation it must re-create, according to the anthropologist Gayle Rubin, is sex, for sex constitutes a fundamental principle of order. But, let me emphasize, family and society embroider on sex; they do not accept it as it is. Although the incest taboo, for example, is fundamentally a biological issue, it must become encoded into cultural systems if it is to be transmitted to the young. For to be transmissible in human, i.e., symbolic, communication, it must take on symbolic form and value.

If the family is the social crossroads where biology, culture, and psychology meet, then kinship is the symbolic one (and it is no wonder that in the original myth, Oedipus killed his unrecognized father at a crossroads). Through kinship's interpretation of the incest taboo, according to Rubin, the family communicates cultural meanings about how to become an adult of the appropriate gender. She suggests that kinship terms function as symbols to organize sexuality. They transform sex, or genital differences, to create gender, or social differences. Each kinship thus contains, in addition to other things, a sex/gender system which makes males into men, females into women, and sex into love and marriage.

Kinship is the symbolic system that absorbs the incest taboo most easily not only because the roles of descent, marriage, and incest are all learned so early, but because all these rules converge on sexuality. In fact, kinship ideology often does not distinguish between incest prohibitions and exogamic prescriptions. This fusion led Mauss and later Lévi-Strauss to see incest prohibitions and marriage prescriptions as constituting the elementary principles of social integration. For them, exogamy is the earliest and most widespread human means of social cohesion: Men exchange women and thereby create alliances with one another and their kin groups.

This structural theory of incest and exogamy follows the Freudian tradition in positing sex and power as the universally dominant motivations for human behavior. The theory makes of marriage a means of alliance, and of the incest prohibition a dynamic to keep the exchanges going: If a man must renounce sexual access to, and therefore power over, his real and classificatory sisters and mothers, he is forced to find sex and spouses elsewhere. He conceives his exchange rights to kinswomen as a return for their sexual distance and uses them to negotiate for spouses with other men, who are, in turn, the real and classificatory brothers of other women.

As elegant as this model is, it is not a universally valid one. It operates quite starkly among the Yanomamö, perhaps more subtly in other cases. But do men control all marriages in all societies? Does exogamy, which links families, have to be forced by an incest taboo? Is there an innate unwillingness to leave the family group? Is there no autonomous drive to link up with others? Like Freudian theory, this structural one does not question its cultural premises. It captures not the actual means of social integration, but a widespread interpretation of it, which coincides with an individualized ideology of male dominance. It reduces the social to the individual. At least in the Euro-American experience, the learning of the incest-exogamy rule is the first time the individual learns that, in order to make her or his own life, she/he must make a relationship with a new person, i.e., with someone not of the parent-child triad, or family, or kin group. It is, then, the earliest form of social cohesion for the person, but not for culture.

Indeed, one might suggest that the incest-exogamy rules have less to do with sex (and marriage) and more to do with the creation and overcoming of boundaries between people. Recent psychoanalytic theories of the interpersonal and object relations schools suggest that the capacity to form new relationships requires having an integrated sense of self. The development of the ability to be a separate person who can simultaneously unite with others may be more crucial to mental health, or personal integration, and to the evolution of *Homo sapiens* and culture, than the management of sexual or aggressive impulses, or the overcoming of repression, in and of themselves.* It may be that the development of the individual, as idiosyncratic as it is,

*According to these theories, the failure to distinguish the boundaries between self and other constitutes one of the major symptoms of many neurotics and psychotics. The resultant merging impedes the development both of personal autonomy, or a self, and of the recognition of the separateness of the other, which are two fundamental prerequisites for genuine connections between self and other.

emerges only through confrontation and interaction with others.

I want now to turn to the fact and ideology of male dominance which the Freudo-structuralist theory of incest-exogamy rules reflects. This is an issue of contemporary concern in our culture and of long-standing concern to me. In all cultures, men generally control public, political power, the creation of symbols, and therefore most other people, things, and acts. But no innate biological differences dictate this virtual universal inequality between females and males, as is shown by the wide variation in male and female personality characteristics and social roles. Margaret Mead, for example, studied three cultures in which what is typically female in one becomes typically male in another. Among the Tchambuli of New Guinea, women handle trade and domestic affairs, while men specialize in ritual and the arts. The neighboring Arapesh have cooperative, complementary male and female roles. The third group, the nearby Mundugumor, have a division of psychosocial labor similar to ours, in which men dominate the economy, women the household, and men are seen to be rational, women emotional.

This is not to say that women share nothing cross-culturally; all women learn that they can bear children, and many share the experience of raising them. But all this is learned; there is no "maternal instinct." According to the anthropologist Nancy Chodorow, the nearly universal assignment of early childrearing to women results in a maturation experience shared by all women. Since girls are first socialized by their mothers, i.e., by women, they have their role models at first hand and early on. The immediacy of their learning how to be women contrasts with the distance between boys and their role models. Raised first by women, boys only later, at or around puberty, pass into the hands of men from whom they receive the rest of their education. This transition, and not adulthood per se, may be what puberty rituals usually mark; puberty rites are more common for males than females.

Finally, Chodorow indicates that there seems to be some evidence for women's psychic boundaries to become more "permeable" than those of men and for women to have a more immediate ability to join with others. Men develop a clearer sense of self and become less able to merge. The firsthand quality of girls' learning of their gender and sex roles may result in their understanding the world in more particularistic, affective, immediate terms. The remoteness of the boy's role model contributes to the cultural assignment to men of a more abstracted, analytic, remote view of the world. Now, in our culture, this "feminine" way of relating to and viewing the world merits contempt, the "masculine" one prestige. Both positions, of course, have advantages and disadvantages in any culture. In ours, too much merging precludes autonomy; too much distance results in mad isolation.

The question of values aside, it is clear that women and men, and their asymmetrical relationship, are made, not born. In particular, it may be that since women tend to be relegated to the household, they remain in the private domain, away from public power. Their exclusive tasks of household work and child-rearing tend to contribute to their second-class status. Yet even in those societies in which women have some economic and political power, they are deemed somehow less than men. In our culture, certain things, like emotions and intuitions, or housework and child care, symbolize femaleness and triviality. They contrast with rational sense perception, going to work every day, and serious considerations of the cosmos, which all are associated with maleness. The economically dominant Tchambuli women are thought to be morally and intellectually inferior to men; otherwise equal Arapesh women are like "daughters" to their husbands.

The second problem now arises, the professional one about the cultural meaningfulness, or function, of an ideology of innate human and male-female behavior. In answering it, I will depend for ethnographic examples largely on our own culture, for two reasons: First, data on this question are scarce, and investigations have just begun. The second reason has to do with problems of inference such as I have already discussed. Symbolic structuralism, in whose terms I have couched this chapter, does not provide us with a way to know when we have found a symbol, but we can intuitively agree that in our culture, males and females symbolize different things. Similarly, we cannot know with certainty the unconscious meaning of symbols in another culture, but we have some basis for agreeing on its likelihood in our own. In other words, here I depend on the intuitive, though not demonstrated, validity of the insider's view, on the view from familiar everyday life, to which I will apply the perspective of the specialist, or outsider.

As I suggested in Chapter I, an ideology of a unitary human nature reaffirms the self-evident validity of a culture's ethnocentrism. So, then, would a belief that some things are naturally male and others naturally female. But I think such a belief might do more. I think, following the kind of interpretation the anthropologist Mary Douglas has offered for certain other polarities, that this division is one way that a culture can create order out of chaos, as, we have seen, ideology in general and ritual in particular try to do. Thus, though some females are taller than some males, and some males have larger breasts than some females, both males and females resemble each other more than they do, say, parakeets or the sky, as Rubin points out. Yet they differ regularly enough for a culture to make them part of, or even the dominant components of, binary sets that neatly divide up the world. The separation of male and female comes to symbolize order. They join with many other things, like food, utensils, or ritual objects which have to be kept in their proper places if the social order is to survive. Among other dichotomies are pure/polluted, clean/dirty, sacred/profane, public/private, thought/feeling, and reason/emotion. In Douglas's theory, any transgression of these dichotomies can suggest disorder, danger, pollution. It is no surprise that unisex hairstyles and clothing disgust or anger some people.

But the ideology is not merely about "separate but equal," for all the first terms of the contrasts, including men, are culturally viewed as qualitatively better than the second terms, including women. Furthermore, in our own ideology, women do not even keep to their place: They also symbolize the crossing of boundaries. As Sherry B. Ortner has suggested, where men, in ideology, represent "Culture," women often represent not "Nature" but something in between. In Ortner's view, ideologies create everywhere a distinction between Culture and Nature. Culture represents humans' transcendence of the givens of their existence; it is therefore higher than Nature. The position of women in this hierarchy is universally in the middle. Their association with childbirth and childrearing, and their greater embeddedness in everyday private life, make them seem closer to nature than men who, in engaging in public relations between private households, participate in the creation of Culture and so transcend the givens of Nature. Women, though part of Culture, transcend Nature less than men.

Secondly, women also are seen as synthesizing Nature and Culture by converting infants and children into enculturated human beings. Indeed, women's performance of what is recognized, though not always honored, as a crucial function for society may lead to the frequently severe restrictions on their sexuality and on the knowledge and power to which they are allowed access. Finally, women can be symbols, pure and simple, of the ambiguity and paradox of the universe. Woman appears as the Giver and Taker of life. The "feminine" mode of relating has two forms: Its particularistic, everyday aspect is seen as lower than the remote, social relations between men; but its quality of intuitive, boundary-crossing, mother-child communion is seen as higher, transcending daily life and symbolizing a desired merging with that which is higher than human beings.

A complete explanation for women's secondary status will emerge only from the study of the specifics of any separate cultures. But the issue's lack of clarity, combined with the power of its symbols, infuriates many. For the ideology's unequal division of psychosocial labor between males and females purports not only to describe the world, but to prescribe for it. Feminists question the description's validity, for it distorts what it supposedly reflects. Feminists also challenge the prescription's morality, for it serves the interests of an ongoing social structure by oppressing one group in it.

One might think the problem was one merely of people changing their minds: If we believed and acted as if women and men were equal, some think, then they would become so. But the problem has both a material and a structural base. Ideology does not float independently above the life we live daily. It creates a vision of a particular reality in order to serve that reality. The division of the world into male and female things interlocks with a particular economic system and its world view.

Let us examine this interlocking briefly as a way of summarizing this chapter. Our fundamental psychosocial philosophy, partial and conflicted, presumes a universal "Economic Man." It defines humanity by a desire for personal gain, instincts for aggression and territoriality, and a search for monetary and emotional profit. But "Economic Man," though meant to be universal, turns into "economic male." Euro-American ideology both perceives and values human beings as independent (or isolated) takers and disparages connections in which individuals receive help from others. It then transforms this ethos into the symbolic system just described: Men, it supposes, are instinctively independent, aggressive loners and women the dependent, tenderly nurturant socializers; the former are praised, the latter denigrated.

In reality, no such split occurs: Men work interdependently in corporate groups and also love and give; women toil in isolated nuclear family households, and also take and hate. In reality, too, organized cooperation and sharing, not chaotic grabbing, are the human means of survival; all people in our culture (and, in fact, throughout the world) are economically interdependent. Phylogeny, the evolution of organic life, partakes of matter's progression toward increased integration at higher and higher levels of organization: Organisms can be arranged from amoebas to humans, from the less to the more structurally complex. The complex organisms have their parts more interdependent and the incidence of their social ties more prevalent. In this sense, Mauss was correct to postulate "the Gift"—the obligation to give, to receive, and to repay, of which the exchange of women is but one example—as the mark of society and humanity. The need to exchange with others is the specifically human form of increased social complexity and integration.

Though in our ideology the exchange of services between women and men is central to the formation of any and all culture, it really is auxiliary to our particular economic and political orders. Because of this, our images of men and women become partial and abstracted. Our ideology splits up a total human self into two parts, assigning one to males, the other to females. Masculinity symbolizes the adult status of active domination in the outside world of work. Work becomes important not only for its material reward but because it reciprocally symbolizes power and adult responsibility. When men lose their jobs, they feel they have lost their masculinity. Femininity splits. It represents both the mother, keeping the house comfortable, and the child, passively receiving money and consuming it on leisurely weekly or daily shopping trips. If a woman must go to work, she feels she loses her femininity. The social definitions of genders thus lie outside the person's control; they have become reified, and depend on the acquisition of paying work.

The total human being constructed from these two halves is a contradictory, disjointed creature. Its chaos is but part of the fragmentation of our social and family structures, which appears in the way our secular institutions take control of our lives and rituals. Our ceremonies become "ritualistic" because we rarely participate actively in them. It is not just that most of us are usually passive spectators of ceremonies. We rarely join in creating and maintaining *any* of our ideology, because only a few specialists like clergy, politicians, academics, and advertisers, in their appropriate specialized institutions, have the honed social self-awareness to do so. And they reap the rewards of these skills, like the others in power who try to keep these skills from the rest of the population.

In contrast, the Arunta in their whole culture and the Greeks in their exorcism are, I think, pesonally more integrated than we are. The Arunta men actively create and perform their ritual and interpret their beliefs; they similarly control their economic and political life. The Greek women, in their exorcism, are also in control; Maria's sons were close, eager observers who clearly identified with the role of the afflicted. They are true believers, in that they participate fully with spirit and body. Ritual for them is a total experience, an intellectual, esthetic, and personal realization. For the noncynical believer, ritual renews the belief which brings it about, and the belief in turn sanctifies the ritual. But their belief is possible also because it rests on a solid integration between social form, social function, and social control. In contrast, the individual's loss of control of his/her own life experience, including rituals, typifies complex societies. In our culture, and perhaps sometimes in the Greek one, most activities are organized so that only part of one's self is engaged. At our work, for example, only that part that contributes to the interest of the firm is relevant; at play, only that which is fun-loving; at church, only the reverent. In church, indeed, the Greeks resemble us, for there the control lies in the specialists' hands.

Splitting is the psychodynamic correlate of specialization and lack of control. We do not split ourselves usefully in the sense of experiencing and observing ourselves, but painfully in the sense of realizing only one set of possibilities. As corporations and other institutions come to specialize in the family's functions, so, as our definitions of male and female show, do people specialize in parts of being human. Such unintegrated beings grow from and also produce a certain set of political and economic conditions. As the late anthropologist Jules Henry said in 1963, we are part-persons. Though enculturated to seek self-realization and to live up to and even beyond our potential, we find in our narrowly specialized work only limited scope for our creative energy. Our economy encourages not the realization of self, but only its development along single dimensions. As consumers, we unconsciously substitute our increasingly rich standard of living for an increasingly impoverished personal experience. With diminished selves, we have a hard time securely integrating with others.

Work and leisure, though alternating phases of one human existence, become split like the self. They too become reified, for they escape the individual's control. It may not be going too far to say that they become rituals celebrating the cultural ideas toward which enculturation conducts the young: They celebrate an ethos which makes rational sense (one must, after all, work and consume) and a world view that is emotionally persuasive (it is morally good to work; it feels good to buy). Male and female, locked in their union of heterosexual monogamy, summarize this ideology. Their fulfillment of standard roles enables the economic system to survive by having the male work and the female provide homely, leisure comforts.

Yet the facts that we have lost an unquestioned belief in ritual and that our culture assures its own self-examination, contain within them the possibility that neither ritual nor ideology need blindly dominate us. The fact that we split the human self into two parts raises the possibility of a new joining. The fact that we can know, not believe in, our culture, gives us the chance to control it. To take this chance, we must also control the material and political conditions of its existence. These are the subjects of the next chapter.

VI.

Energy, Work, and Power: From the Frying Pan into the Fire

Modes of Production

Sociality, or the human tendency to cooperate, does not happen naturally, without order, plan, or consciousness. It is made. Human survival requires cultural form which aligns the behavior of diverse individuals and groups. Kinship is one such form, the division of labor another, bureaucracy a third. The control of this vital process, i.e., of the continuing re-production of social life, is the essential basis of power. Does this fact mean that power inequalities are embedded in the human condition? Can coordination ever be automatic, or self-regulating, without some inordinately powerful person or group controlling it? Or do power differentials inevitably emerge from the necessities of administration? Unanswered questions like these provoke the considerations in this chapter.

It may seem odd to begin a chapter concerning power and inequality by referring to cooperation. Yet as true as it is that power often entails conflicts and that "power comes out of the barrel of a gun," it is also true that conflict and combat grow from the difficulties met by the progressively increasing integration that has typified the evolution of culture. This integration involves the elaboration of the ways social life is created, and their increased coordination. As Chapter V showed, the family re-creates social life by reproducing human beings, shaping their sexual strivings into gender, their social tendencies into roles, their asocial urges into a sense of self and a desire for new unions. Other organizations also re-create social life by using the raw human substance. The economic system produces material and mental means of survival by coordinating human actions in systems of exchange. The political system makes the production and use of these means possible by organizing concerted group action to achieve group goals, and by reconciling the conflicts within and between groups.

Economics and politics are the twin subjects of this chapter: What links them is power. Quite briefly, since volumes can be and have been devoted to it, *power* is the capability of getting things done, with respect to people or to objects or to social structures or to ideas; it may rest in individuals or collectivities. Power occurs universally, and emerges at different levels of organization—psychological and cultural, intra- and inter-societal—and in different forms—material and mental, structural and symbolic. Power exists because some people are older or bigger or smarter than others; because some populations are larger than others; because some cultures have more efficient relations to their environments, more effective weapons, more persuasive ideologies, and/or more centralized and efficient administrative organizations.

But these differences do not necessitate inequalities. Among humans, the strong do not have to kill the weak, the smart mock the dull, the efficiently adapted drive out the less adapted, or the more organized and armed subjugate those less so. Culture transforms differences into inequalities and, in turn, creates new differences. Inequality in power is a social relation whereby one person or group has an advantage in realizing desires and getting things done, although and perhaps because others lacking that advantage can't. The question is, then, what enables political or economic power to crystallize in one part of a society and not in another? And why does this happen?

This chapter, promising no answers, examines the issues and problems that arise in grappling with these and other questions. Some issues have arisen before, such as the relation between individual and culture or between mind and matter. For example, How do some people get power over others, even if the others don't want them to? We might answer that although people don't consciously want to be subordinate to anyone else, perhaps unconsciously they do. Yet this psychic contradiction is insufficient to explain power differences: It permits, but cannot cause, inequality; it can only fit in with another action. The cause lies in the interaction of psychological and social processes. Let us say, for example, that some person or group takes over material things, like land, which others need. The conqueror can then maintain this power through continual, though veiled, threats of physical punishment, which stimulate and reinforce the others' psychic dependency.

Yet even this example is far too simple. Apart from outright theft and physical coercion, the processes by which some gain power over others are not only subtle and long-term, but also complicated. They might involve, for example, the use of cultural ideology as propaganda to play contradictory conscious or unconscious desires off against one another in order to secure or to maintain control without a continual show of force. The means to power come from all domains of human activity. The economy, for example, is a major source of power, even though our own cultural world view distinguishes it from political power proper. Indeed, the social sciences traditionally conceptualize it as a virtually autonomous subsystem, little affected by the rest of its culture and expressive of self-evident, "natural" laws to which it is subject. Yet even in the simple example above, economic organization and political power are contingent upon one another, as, indeed, holism postulates. Though economies are subject to laws, these laws are the products of the interaction between nature and culture, not of one self-propelled segment of either.

Given this criticism, the usual social science definition of *economy*, the "production, distribution, and consumption of goods and services," needs amplification. It is too narrow. This conceptualization triply segments a continuous reality because it reflects the particular historical circumstances from which it comes: The capitalist economic system is triply segmented into producers (e.g., firms or corporations), distributing institutions (e.g., banks, stock exchanges), and consumers (e.g., households, businesses). The definition comes from the theory of bourgeois or capitalist (as distinct from Marxist) economics, whose concern is to explain and prescribe for capitalist economy. Since the anthropological concern reaches temporally and spatially beyond capitalism, it cannot take these economic arrangements as constants. Only a more universal definition can encompass cross-cultural variation in economic systems and perhaps make more sense of capitalism than its own definition. In its broadest sense, economy, or as it is sometimes called, political economy, is about the creation not merely of wealth, but of human social existence itself. This formulation suggests the contingency of all parts of the economic system and posits the economy as an integrated part of a whole culture.

This broad definition enables us to revise the standard one so as to take into account the unity of the three segments. With the French structural-Marxist anthropologist Maurice Godelier, I would say that the economy consists of both a particular set of activities composing one part of the structure (production, distribution, and consumption) and a particular feature of all activities, the exchange and use of material means. The economy depends on and produces services and intangibles by means of the material goods which it produces. The economy thus rests on the physical environment, though it is not reducible to it. Rather, through physical and mental work, humans create a series of connections between culture and nature that together are called the *ecological adaptation.* The character of the ecological adaptation, like that of all social life, shapes and is shaped by the process of production.

Energy, Work, and Power

In Marxist economic thought, the productive process is central to an understanding of any economic system. Labor-power, in conjunction with material means, yields all wealth and satisfies all needs. This work that human beings do creates all wealth and value in a society; all their actions re-create the society.* Once said, this is obvious. The questions are, then, What are the needs? What actions meet them? And how do they reproduce the society? First, in the course of satisfying physiological survival needs, the production process quite literally enables people to stay alive. In order to get food, they must work; they expend energy that they must restore if they are to live and work another day. So they must procure or produce replacement calories and nutrients. In addition to thus reproducing individual flesh, the economy also supports biological reproduction, by providing energy for sexual intercourse, and for the needs of infants, young children, and pregnant and lactating women. All these activities require objects or tools, and these too are created and replaced.

The economy also supports, and therefore re-produces, the rules, institutions, and values by which people create, exchange, and use objects and actions. We usually think of needs in a utilitarian sort of way, reducing them to bedrock surivival goods. But human beings, who are not merely biological organisms, also need intangibles and luxuries to stay alive. They can work only in the context of a particular organization of people, activities, and things. They can mate and procreate only within rules and institutions. And they need a "ceremonial fund" to mount the public rituals that demonstrate world view and morality and thereby secure acceptance of rules and institutions.

* Gold, for example, becomes valuable only because of the effort involved in extracting it. Such effort is expended when the relations of production require people to compete over scarcity, i.e., when one of the principles of the economic system is scarcity. The natural rarity of "precious" metals is thus utilized by a particular social system. Their "preciousness" does not come from their scarcity, but from the view of the society, from a cultural ideology which values that which is scarce.

Although our culture classifies such social relations and ideological systems as noneconomic, without them no economic activity would take place. Here is a simple, homely example: A man earns money to support his family, i.e., a social institution; in turn, his family supports him emotionally and physically, by giving him food, love, companionship, and a reason to keep on slugging. Curiously, our culture downgrades these emotionally-supportive activities, unless they are remunerated, in which case we call them services like those of educators, psychotherapists, or prostitutes. But unpaid work, like raising children, arguing with spouses, or visiting friends is fundamental to economic action. It produces things that are of use, though not utilitarian, things such as enculturated children or a more secure framework for social action. Likewise, people need leisure to relax, reflect, and speculate about self, others, and the world, and to rethink their world views. Humans with no playtime for creativity may survive biologically, but they work poorly, and if they do not revolt, their apathy reduces reproduction, and they die out.

The form of economic activity shapes the quality of life. This form is called a mode of production. A *mode of production* consists of the material forces of production and the relations of production. The *material forces* or factors are basic resources, like water and land; labor; and technology (which ranges from tangibles, like tools or elaborate machines or money, to intangibles like knowledge of hunting territory or "pull" in getting lower tax assessments). The *relations of production* are determined by the distribution of control over political power, productive forces, and people; they are the relations of appropriation between people. Together, the relations and forces constitute the process of production, i.e., the organization and hierarchy of work, the division of labor, and the aims of production. Chapter III discussed some of the relations of the capitalist mode of production;* other familiar kinds are the feudal and the socialist modes, and we will see two or three different ones below.

* Private property; privately owned labor which is regarded like any other commodity and can be sold for wages; the acquisition of all goods

Energy, Work, and Power

A crucial distinction among modes of production lies in their aims, which determine *distribution,* or how products, or goods and services, get from producer to consumer; the aims, in turn, are governed by the rules of access to resources given in the relations of production. The crucial distinction is between production for use and production for exchange. *Production for use* means that something, a good or a service, is made to satisfy a specific need of a particular person or group; in our culture, a housewife's cooking of dinner for her husband and children is an example of production for use. *Production for exchange* means that a good or service is created to be traded for something else, usually money or some other valuable object; hence, the production of meals in a cafeteria is production for exchange.

Use-production involves nonremunerated labor and a price-less product; it is of value only to those for whom it has been made or done. Our culture defines the production of such *use-values* as noneconomic; for example, when the Federal Government tallies the Gross National Product, it omits housework. In other words, our cultural ideology defines as (adult) *work* only those activities that are transferrable for money. Such activities and their products are called commodities and have *exchange-value:* another way of saying this is that the use-value of commodities lies in the fact that they are alienable—someone will pay money in exchange for them. Most of our production is based on exchange-value, and any proper use-values are ignored, sentimentalized (like, recently, home-canning), or mocked. Although some praise mother's pot roast as "priceless," the adjective is double-edged, for if something has no price on the market, then it also is very often "valueless." We value things that are alienable, therefore "alien" to our personal, particular identities. This is the meaning and source of the psychological sensation and social

---

and services through money purchase; the aim and need to make a profit; the assumption that each economic actor acts in her/his individual "self-interest"; and the ownership by one group of people of money, land, and technology, and by another of labor only, so that the latter must sell labor to the former.

fact of *alienation*, which characterizes economies based on exchange-value (as well as their institutions, as we saw in the case of college graduation in Chapter V).

The mode of production is a concept that encompasses the economic system as a whole, and we will examine different varieties of it below. But we also have to connect it to the micro-level. In any mode of production, from the individual's viewpoint what she/he is doing is making a living, by expending a certain amount of energy and resources so as to realize some goal, be it food, the manufacture of an object, or anything else that will enable one to continue living. Thus, all people economize; this means that all people match their resources or means to priority-ordered goals. For example, in our culture, if one has only one thousand dollars ("scarce" means), one must ration it. As an entrepreneur, one might add it to savings or loans to open a restaurant, build a factory, or start a new line in an established factory. As a consumer, one might save for a child's education, buy a used car, or splurge on a fur coat. But one must divide the thousand dollars among the alternatives. Therefore, one must rank one's desires; the order one chooses depends on the immediacy of any one need/want, and on one's social position or personal history.

This behavior is technically called maximizing. It has sometimes been thought that people in other cultures do not maximize as we do, preferring to spend money on, let's say, pilgrimages or transistor radios instead of saving it. The difference between us and people in other cultures is not that they don't ever maximize, but that they maximize different things. For example, one Greek tailor we knew maintained that he earned enough both to support his family and to close his one-man shop for a day whenever he felt like it; he traded a day's earnings for male companionship in the café. He was interested in satisfying known and finite demands, not in accumulating cash to invest in some larger project.

In other cultures, too, neither the goals nor the means are as unlimited as ours appear to be. We are victims of a culture of plenty that allows us to think that we can be whatever we want and makes us want everything, including the unimaginable.

In contrast, to be a Nuer male means simply to herd cattle. The Greek village men I knew could become only herders, farmers, tailors, or construction workers, according to their fathers' occupations. The Nuer have no choice, the Greeks' range of choice is narrow. But paradoxically, the more the choice, the greater the uncertainty.

Finally, such economies offer fewer consumption choices. Greek rural people rarely go to college, drive cars or wear fur coats, though they do buy transistor radios when they get the chance. In general, the object or goal for which they spend money is limited by immediate survival needs or defined in advance by social and ceremonial needs. This is not to imply that the Greeks are "slaves to custom," for they do indeed make economizing choices: Our seventy-two-year-old landlady, who perpetually told me how she "made economies," would bargain for slightly spoiled vegetables in the market, and others would save for tuition at secondary or technical schools for their eldest or most able sons.

Economizing, then, is a universal process, but its content varies with the *substantive economy*, i.e., with the work people actually do.* The most common types of substantive economy are foraging (hunting, fishing, and gathering wild vegetables), domestication (agriculture, horticulture [the raising of domesticated plants using only human and no animal labor with simple tools like hoes], and pastoralism), and industrial manufacturing. Usually none of these occurs alone. For example, people in cultures like

* There is a now-moribund debate in the subfield of economic anthropology over the meaning of *economy*. The formalists hold that a process, that of *economizing*, lies at the heart of any economy. The substantivists hold that economizing occurs only in market economies and that the substantive definition is the only cross-culturally valid one. The latter are relativist, insisting on the diversity of means of survival, the former, universalist, insisting on the unity of economies. Obviously, both similarities and differences must be taken into account, preferably by the same theory. Since these provide neither such a theory nor an analysis of production, I have chosen not to take a position in either camp. However, I do use three major concepts developed by the creator of substantivism, Karl Polanyi; these are reciprocity, redistribution, and market exchange.

those of the /Kung or the Australians, who hunt game for their animal protein, also gather wild roots and berries, which constitute 70 percent of their diet. Pastoralists, such as Saharan camel herders, barter livestock for grain in settled villages on the edge of the desert; blacksmiths and merchants travel into the desert to sell them metal pots and other craft objects, and the nomads pay with money from hides they have sold in a regional market-place that they visit occasionally. Economic systems like ours, most of whose activities consist of manufacturing and the production of services, require a solid agricultural basis, lest the factory and office workers starve.

The way that things are produced in one area of substantive economy may affect the way that things are produced in another. For example, American agriculture was once organized primarily into family farms that produced some for use and some for exchange. As most of the rest of production came to be industrially organized, so farming became industrial agriculture, based on the cultivation of thousands of acres. Run to increase the rate of profit, and not at all for use-values, agribusiness is an investment that its owners will sell if they can get a higher return in some other sector of the economy. Its patterns of production and sale depend on the needs of profit, not of nutrition. Thus, owners act in the same way as manufacturers of cars or cribs.

This example suggests that two modes of production, such as family farming and agribusiness represent, may coexist in one society, but that one will dominate or eventually take over. For example, one area of use-production that continues to thrive in our economy is the household; but if monetary values are assigned to housework and child rearing, they too will go the way of all labor, gaining the respect accorded paid work and its alienation as well.

All theorists do not concur that different modes of production can coexist in one culture, but the French anthropologist, Claude Meillassoux, makes a good case for it in his analysis of the Gouro of the Ivory Coast. Let us examine their economy in some detail so as to see what a mode of production is, how two can coexist, and why they do so. The Gouro's substantive economy includes hunting, animal husbandry, wild-food collection, horticulture, and the manufacture of small handicrafts. Their villages are sectioned into patrilineages, the elders of each forming the village council; the overall structure of their society resembles that of the Nuer. The Gouro have two modes of production, the village mode and the lineage mode, each organizing different activities, products, and processes of exchange.

The village mode is collective and egalitarian, and produces for use. Based on the hunting of small game (e.g., deer) by males, its material forces consist of hunting nets, spears, and the village fallow land. Birth in the village confers the right to hunt, because the land is held in common, as are the trees of which spearshafts are made. The iron for spear points, however, must be purchased by the elders from blacksmiths of another society. Finally, the hunting nets belong to lineages, and the larger nets require several men to work them. The distribution of control over the means of production—common land and net ownership—and the technical requirement that nets be collectively handled, mean that the work of the hunt is also organized collectively. It can be initiated, however, by any individual who is willing to recruit and direct others in his village for the hunt itself; he does not command the hunting but rather integrates its various activities.

The distribution of the catch follows collective, egalitarian principles, echoing those which regulate control of the means of production. Although the leader will sometimes receive an extra leg for his administrative services, the products of the joint effort are otherwise shared equally, according to a type of exchange called by anthropologists *balanced reciprocity*. This means that two individuals, or two groups, of equal social standing, exchange or partake of equivalent agreed-upon amounts of specific goods and/or services. This material equalization parallels the egalitarian structure of the production unit: The hierarchy dissolves when the hunt is over, and a new one will form for the next hunt. The organization of work in the village mode thus prevents administrative control from crystallizing into entrenched hierarchical power.

The lineage mode, however, has a more permanent hierarchy, based on the power of lineage elders over junior males. Organized primarily for use-values, it produces some exchange-values as well. The patrilineage is both production unit and consumption unit. It organizes horticulture, of which the factors of production are wooden and iron tools, land, and labor. The wooden tools belong to individuals, but are freely borrowed and lent. Only the elders can personally own iron tools, but they have enough for use by the men and women under their direction.

The control of land follows the segmentary integration of Gouro society. As among the Nuer, kinship and territorial principles combine to produce equal, cohesive residential units, which sometimes join together along a hierarchy of patrilineal descent. The arable land belongs to the lineage, but since it is also part of village land, it will be protected by the village as a whole against trespassers. The village cannot keep the lineage from its land, just as the elders have no right to sell the iron tools. Reciprocally, the lineage cannot take its land away from the village, or the village, its land from the tribe (which has residual rights to it). The Gouro, therefore, have no private ownership; all resources and goods are for group use, are included within successively higher levels of organization, and have only use-value, at least within Gouro society.

The elders coordinate cultivation and the distribution of the harvest, but this yields them no great power since everyone knows the routine. Elders allocate plots and supervise the division of labor. Work teams consisting of several households coordinate their efforts to plow, plant, and harvest seasonal crops. Smaller teams of one or two households maintain fields and pick crops daily. Labor in their *slash-and-burn*, or *swidden*, cultivation is generally divided according to sex: Men cut and burn forest and secondary growth, following which the women plant the crops on the cleared land (maize, manioc, taro, rice, etc.); during the growing season, women and men together tend banana trees and plants; finally, women do most of the harvesting.

The elders also administer distribution, by means of *redistribution*, in which a central authority assumes control over goods and services, and decides how much and to whom it will later return them. Here, junior males and the females deliver the crops to the lineage granary that one elder, or the senior elder's wife, manages. The main meal of each day, made from granary stores, is eaten communally in the evening by members of the lineage. Each household forms a smaller consumption unit within the group, and receives food according to its size.

The lineage mode, unlike the village mode, also regulates production for exchange. Classificatory lineage brothers hunt elephants and give the ivory tusks to elders, who also receive harvests of kola nuts from women and children. Livestock, grazed on lineage fallow land, belong to the elders. Finally, artifacts such as baskets or loincloths belong to the community in the person of the elders; the craftsmen receive their food with their domestic group, just as if they had been doing joint cultivation. The elders barter these commodities with tradesmen from other societies for the guns and other metal products which the Gouro want for bride-wealth. Thus, the Gouro economy, which is geared primarily to the production of *subsistence,* i.e., to the satisfaction of the needs/wants of its members, is linked secondarily to a market economy.

A *market economy* is an economic system in which the factors of production are acquired, or distributed, by price. They are for sale to anyone, not inextricably wedded to a corporate group. The means of production therefore have exchange-value. Their value, like that of other commodities, lies not in their use to a particular person or group, but in their utility to any person who can consume them or use them in a later exchange (for other goods or money); part of the meaning of "price" lies in this value. The goods brought to market are those things defined by their producers as not immediately necessary for subsistence or ceremonial needs; they are, relative to the needs/wants of the production unit, "surplus."

Whereas most economic activities in a use-value economy concern production and consumption, distribution activities assume an equal importance in a market economy. People completely enmeshed in distribution, like merchants, make their living from money. They buy in order to sell, i.e., in order to make money, in contrast to people like the Gouro elders who sell in order to buy, i.e., in order to satisfy consumption needs. Merchants, of course, must also feed themselves, but their participation in the market has a special quality. It is especially affected by the way market exchange depersonalizes the exchangers. They become anonymous and may, if necessary, haggle without the moral obligation to look out for the other's well-being, which is one of the bases of use-value economies.

By eliminating this concern for the other, market exchange might make possible the transformation of the Gouro hierarchy of administration into one of unequal power. But the culture is in principle protected from this by structural and ideological mechanisms that keep the external market economy and the internal use-economy separate. Only elders may trade, and their use of goods is prescribed according to the Gouro's three *spheres of exchange,* or areas of distribution. These are the subsistence, the market, and the marriage spheres.

The spheres are spatiotemporally, structurally, and ideologically separate. The subsistence sphere has the least moral worth, and includes everyday food, clothing, and shelter; the market sphere is midway in worth, involving the exchange of commodities on the market; and the marriage sphere is morally superior, containing bride-wealth goods and brides. The items of the marriage sphere and the commodities traded for them constitute prestige goods, which the elders must use on behalf of the lineage to marry off its young men. Since marriage is exogamous to the lineage and village, and the elders control intervillage and other political relations, they also arrange matches and negotiate bride-wealth. Their control over the matrimonial process in effect also gives them some power over junior males, while insulating the everyday subsistence activities in which the juniors participate from the rules and values of the varket.

The lineage mode, not the village mode, integrates the economy, so that the principle of kinship dominates over that of territory. First, the lineage mode centers on the subsistence sector which ensures the daily continuity of life. Subsistence production absorbs the bulk of labor, energy expenditure, and daily concerns, and the subsistence economy is organized largely by kinship. Kinship, in fact, organizes access to natural and produced resources, the division of labor, and inter-economy relations. Kinship ideology links the two modes symbolically as well: Like the Nuer, the Gouro speak of villages as patrilineally related lineages. Furthermore, segments of hunting parties and intravillage residential areas, are based on lineage membership. Finally, the village council contains all the elders of all the lineages, so that the lineage mode colors even peacetime politics.

Secondly, since the elders regulate marriage, the lineage mode controls labor. The economic aspect of marriage is its organization of labor: A marriage adds a worker to the community, one of whose jobs it is to produce other workers, i.e., children. Although membership in the corporate lineage makes other factors of production like natural resources and tools (except metal) equally available to all, labor, being human, has a mind and will of its own. Since survival depends on human energy, the control, or at least the organization, of people is crucial. Therefore, as the French structural Marxist anthropologist Emmanuel Terray saw, kinship becomes crucial, because its function is precisely that, to create, out of raw human flesh, social beings who will cooperate. The power of kinship to do this, like its power to organize the sex/gender system, comes from its ambiguity: Not biological, its basis in biology makes it appear arbitrary and unquestionable, like a commandment from outside society itself; but, since it is also made by humans, it can be bent and shaped as needed.

Since kinship is the logical dynamo of economic and social reproduction, it therefore makes sense that the lineage mode extends to noneconomic social life as well. Lineage elders thus oversee the reproduction of society, physiologically through food production, and biologically through marriage. They also administer the reproduction of social structure, for they enable new households to form. Finally, as the repositories of lore, myth, and genealogies, and as controllers of ritual, they participate in the village council, arrange intervillage marriages, and thereby recreate the political structure.

What, then, is the function of the village mode? It has two major characteristics: only males participate in it, and its activities, group hunting and warfare, are not daily affairs. Furthermore, Meillassoux tells us, hunting and war have attached to them more ceremonials and prestige than any lineage mode activities. The village mode thus seems (though Meillassoux does not say this explicitly) to function for extraordinary and future political needs: It organizes people so that they may defend themselves in war, and socializes them by creating interlineage ties among the juniors who will eventually work together as elders on the village council. Its association with ceremonial is based on ritual's function to re-enact and reinforce the fact and process of the village's long-term unity. Its function then is a "between" one, for it connects otherwise self-sufficient lineages and villages in political action.

Exchange and the Market

As self-sufficient as primitive or subsistence economies are, producing most of their required goods and services themselves, what really distinguishes them from the market economies of complex societies is the relatively *unmediated* character of their activities. This means that little stands between the human being and the material forces, or products, of her/his work. For example, among the Gouro, the producers also control the means of production, and the elders, whose interests are nearly identical with the workers', organize the work. The lineage mode's production unit is the same in personnel and structure as its consumption unit, so that decisions about production and about consumption are one and the same, and there are no distributors, or middlemen, to come between them. Finally, and crucially, the dominant factor of production is labor, whose material substance, human beings, is the same as that of society itself. Kinship organizes both labor and society; the human body belongs only to the group and to the individual, and the only people who can withhold its power are those whose interests are fused by the arbitrary fiat of kinship. Within the confines of their culture's limited control over nature, and of the elders' limited control over juniors and females, people in primitive societies control their own destinies. Power is relatively equally dispersed among them.

A subsistence economy begins to disappear when some thing or person comes between producer and means of production. When a major factor effectively escapes personal or kinship control, people must work not only to provide subsistence, but also to acquire the needed productive factors. Those who control the means of production also control the producers. *Peasants* are people who produce primarily for their own needs, but need to acquire the use of land by paying rent, taxes, or tribute to some other social group. Peasants, therefore, have to produce for exchange. Peasants are at the bottom of a structure of power, and landlords, government officials, and the like are on top, usually organized in a different mode of production from the peasants.

In peasant society, production and consumption units partly coincide and partly split apart. Let us look at the nineteenth-century ancestors of the Greek villagers whom I studied. They had what might be called the domestic mode of production.* The patrilineal extended family household was both production and consumption unit. Shepherds, for example, would raise sheep and goats, make cheese from the milk, weave fabric from the wool, and make clothes of the woolens. Since the household worked for its own wants/needs, the producers were also the consumers. Distribution followed both reciprocal and redistributive processes. In order, however, to satisfy its needs, the household also had to produce for the market economy. People needed money to buy things like olive oil, flour, coffee, sugar, and metals,

* Marshall Sahlins created the idea of the domestic mode more for societies like the Gouro than for peasant societies, but A. V. Chayanov's original application, from which Sahlins derived his model, was to Russian peasants. In any event, it may be that the domestic mode, in the absence of a mediating central authority, could be equivalent and alternative to a lineage mode. The conceptualization of types of modes of production, other than capitalism and socialism, is just beginning; I expect other modifications to emerge.

and to pay taxes. They would sell cheese, stock, and clothing in the village or in those marketplace bazaars in county and provincial seats where they bought their staples. With each new wife or child, they would increase the size of the herds, the number of cloaks made, and so on; they would increase production to build up trousseaux and decrease it when daughters married and left home.

This participation in a market economy continually threatened the unity of production and consumption. Like the Gouro, the peasants separated the domestic and market domains; for example, only the eldest male of the household would deal with merchants and handle money. But the domestic mode was not as insulated as the Gouro economy, for the Greeks used the money for everyday as well as special occasions, thus allowing subsistence to become subject to the rules and vicissitudes of the market. Furthermore, the members of the household were caught in a contradiction: They worked for each other, but could realize these use-values only by producing for exchange, the control of which transactions belonged to higher levels of organization. The village owned the land and pastures corporately, and paid tribute to the then-dominant Ottoman Empire. The village raised this tribute by taxing the livestock of the individual households. Ultimately, then, the power to decide on the household's production lay not even at the level of the village government, but at that of the Empire.

And even this power was based on more distant origins, and its strength and remoteness increased throughout the twentieth century. Since the financial needs of both the Ottoman Empire and, after 1913 (when the geographical area in which the village is located became part of Greece), the Greek government were affected by world market prices, inflations, and wars, taxes perpetually rose. Taxation, in turn, increased the proportion of labor and energy the peasants had to devote to working in the market in order to earn money, and decreased proportionally their production of use-values. The distance between domestic and market domains lessened until now all production, except that of keeping house, cooking food, and making woolen underwear, blankets, and rugs, has come to be for exchange. All other needs can and must be met by spending money. As in other complex societies, kinship and use-production now coincide only in the household.

The processes which brought this about, here and elsewhere, involve money, specialization of labor, and changes in the relations of production. Now, not all economic systems depend on money: Exchange can be carried out by barter (as between Gouro elders and tradesmen) or by conventional amounts (Greek trousseaux sometimes varied within a fixed range of value). No intermediary objects are needed where production is for use, and people know what they need and when they need it. But when the aim of production is to acquire not products but their exchange-value, and thereby to purchase something else or to realize a profit, then objects which have no intrinsic, but only symbolic value, which are portable, which can be subdivided and standardized, and of which accounts can therefore be kept, become very useful: These objects are *money,* and they symbolize the exchange-value produced.

The use of money as a medium of exchange allows commodity production to take over use-value production and the principles of market-exchange to eliminate reciprocity and redistribution. For example, the Gouro's participation in a market economy has begun to merge their three spheres of exchange. Though symbolically separate, the spheres are nevertheless linked both in structure (for the elders regulate all three) and in substance: The subsistence sphere produces the goods that the second and third require; for example, the maize grown feeds the weavers (subsistence), whose loincloths are traded in the market (market), for funds to pay for brides (marriage). Now, one of money's functions is as a universal equivalent; since everything becomes translatable into it, it can symbolize and so make meaningful the concrete transformations among the spheres. It thereby enables the market economy to penetrate the subsistence economy completely, i.e., materially, structurally, and symbolically, by enabling the possessor of money to acquire things from all spheres.

But before money can put a price on people's physical and

social well-being, hunger and other survival needs must be reliably satisfied by the market, and the market must also consistently make available the factors of production. This means that food, clothing, shelter, technology, and other necessities must be regularly produced for exchange. Such regular production requires specialization. This means that, in the society-wide division of labor, individuals, households, or villages are not self-sufficient, but rather produce one good or service for sale, and depend for most or all of their subsistence on the market. Storage and transportation facilities combine with money to enable people to rely on the provision of subsistence and to plan on the basis of it: If producers or consumers need something that is not available at a given moment, they can wait; if producers, for example, are specializing in beef and the consumer wants veal, the consumer can wait because money "stores value" (and, unlike the meat, will keep). We do not have to spend our imaginary one thousand dollars immediately, for it will buy something (though less) next week or next year. Money and market exchanges thus make specialization possible by integrating the separate, diverse actions and desires of different producers. The Greeks in the domestic mode participated to some extent in such a specialized economy, by providing, for example, a regular source of sheep milk to cheese merchants, or specialized tailoring, and in turn buying olive oil and other consumption goods produced elsewhere.

For specialization to flourish and for market-exchange to dominate subsistence activities, most or all of the means of production must also become available for purchase, or new means which are so available must emerge. For example, in the capitalist mode of production, which is the most developed form of market economy to date, the relations of production become such that goods are alienable from the individuals or groups who control them, e.g., private property. Similarly, labor-power becomes a commodity, and services are for sale. Even intangible ideology can become a commodity, as in the case of contemporary publishing companies that own their employees' ideas. None of the Gouro factors of production is so available: Land cannot be sold by either village or lineage (and no one would think to buy it), nor are iron tools and labor alienable. The land of the Greek village was likewise corporate village property (and it still cannot be sold); in the domestic mode, the household had rights to the labor and products of its members, and could sell the products. In contrast to the Gouro, however, individuals could leave their households, but they rarely did so since the possibility of making a living elsewhere was limited.

Nonetheless, labor was alienable, thus permitting individuals to become independent of each other and of the corporate production unit. This meant that in twentieth-century Greece, when the scope and specialization of the market economy grew and money became a more important means of production than, let us say, inherited rights to inalienable mountain pasture, the conditions were ripe for market principles to dominate the domestic mode. First, it is likely that production decisions came to be controlled more and more by market principles and government needs, and less and less by the household's consumption needs. Since money was a basic productive force, the peasant cultivators or shepherds could, and had to, acquire it not only for rent as in the past, but now also for seed, feed, and other factors. They did so by selling to the market and also by buying it (i.e., borrowing at interest) from its owners, the government-run banks. The need for money ultimately decreased attempts at household self-sufficiency. Whereas formerly some joint family shepherd households had tried to cover several areas of their specialty, by raising stock, making cheese, and making and selling woolen products, as the twentieth century passed they cut back. In such households, all the men became shepherds, or the merchants left and specialized fully; or some herded while others worked for wages in Greece or abroad. The women continued their maintenance tasks until the second half of the twentieth century, when they too added wage-labor to their repertoire.

Wage-work diminishes the household's control over labor. The individual's experience of this process is that she/he can choose to use her/his labor-power either to satisfy a household need/want, or to provide wage-labor for someone who can buy it, or to work as an independent entrepreneur. Ideological change widens these fissures in the edifice of joint family interests; the individual comes to see her/himself as working for her/himself alone, and is reinforced in this view by practices such as government-kept vital statistics on each person, taxation on individuals' income, or individual military responsibility, in contrast to the individual's previous identity as just a member of the household. If the individual finds that her/his interests differ from those of the others in the household, she/he can and may leave. The household's unity fragments as its joint access to the means of production and survival erodes, and so the domestic mode disappears.

In Greece, individuals often welcomed this change. Kinship responsibilities, though providing security, had limited individual self-realization in many ways: Young men were subordinate to despotic old patriarchs, women to men and to domineering mothers-in-law (as Gouro junior males were subject to elders). People left the village for the cities, or took up other occupations in the village. Thus they freed themselves from multiple personal commitments and escaped from the enveloping totality of the productive process by specializing in one activity, such as cheese-making, or one job, like construction work. Ultimately, the individual's labor has become an even more minute part of the whole, as when she/he caps bottles in a soda-pop factory elsewhere in mainland Greece.

But this independence from previous constraints has another dimension under the capitalism that has been one of Greece's modes of production since the seventeenth century and is now the dominant one. With the new independence, in any culture, the individual loses responsibility for and control over both product and productive process. One explanation for this is Marxist: What the employee does is to sell her/his labor-power to an employer for a certain period of time, labor-time, because she/he takes *surplus-value* from the employees.

According to Marx, the concept of surplus-value is historically specific to capitalism, and its existence distinguishes that mode of production from others. However, lack of data prevented Marx from analyzing noncapitalist modes of production sufficiently to know whether there is surplus-value in them or not, and no one else to date has done so either. Nevertheless, there is probably some relation between concrete surpluses of production in precapitalist societies, and the intangible surplus-value of capitalism, which might work in the following way:

When the individual works to provide her/his subsistence, the value of her/his labor and products lies in their use. Anything above and beyond these use-defined wants/needs (including social and ceremonial, as well as physiological, needs) is *surplus.* If such surplus can be produced (and, as I discuss below, surplus is culturally relative), it becomes possible, after satisfying subsistence needs, to make products or perform services for exchange. To their original use-value is added their exchange-value. Now, if the producer sells the surplus, she/he both satisfies subsistence needs by use-values and realizes what, in capitalism, becomes surplus-value, or the monetary return of the exchange-value. But she/he uses this return for consumption, not further production; subsistence producers do not go into business. This is what occurs among the Gouro.

But in a capitalist market economy, people are in business to make money which they then keep to reinvest in production, as well as to satisfy whatever consumption need crops up in the future. The employer buys the employees' labor time in order to sell its results. And the employer can profit on this because all she/he need pay out is the equivalent of the subsistence the employee needs (for self and family). The employer can then take the produce and sell it for a price that consists of the employee's subsistence (the former use-value) plus its exchange-value. The employer's profit comes from the latter and therefore consists of surplus-value. Surplus-value, unlike use-value that can be consumed or used up, can accumulate in the form of *capital,* i.e., as money or, let us say, inventory; these are the concrete, or congealed, forms of surplus value, and represent all the labor which went into producing them.

The capital is the employer's private property, and she/he thus has the right to decide how it is to be used. She/he therefore has a power which the employee does not and this, of course, affects the life of the employee who, owning only labor, has no reciprocal or parallel power. There is then, a third source of power over the Greeks, the employer. It may be the village Greeks' sense of this power that makes them desire fiercely to be independent entrepreneurs or to be willing to trade a day's wages for a day of leisure at home or at the cafe.

In capitalism, production and consumption of subsistence goods come to be performed by different, unequal groups. The production unit may be the firm or the government, the consumption unit our lone employee, or the nuclear or extended family household. In any case, their structures differ, their activities are physically separate, and, as I have just indicated, their interests are likely to be antagonistic. All that connects them is exchange, both between employer and employee and between producer and consumer. On a societal level, this means that need satisfaction of the weaker group, i.e., the consumers, dwindles. They lose control not only of what they produce, but of the power to fill their needs. Alienation characterizes market-exchange, because the market mediates between needs and their satisfaction, worker and product, producer and consumer.

In taking the Marxist tack of beginning with production, instead of that ordinarily taken by economists and anthropologists of starting with exchange, one asks not only what is being produced, but for what and for whom production exists. In other words, one immediately begins to consider distribution and consumption. One also quickly gets to specifics, for production in particular instances means production for certain needs, for certain people with a certain distribution of control over resources, and so on. And one gets a view of the overall character of the economic system by understanding its handling of use-value and exchange-value. These kinds of value and their social structuring of work and material represent two kinds of freedom. Though neither appears separately, one usually dominates. When it is use-value, the individual is always guaranteed food, if there is any at all, and a job, and is thus freed from uncertainty; but one's range of choice is very small. With exchange-value, one may choose where one will trade one's labor, but one never knows whether one will be able to do so. The two types of value also represent two kinds of social integration: Use-value implies a fine, though inflexible, attunement between needs and the objects made to satisfy them; exchange-value means that the objects made often have nothing to do with the needs requiring satisfaction.

In the production of use-values, work depends on specific social relationships, usually defined by kinship, familial, or domestic obligations that clearly define one's self-hood, but also subordinate it to the tyranny of age or sex roles. In the production of exchange-values, goods and services are anonymous and dissociated from self. The individual's labor has only an abstract meaning on the market, where she/he produces goods for whomever has the cash to buy them. In the first instance, the producer has pride in the products of her/his labor because they satisfy known recipients; alienation replaces the craftsman's pride when there is no one in particular to produce for.

But if goods can be produced for no one in particular, then they can, potentially, be produced for anything or anyone, for whatever people choose. The dominance of exchange value frees the kind and amount of products from the limits arbitrarily imposed by kinship. Beyond exchange value lies a third kind of freedom, not yet seen in any economy, in which the unique needs of each individual are satisfied at the same time as are the shared needs of all individuals; in which the producer identifies personally with product and consumer, and yet retains an identity distinct from the group; in which there is an alignment of production with the capabilities and needs of its technology, population, and resource base.

ECOLOGICAL ADAPTATIONS

Use-value has usually been associated with technologically simple societies, whose control over nature is skimpy. The growth of exchange-value has both fed on and nourished the increasing transformation of the physical environment by culture, which has been made possible by the industrial means of production, i.e., by machine technology run on fossil fuels, operated by people working in hierarchical groups in centralized places. Technology, now the dominant factor of production in both capitalist and socialist societies, not only yields a greater rate of profit than human labor, but produces more goods and permits an absolutely higher standard of living. In scientific as well as everyday thinking, we therefore tend to see technology as both the solution to all our problems and the cause of all our ills.

As so often happens, cultural reality blinds us. Our particular need for technology makes us forget that it is but a means of using the physical environment, which is the source of all our tools, produce, and life. Technology is our link to the larger system in which all cultures survive, the *web of life* or the *ecosystem.* Humans, like other species, occupy an *ecological niche;* this refers to both the physical location of a species and the resources the species uses for survival. *Homo sapiens'* niche is the whole earth (and, perhaps, if this is not too grandiose a presumption, the universe). Culture, at its broadest level of abstraction, is the means to adapt to the niche.

On the level of abstraction of particular cultures, niches are narrower and more specific. Just as economic activities are embedded in social structures and values, so each economic system transacts intimately and intricately with its niche. The niche limits but does not determine how the society survives. Productivity, for example, does not vary directly with either technology or environment alone, but rather with (1) technology, in (2) a particular environment, used by (3) a particular organization of labor, for (4) particular purposes. In other words, the features of each ecological adaptation, as well as of each economy, emerge from a set of relationships, not from single factors. There is, then, no "natural" environment: When humans occupy a particular space on earth, they remake it to fit their own needs and desires, as structured by culturally conditioned living arrangements, social relationships, and beliefs. They dig into it, cut vegetation from it, build structures on it, scatter garbage over it, and bury their dead in it. These actions change the landscape, and this alteration eventually forces the society itself to change.

Energy, Work, and Power

The most important one-way transaction for any living creatures is the acquisition of energy from the environment. The sun is the ultimate source of energy for the food chain of which humans are the highest and most complex link. The other links in the chain, however, must thrive if humans are to survive. Once said, this is a truism; but in our culture we often forget it because our culture's technical mastery makes us think that we have mastered nature, when we are but a dependent part of it.

The corollaries of this truism are equally obvious and equally ignored. First, all culture requires the intake and expenditure of energy, from the production of food and tools to the administration of labor, from everyday social relations to ceremonial ritual, from a spanking to the political construction of domestic and foreign relations. Human beings, as distinct from other animals, do not transform this energy immediately into flesh: They domesticate plants and animals so as not to have to go after them; they harness the wind's power in mills and boats; they create steam and internal combustion engines, nuclear reactors and solar cells. They thereby increase the amount of energy, or power, available to them and so can reproduce more goods than they could if they relied merely on their own muscle power. The more energy a culture captures, the more complexly organized it can be; conversely, the greater its organization, the more energy it can take in. The main process of cultural evolution has been this mutual amplification of energy capture and organizational complexity.

A second corollary is that culture must care for nature. Each human community needs various materials, like earth and water, or animals, plants, and minerals, to survive. But as each economic system takes from its ecological niche, it must also return something, for the niche has its own life requirements. The disposal of human organic wastes, for example, returns nutrients to the soil where microorganisms decompose them, thereby fertilizing the soil and making the nutrients once again available to other organisms (and eventually to humans). But there are other, more indirect ways in which balances are achieved between cultural and environmental systems.

For instance, the Greek shepherds, like the pastoral Nuer, migrated seasonally between uplands and lowlands. Their winter season began about November 1 in lowland areas; around May 1, they traveled for two weeks with the sheep and goats up to their mountain village where they would summer until mid-October. Then they would begin their downward trek again. This simple, two-move transhumance satisfies cultural, animal, and environmental needs. It allows both mountain and lowland pasture to rest and regenerate. It also maintains the stock, for although the sheep and goats might withstand the annual two meters of snow in the mountains, they cannot survive the summer heat of the plains. Their survival provides the human population with products for use and for sale.

Longer-term balances are also achieved. Slash-and-burn agriculture, although it was the first form of agriculture in the temperate zones of western Europe, usually occurs in tropical areas, as among the Yanomamö and the Gouro, where the soil's structure is relatively fragile and susceptible to being leached out by rain and overuse. Since the only fertilizer applied is the ashes from burned vegetation, the soil's nutrients are used up quickly. After one, several, or many years, a community or village will have to move to a new, more fertile plot. Swidden farmers, aware of this necessity, in some areas annually open up a bit of new land and abandon parts of the old; in others, they move abruptly. In either case, they do not return for seven to twenty-five years, when second-growth forest will have renewed the old area's fertility. If, as sometimes happens, anything prevents their migration, the plant and animal environment will become degraded beyond repair.

Semiannual migration and the regular abandonment of swidden sites exemplify the two primary processes of any ecosystem, the flow of energy and the cycling of matter. Here energy flows, and matter recycles, through environment and culture. The processes therefore have a cultural form, ecological adaptation, whose nucleus, in the theory of the late anthropologist Julian Steward, is called the "cultural core." This consists of the relationships among (1) the parts of the environment necessary for a culture's survival (plants and animals, water, and raw materials for tools), (2) the tools used to acquire these, and (3) the social means for using the environment and tools (work processes and the division of labor). This complex of things, activities, and relationships is actually the means of production as seen from another angle. This perspective grants to natural resources and the organization of labor the attention economics usually reserves for money, technology, and land. It is this view that revealed, for example, the role of kinship and marriage in regulating Gouro labor.

Ecological theory also interlocks nature and culture, and creates a separate subsystem from parts of both. It emphasizes our animal nature and oddly returns us to the peculiarly human, like personality structure and war, which it explains in terms of the relationship between human populations, their resources, and their needs. Let us see how this works for the Yanomanö. Like the ecological study of animals, ecological anthropology takes the local population as its unit. It measures evolutionary adaptation, or survival, by the adjustment of population size to its niche. Typically, there are population minima and maxima with which the organization of labor can operate and which the techno-environmental aspects of its adaptation can support. The population range of a Yanomamö village is between 40 and 150, with an optimum of 75–100.

This measure provides an unambiguous standard for cultural survival: Anything that keeps the population within a certain range is, according to this theory, functional. As among animal populations, when the population approaches either end of the range, something, usually a social event, occurs which rights the balance. Among the Yanomamö, quarrels and warfare are the events, and rivalries and alliances the mechanisms for keeping the population within range. The model for understanding how those mechanisms work is that of a self-regulating system, or *homeostat,* each of whose parts affects the other and whose aim is to maintain a variable factor within a certain range of values. The simplest model of this is a thermostat: The variable is the room temperature, and the thermostat functions to keep it, let us say, at about 68°F. The heating system is at rest until something outside the system lowers the temperature below 67.5°; the oil burner then starts and operates until the heat reaches 68.5°. Everything in the system thus works to keep the temperature between 67.5° and 68.5°.

When a Yanomamö village begins to near its maximum, then, conflicts ensue. Yanomamö males have learned that wounded feelings legitimately motivate quarrels, violence, and warfare. Classificatory brothers begin to quarrel over women, gardens, and insults. Or the quarrels between two villages will have graduated beyond temporizing measures, and one will raid and rout the other. But at the same time affinal alliances provide a social structure that can realign population and resources. These can create new villages out of one which has been split by internal dissension or by warfare: In the former case, the old village bifurcates; some men stay and take in affines, and others leave to reside with their in-laws. In the case of war, one affinal faction will form its own village on the old land, or settle in a new area; a second will perhaps join another allied village whose own population has fallen very low.

Ecological adaptations, then, have shifting balances. Here, systematic social mechanisms reduce population density when it becomes too great for available resources, or increase it when it becomes too small for the mode of production. According to Harris (though Chagnon does not agree), the factor that becomes scarce in relation to population increase is animal protein. He suggests that its scarcity is techno-environmentally caused. The Yanomamö cannot get enough of it because their population has increased relative to it and their technology is limited. Footpower and crudely-made dugout canoes restrict the amount of hunting territory each village can control and therefore the amount of game it can capture. Harris and others have hypothesized that the absence of protein, a nutrient essential to physical and mental development, often underlies social conflict, which then works homeostatically to regulate the size and density of population and the distribution and intake of protein.

The homeostatic model, as created by the ecological anthropologists A. P. Vayda, R. A. Rappaport, and others, clarifies the self-regulating dimensions of this process, but applies only to the internal operation of systems. It explains neither what makes the demographics go awry nor the non-demographic dimensions of the regulatory mechanisms. The model's structure, its functional circularity, mimics the mutual influence and vicious cycle among variables, like warfare, social relations, and psychological dispositions in an ecological adaptation. Here ecological theory shows that warfare (1) checks environmental degradation by decreasing population absolutely and lowering the number of hunters, and (2) improves the culture's survival chances by creating relatively smaller and more dispersed villages, thereby lowering density and raising per capita protein. But the model does not explain why all this happens to the Yanomamö, for its avowed teleology ignores anything unconnected to these ends or outside the system.

Causes, as in the thermostat model, lie in *mutual causality*, in the connection or interaction between systems. One model which fits this definition of cause is called deviation-amplification, and contrasts with the deviation-counteracting homeostat. In this model, an accidental change in one direction in one element positively influences the agent of change, increasing the likelihood that the original influence will recur; this in turn increases the probability that the changed element will continue to change. To use Magoroh Maruyama's example, one can imagine a rock in which accidents of climate and geography bring about a crack. With time, water collects in the crack, widening it and thereby permitting more water to collect and further widening to take place. Soon, microorganisms come to live in the water, eventually producing sufficient organic waste material so that at some future time a plant is able to take root and ultimately to split the rock. The original rock system is thus totally changed.

The Yanomamö system of population, technology, and protein capture, then, goes out of alignment because it interacts with, or is part of more encompassing natural and cultural systems in which change is occurring; changes in all are mutually reinforcing or amplifying. Under conditions of environmental change, animal populations will grow to the limits of their resource base, and this growth generally underlies ecological swings. Furthermore, the continued occupation of a niche by a species also will change the landscape, which in turn forces the species to change its way of coping with it. In effect, the species changes even while trying to survive and to remain the same. The Yanomamö may be undergoing some other change, of which population growth, warfare, and so on are expressions.

As Harris suggests, the Yanomamö live within bigger, autonomous political units, or nations, and the relations between them influence Yanomamö culture as well. As the North American pioneers once did, Brazilian and Venezuelan prospecters and colonists have for decades now been pushing forward the frontiers of their developing economies. Their technological and organizational power may be squeezing the Yanomamö onto a smaller resource base, which decreases the population that the factors and relations of the Yanomamö productive system can support. The very crudeness of their canoes, a means to fish for a new protein source, suggests to Harris that they have just begun to cope technologically with this change in environment and that, therefore, the problem itself is quite recent.

Institutions like warfare can be adaptive and respond to distant impingements without the people themselves subscribing to any of these explanations. They may be conscious of them; Greek shepherds will readily explain that the sheep's temperature tolerance requires migration. But the Yanomamö do not talk of scarcity of protein; they will tell you that their villages disperse because of land shortage, or sibling rivalry (and thus they replicate the psychological explanation).* The homeostatic and causal models are etic; emic explanations may differ. But none advanced so far tells us why humans lack the mechanisms which other animals have to reduce population before killing becomes

* Indeed, in the *Iliad* of Homer, in our own tradition, some Greeks and Trojans thought they went to war over Helen of Troy, although in another ancient epic poem known as the *Kypria*, the war was said to have originated as a plan of Zeus to relieve the burden of the earth's overpopulation!

necessary. Nonhuman animals kill their own only rarely; we engage in sporadic, but endemic intraspecies hostilities. I think the answer has to do with power, a fact of human life which, like energy or love, humans have not yet learned to manage.

DOMAINS OF POWER

The preceding discussion of the material bases of economy and polity, the means and structure of making a living, and cultural interactions with nature, has consistently touched on their implications for power. It should be clear that, in this analysis, material and mental bases for power are mutually reinforcing, not mutually exclusive. The Gouro elders' power, for example, rests on the control of objects, people, and the symbolically separate market and prestige spheres of exchange. Power is, therefore, encoded in symbols, enacted in relationships, and grounded in things.

The relations of production, i.e., the structure of distribution, reveal the basic power relations of a culture, for they contain the rules by which people acquire the means to survive. The political part of the political economy of any society has partly to do with the nature of control over the means of production, or, as anthropologists have phrased it, access to "scarce and demanded (or strategic) resources." This revision of traditional Marxian terminology is useful, because, as we have seen, it is not always the means of production as we know them in capitalism, that are crucial; they may, for example, be natural resources, like type of game, or social relations, like marriage.

Power, then, exists in different domains within each culture. It has material, psychological, and social dimensions, and its constitution varies accordingly—strength in rape, tools in production, "pull" in getting a job, charisma in group leadership, decision making in politics, or the manipulation of myth in propaganda. Its psychosocial dimensions include awe and noblesse oblige, respect and contempt, and sadomasochistic relationships, among others. Its behavioral expressions vary. The young defer to the lineage elders who arrange their marriages;

the peasant gives the first fruits to the feudal lord who owns the land; and the urban female on a lonely street walks with lowered glance and tensed muscles past the menacing male stranger.

The more difficult it is for power to be translated from one domain to another, the less power any one individual has over another. For example, Gouro elders monopolize decision-making about the daily division of labor, and also about the more occasional issues of marriage and intervillage relations. Their authority has material bases in their trusteeship of the lineage territory and their control of the market and prestige spheres of exchange. The social bases of their authority derive from their control over marriage and therefore over labor, and from their representation of the lineage to the outside. Elders thus have more direct access to strategic resources than others. But they do not use this power to become rich or exploit others, not because they don't want to (they may or may not), but because they can't. Although the elder controls the matrimonial goods, he cannot use them to produce wealth. They can only be exchanged for women, so that the only riches they create are women, or labor.

And this labor ultimately belongs to the whole lineage community, which really owns the means of production. The elders' control of the lineage mode is a managerial service they perform for the young men, who give in return labor, subsistence and prestige goods, and respect. Between each elder and each junior, in fact, exists a kind of delayed balance reciprocity. Since each youth will someday be an elder, he will inherit the rights to power once exercised over him and to the services he provided. But if an elder does not redistribute women to the young men, or if he appropriates matrimonial goods for his own use, he will lose his office or even be abandoned by the lineage, without which he could not survive.

Interlocking structures and equal access to equivalent, though not identical, resources check the expansion of the elders' power across domains. The elders rely on the married and unmarried juniors' physical strength not only for food provision but also for warfare, both defensive and offensive. This strength is socially structured by the village mode. Success in war depends on the juniors' dominance in the village mode, which in turn permits them to acquire personal power through military prowess or skill in hunting, independently of the elders. The village mode connections also strengthen the juniors' independent intragenerational ties at the expense of their vertical ties to elders, for village mode ties cut across lineage mode ties. The elders, therefore, lack control of at least one area where juniors develop a sense of self-worth and the social reputations which bring them power. Elders thus cannot exploit juniors the way employers can do to employees.

But reciprocally, juniors cannot steal elders' power because its bases are scattered. Elders control some but not all aspects of people's lives, and some but not all goods, for some but not all purposes. They teach the younger men only gradually their technological and social skills and knowledge. Finally, the village mode loyalties also unite elders of different lineages and villages, for they too were once young hunter-warriors. These loyalties constitute social power that maintains the juniors' respect and subordination, for elders will arrange marriages, the real source of power, only with each other, and none would give his lineage kinswoman to a young man, even if the latter somehow got hold of the bride-price on the market.

Power among the Gouro is personal and ephemeral. For example, a particularly skilled hunter earns a reputation as such and commands others' hunting loyalties. But the prestige they accord him nets him a larger catch only at those hunts he leads, not at every one; similarly, superior warriors get more booty, but have no permanent rights to more wealth. And their children do not inherit these positions; they can achieve esteem only by their own acts. Indeed, qualities like belligerence, though useful in battle, handicap daily conduct; an aspirant to the village council is better off learning conciliation and humility. The social structuring of power is relatively egalitarian, at least among males. Personal prestige disappears with the person who achieves it and the circumstances which promote it. No intergenerational classes can, therefore, be created.

In Gouro society as a whole, the number of prestige positions is infinite, expanding or contracting with the number able to fill them. In other words, each male becomes a respected, powerful elder when and because he ages. No male dominates internal political affairs, though one man may represent his lineage as a head man to other lineages, his village to other villages, or his society to other societies, his group sees him as merely "first among equals." As with the Yanomamö, no one can command anyone to do anything. As with the Nuer leopard-skin chief, power is moral, not physical.

Permanent intrasocietal power differences and the transfer of power from one domain to another depend on intrasocietal differences in access to strategic resources and the distancing of private and public. These in turn are consequent on the development of inter-societal relations. So long as production is for use, specialization minimal, few goods obtained by exchange, and surplus production low, differential access to resources is unlikely to develop among individuals or groups; therefore, power is less likely to crystallize around any one of them. So long as production and consumption units structurally coincide, so will private and public interests, and therefore domestic and political sectors. And so, paradoxically, will power remain diffuse. For example, the Gouro household is the most private sector, the village the most public, the lineage in between. Since the lineage is the daily political arena, and since the household's survival depends on that of the lineage, the domestic and the political are, in effect, completely merged for most activities, people, and time. They split when intra- and inter-village activities dominate; but this occurs either intermittently, in the case of hunting, or rarely, in the case of war. Therefore, most decisions taken by anyone in public political power mesh with private needs. These are elders' decisions. But as the market economy has increased in importance to the Gouro, the lineage mode and the village mode now vie for public power. As power comes to rest on money, the elders' behavior becomes arbitrary, and the juniors, able to earn cash wages, have begun to act more independently.

As soon as exchange becomes important, a public arena emerges; a space develops for the creation, acquisition, and manipulation of power in the area between producers, in a public domain. The political/public begins to separate from the domestic/private when relations with those emically defined as "them," e.g., nonkin or another society, become prominent. Etically viewed, this occurs when such relations as trade, diplomacy, and war become necessary to the social system, and require permanent institutions to carry them out. For example, let us return to the Trobriand Islands, whose matrilineal, matrilocal households raise yams and other tropical crops in the domestic mode of production. Clustered in autonomous villages, the population is stratified, divided into two strata, or layers, of chiefly and commoner lineages. The chiefs are relatively few, and inherit their positions matrilineally. Each chief's position as village leader depends on his fulfillment of certain obligations. His power lies in the loyalty of his followers, for whom he must acquire prestige. In so doing, he links the public and private domains.

One source of prestige is the display of abundant yam harvests to members of his own and other communities. He accumulates yams first from his own gardens; secondly, since he, like each man, must receive from his wife's real and classificatory brothers a certain proportion of their annual harvests (and must give the same to his own "sisters' " husbands), and since a chief may have as many as forty wives, he receives large quantities of yams annually. He also tries to ensure large harvests by personally, or through the village's garden priest, exhorting each cultivator to compete. At the feast, which follows the harvest display, the chief must also redistribute the food to his villagers, in-laws, and other followers.

The chief must keep on acquiring prestige, but the ways open to him do not allow his political power over others to increase. He uses the prestige from abundant harvests as a means to acquire certain shell bracelets and necklaces through the *Kula Ring*. This Ring is not a piece of jewelry, but a system of ceremonial exchange containing ritually polite bargaining usually between chiefs of different villages or different islands. Each chief has a set of trading partners; with any given partner, he gives bracelets and receives necklaces, or vice versa. On the map, necklaces go clockwise, and bracelets counterclockwise. On each occasion, each man aims to get a more prestigious ornament than he has given; an ornament's reputation grows with the frequency of its transfer and the number and prestige of objects given for it. The greater the object's reputation, the more prestige for the chief and his village. The prestige, however, erodes if the chief does not soon trade his newest possessions for others.

These ceremonial valuables function as symbols, like the Crown Jewels of England. Their ritual display has use, for Trobrianders do not live on yams alone. They bring prestige to people, and validate the chief's leadership. If nothing else, they make people feel good about themselves. But in fact they do more. According to the contemporary theorist M. Sahlins, ceremonial exchange generates prestige, by means of which social action can be mobilized, public power can be consolidated, and both action and power used in the achievement of group political goals like the pursuit of subsistence goods, the regularization of diplomacy, or the prosecution of war. The Kula's framework gives to potentially hostile island societies, who may communicate directly only once a year, a routinized basis for interaction which will work smoothly so long as one just follows the rules.

Like Yanomamö marriage alliances, the Kula functions politically but has additional economic and ecological roles: For, side by side with ceremonial exchange goes market trade in utilitarian goods. Since, on inter-island sections of the Kula, the chief must sail dangerous seas, he needs sailors and warriors. Commoners crew for him, in return not only for the prestige he will acquire, but for the goods they can get themselves. Each bargains hotly with other commoners to trade goods he has brought from home or other ports for goods which the host islander controls. The Kula Ring thus does what marketplaces do in, for example, North Africa or Mexico: It allows exchanges between ecologically diverse areas and between different craft specialists. And it remains structurally, as well as spatially, separate from the subsistence production of use-values, probably because it operates without money.

Energy, Work, and Power

The Kula simultaneously satisfies material wants, fills psychosocial luxury needs, and integrates different societies in the absence of a formal governmental or international structure. It is a public activity, drawing private individuals into a common endeavor. It also connects the domestic and politico-economic sectors within the society. For, public power systematically increases the production of essentially private households by encouraging each man to expend more energy on his garden, in order to build the chief's and village's prestige on which the whole structure is based. And, in thus causing production in excess of normal requirements, the Kula is ecologically adaptive, for it buffers a society whose simple technology provides no means of storage against natural disasters which from time to time wipe out large portions of the crop.

The status of chief, around which the power to link public and private crystallizes, also transforms power among the several domains: In order to bargain well in the Kula, the chief needs prestige. Prestige depends on loyal followers, whom he attracts, or creates, by redistributing large harvests and by marrying carefully. He exacts the large harvests by means of the great prestige he has accumulated from the Kula valuables he has astutely and diplomatically bargained for. If he fails in any part of this circle from private to public, from kinship to politics, from production to exchange, he falls from power.

By the same token, any man who can break in on the circle can create power for himself. Part of Trobriand political structure is based on *ranking*. This means that positions of leadership are defined by the esteem socially given them. The number of such prestige positions is fixed and is therefore fewer than those potentially able to fill them: There are just so many chiefs. On the other hand, apart from the chiefs, ranks within chiefly lineages are not entirely fixed, and men can move up or down. Furthermore, not all villages have chiefs, so that there is room in some for commoners to become powerful. They do this by generosity: An up and coming young man can give grain and yams to others without overtly asking for anything in return. Tacitly, a return is expected, not in kind, but in loyalty. By means of this *gen-*

eralized reciprocity, a man can build a following and therefore a name. Such "big-men" check chiefly power. If a chief shows signs of stinginess or autocracy, his followers will desert him for a more generously democratic big-man. And the same fate awaits any nonchiefly big-man.

We see here two structural limits on exploitation. No man permanently can arrogate power to himself, for none controls the means of production. Although the chief indirectly controls the labor of his commoners, brothers-in-law, and others, his power over them is coextensive with his continual acquisition of prestige, that is, with his perpetually divesting himself of his wealth by giving yams to his followers and Kula valuables to his trading partners. He does have the connections to go on Kula, but he needs his commoners to do so. He can use others' loyalties to become famous, but not very rich; or, rather, his wealth in Kula valuables is a function of his wealth in loyalties.

When the converse obtains, when control of material goods comes to yield control of people and therefore of loyalties, permanent power configurations can emerge and carry over from one generation to the next, resulting in exploitation. This process constitutes the emergence of class society, wherein one group rules over others because it has control over the latter's life-sustaining resources: One class has power over the rest. This structure and process become possible when there is surplus production. We come now to the difficulties of defining *surplus* in a cross-culturally valid way.

As I said when I defined surplus-value, surplus refers to production above subsistence requirements. Now, although organizations like the World Health Organization are able to define nutritional minima and maxima, nevertheless the emic definition of what and how much constitutes adequate subsistence food varies cross- and intra-culturally. For example, in contrast to the idea in the United States that daily meat consumption is desirable, the village Greeks thought that a weekly mutton stew was a reasonable goal and that meat twice a week was a treat. The satisfaction of other needs varies even more; the term *life-styles* conveys the complexly associated values, attitudes, and preferences characteristic of cultures and subcultures, of classes and ethnic groups.

Granted, then, that what one culture deems a surplus, another might call a deficit, it still is possible to establish that surpluses do exist within any one culture at any one time. If Trobriand yams rot, they are surplus, relative to hunger. If some people in New York City wear emeralds and others sleep in flophouses on the Bowery, this is evidence for surplus production which is unequally distributed. Finally, if every North American household buys a television or can afford one, and Indian and Sahelian children die of typhoid or malnutrition, then a maldistributed surplus exists in the world economic system.

This discussion does not, of course, solve the operational problem of determining how much surplus exists. The difficulty, as Harris says, is that there is no such thing as a superfluous surplus; if there were, one could easily measure it. But, as the examples above illustrate, surplus always has use and form: The Trobriand yams usually are converted into prestige and sometimes into flesh. The Euro-American cultures of plenty amidst a world of want reveal that abundance and scarcity are culturally, not naturally, constituted.

This social structuring of surplus comes right out of relations of production that grant differential access to strategic resources and therefore to products, and that create classes. The classes with superior access control the reproduction not only of their own social life, but of the life of those whose access is limited. They dominate the economy, for they can pass their wealth on to their children. Private wealth then becomes a public issue. Since wealth confers control of the reproduction of the whole society and culture, material power can secure personal loyalties.

In these circumstances, one's identity, choices, and control are initially and forever limited by one's share in the distribution of the means of production. The principles of the market progressively encroach on the private domain of existence, until the latter becomes too small a foundation on which to build an identity. As we have seen, exchange-value permits an escape from the frying pan of domestic power into the fire of public existence. One is freed from the overpowering security of the household; one's loyalties follow one's living, i.e., the public, impersonal politico-economic domain. The ability to sell one's labor-power, for a period of time, thus permits one to lose control of one's identity. One's labor, though not actually separable from one's self, comes to seem abstract, depersonalized and alien and then so do identity and self.

This alienation comes from the same processes that divide public and private. The public domain produces goods and services, but consumes the labor, which, as we saw in the case of the housewife's support of her working husband, is produced in the private domain; the private domain, in turn, consumes the products of the public domain. The public becomes so distanced from the private that those in the latter have only the barest sense of what is happening in the former. Furthermore, people acquire bedrock survival goods and services from producers whom they don't know. Therefore, a society-wide economy emerges, managed not by those whose interests even partly overlap with those of the primary producers or consumers, but by those who specialize in overseeing and engaging in exchange. The interests of these middlemen and bureaucrats may not necessarily conflict with those of the producers and consumers, but they are certainly different, for they are geared to the needs of the processes of exchange.

A qualitatively different kind of political structure develops, in other words, when, in order to provide for themselves, people depend on a centralized financial and/or governmental apparatus. Like the nineteenth-century ancestors of the Greek villagers I studied, people may still produce use-values at home, but they nevertheless must purchase goods and services from the market to satisfy the household's wants/needs. They therefore depend on a system that mints and backs money and ensures that trade goods will be imported and reach local markets. The organization that makes this possible is the state. The *state* is a political structure defined by (1) sovereignty over territory and, therefore, over the people in it, (2) the monopoly of coercive force, (3) the exaction of funds from the population in the form of taxes, tribute, rent, and other levies, (4) the regulation of production and exchange, and (5) the creation and manipulation of ideology and ritual. The state is run by a bureaucracy that it pays out of its revenue. It also uses these funds, and may exact labor from the populace as well, to mount public works like roads, irrigation canals, or space exploration, and to carry out public ceremonies validating its power.

Centralized political power can put its officials in a position to get rich, and wealth can put others in a position to obtain offices. Those who run the affairs of the state are frequently richer than those for whom they are supposedly running it. In state societies, a small closed group dominates the arena of public power. This domination has historically taken a bewildering variety of forms: Feudal lords dominate vassals and serfs; an emperor rules with a state bureaucracy over starving peasants; the caste system organizes all Indian economic and political life; capitalists run the economy and control the government in the Euro-American and Japanese cultures, and bureaucrats do so in the Soviet Union; colonialists impose cash monocrop economies on Third World subsistence economic systems. The forms can overlap; thus, the American South has had a racial caste system of black and white as well as a class structure, just as the Middle East economy has traditionally been organized in the ethnic mosaic of occupational specialization, even while each ethnicity is internally split by class.

Whatever its specific form, the state's political structure contains one group of people, an upper or ruling class, with unimpeded access to the resources on which are based the lives and livelihoods of the rest of the population, whose access to the means of production is limited. In other words, the structure of the state involves a crystallization of power around those who control the productive resources. In Greece, under the Turkocracy, these people were first prebendal government officials, representing the Ottoman Empire's mode of production, integrated by state redistribution (sometimes called, by Marxists, the "Asiatic" or feudal mode, and by some anthropologists, the hydraulic mode):* In this, a central government owns and grants agricultural land and territorial protection to men who, in return, guarantee the ruler[s] an annual tribute in kind or cash; the government from time to time helps officials out in building productive technology and in other projects which further its own interests. In the Greek case, these Turkish government representatives, under external commercial capitalist pressure, gradually took private possession of the agricultural lands, as landlords over peasants. Since the nineteenth century, those in power have been capitalists who co-operate closely with, but are not of, the central government.

The structure of the state first transforms economic power into political power, then both of these into symbolic and social power, and back around again. In contrast to the personal achievements of Gouro hunters or Trobriand big-men, members of the government, from bureaucrats to kings, have *official* power: This means, for example, that they can siphon off tax money without total loss of prestige, because the obedience and deference they receive belongs not to them but to the office they occupy and rubs off on them. This guarantees continuity, because even when politicians and kings do fall, the structure continues. Such a governmental structure is quite powerful; it also ensures corruption. Those sharing the power need not occupy the offices; bureaucrats and kings have relatives. Families, moveover, can divide the sources of power, one taking political office, another a major position in distributive institutions, as do Nelson and David Rockefeller.** Our culture's ideological distinction between politics and economies usually prevents us from realizing that this is but an overt example of the real structure of control in the United States.

We have returned again to kinship, which, whether among

* The same considerations apply to the "Asiatic" mode as to the domestic, with the addition that the "Asiatic" has been the center of controversy, not merely academic, but political, which has decreased the attention paid it.

** The classic arrangement of European aristocracy was for one son to go to the military, one to the clergy, and a third to law. Others were then free to devote themselves to high culture or business.

those royal by divine right or among the merely wealthy, maintains power. Inheritance, regulated by kinship, gives temporal continuity to the classes, castes, and ethnic groups that organize stratification. For individuals, this results in *ascribed status:* If one's parents are, for example, in a low Indian caste, then one's life-chances are limited according to the occupation permitted one or the land they own. If one is born higher, then one's life-chances are that much better; high birth makes it less likely that a natural disaster, like a crop epidemic or a run of dowry-requiring female births, will wipe out one's living or life savings. The elite have buffers against misfortune, lower classes don't. Luck really is not egalitarian after all.

The fact that such inequalities exist, and have done so for so long, requires an explanation that takes account of the overt and tacit conspiracies of the high and mighty and the acceptance of the impoverished. On the one hand, a standing military force is perhaps the most obvious weapon in the arsenal of public power that distinguishes the state governmental structure from any other, and is its ultimate support. The state tolerates no other like institutions within its territory; lesser levels of force must obey that of the central government. The establishment and maintenance of such coercive power is therefore in the interests of the rich and powerful.

But the dependence of a political structure on military force for daily order and continuity is expensive. And if, after all, the majority of the population of a state like the United States or Brazil or the Sudan organized to fight the smaller dominant class, the results would not be in doubt. The manipulation of ideology requires less energy and allows for more luxuries for people of all classes. If people can be persuaded to accept, or even to want, a given power structure, then military force can remain as only a symbol of the state's authority.

I am talking about what is called, from another point of view, legitimacy. In Max Weber's sense, all political systems rest on *legitimacy,* or the "consent of the governed." In arguing against the Marxian idea that the rulers somehow concretely wrest power from the ruled, this view infers from the fact that most people in complex societies obey most laws in the absence of immediate physical coercion that people must somehow be agreeing to their own domination.* This, then, is often taken to mean that people are directly responsible for the fact of their being oppressed and therefore can change it at will. Although it is true that force is not used daily on most people in state society, and that at some psychological level, people consent to being ruled, it is more likely that what they are doing is choosing to live rather than to die. If fighting a ruler or ruling class means death, then they consent to the ruler and live.

Another interpretation of legitimacy is developed by the American sociologist, Talcott Parsons, who speaks of *consensual power* which rulers and leaders of complex societies are supposed to have. This is the symbolic granting of compliance by those led in return for an expected and promised future return in economic, political, or other form. Compliance with consensual power, since it is divorced from immediate gratification, is very flexible, enabling a political system that rests on it to make decisions in varied, new situations and therefore to expand.

Such compliance is gained by manipulating ideology, i.e., symbols and ritual, myth and morality, attitudes and beliefs. Ideological control operates on both consciousness and the unconscious. In nonliterate societies, it is exercised by religion and in socialization. In more technologically advanced societies, with literate populations, such control also appears in educational institutions and in the various mass media. This means that the state controls communication. In some cases, the government itself owns or runs some of all media (the Greek government owns the electronic media, but not newspapers), but in others, groups connected to the ruling class do so. Through agencies and commissions, the state controls what may be written or said or shown. Laws concerning national "security" withhold information about

* Similar views on the economy argue that owners of capital and owners of labor meet as equals in the market and agree to exchange their respective goods and services. These views incorrectly deny that employers have any greater power than their employees, and that the former take something from the latter.

government activities at home and abroad. Since they cannot help but reflect cultural ideology, the media may indirectly support the interests of the government and rulers. In general, the media, by what they include and exclude, symbolically reinforce the consolidation of social control characteristic of their state.

The state must pay for each of its powers in kind. To maintain conscious acceptance, if not support, by the mass of the populace, the state must pay, e.g., redistribute taxes and tribute to organize marketplaces, defend its territory, and provide social security for the old and welfare for the poor. But to secure their unconscious acquiescence, it must reserve some wealth for symbolic display, and this is the function of its nonpolitical representatives. In the United States, the media grip our imaginations by showing us people who represent the state, the powerful men and elegant women who command all the luxury of which the rest of us only dream, which only the technological powers of advanced capitalism can produce. Like the Trobriand chiefs, such people must appear "state-ly," so as to convince domestic and foreign onlookers that they and their society are truly powerful and worthy of deference. Kings and queens wear silks and satins; twentieth-century magnates and presidents and their wives collect fine paintings and drink with movie stars. But, unlike Trobriand chiefs who must give away all their wealth, these people get to keep the paintings and only they think that everyone can afford champagne, and strawberries in winter. And all this has the function of keeping power within a small circle of friends.

AND THE POOR HAVE CHILDREN

Through the media, the public domain dominates us even in the privacy of our homes, and we have no reciprocal reach. The private domain, in turn, is ruled over by the most dominated and privatized group of all, women, as it is in all the societies we have looked at. By definition, then, women are at least partly excluded from power. Only where they participate in production with others outside the household, do women have any power at all and attain the status of adults.

In state societies, women's labor and power are relegated to the household and their status to that of children perhaps even more than in other societies. Even among the Gouro, women work with others. Western culture reduces women's collective production to nothing because the organization of industrial production excludes the tasks women usually do: the care and feeding of men and children. Were these to be included, in peace as well as in war, expenses would become too high for profits and social arrangements too complicated for efficiency. For the work of reproducing society requires more freedom and differentiated time than the ruling class will allow under industrial working conditions. So women work for free, and the elite, for whom this is surplus-value, realize a double windfall profit: Labor is daily renewed at no cost to them, and unpaid women constitute a "reserve army" of labor for those times when there is a scarcity of labor. They are then available to be hired, but are also easily, and first, fired.

But the conditions of household work are unique; they provide a built-in potential resistance to exploitation by preserving images of a better life. In being protected from the painful rigor of working for The Man, women have fortunately retained some things that men have had to forget about in order to work for an anonymous bureaucracy and to produce for anonymous consumers. In the household, women still experience the integrated pleasure of producing use-values and of aligning production and consumption. In one sense, housewives know no alienation, for their work and products are connected, in an unmediated way, not only with the satisfaction of the needs/wants of themselves and beloved others, but also with the maintenance of those positively valued relations. Furthermore, work time and leisure time are intermingled, as they are in primitive and peasant economies, not only in space but in feeling.

Thus, the painful division of industrial life into work and play does not completely penetrate the household. But neither does relief from work; a woman's work, as the saying goes, is never done. And the workplace provides something that the household lacks: company. The housewife, though perhaps not alienated, may still be unbearably lonely; a new disparity has emerged since the family has ceased to be a joint production unit, for others consume what only she has produced. And the social result of her lonely production is that she has the status of child, seeming to play while she produces use-values; outside the house, she is dominated by "adult" men, and inside, by soap operas and their advertisements, which continue to stoke her own betrayed desires. The household and its mistress contain, then, the memory of childhood, of pleasurable work, and, for the industrial worker, of the respite of play, which must, in some future time, be realized in adult and socialized form.

Like women, the only area of control the poor retain is the private domain, their personal, domestic lives and their bodies. It is no wonder, then, that they have, sometimes willingly, sometimes not, as many children as they do. In labor-intensive agricultural societies, like India, a high birth rate is adaptive for the society as a whole, since a larger population means higher production. For the individual family, which may lose its infants and therefore workers to the high mortality rate, the more children, the merrier. But in industrial societies, large families function to reduce the wages of the unskilled and to increase the income of the elite, as they simultaneously provide pleasure and anguish to their parents. Although middle-class families have fewer children, the areas they control, leisure and consumption, are likewise privatized. The ruling class are the only ones for whom private and public coincide. They can choose how many children they will have, and how they will spend their leisure, and how much they will consume, because their economic power permits them to do so. And their economic power turns on their participation in public life, not only at home but abroad.

For the power of the contemporary ruling class increasingly depends on external relations, on international politics and economies. Multinational corporations dominate internal economic affairs here and overseas, and their existence is bound up with that of foreign political regimes. Just as the public domain as a distinct and important power arena emerges with the primacy of intercultural relations, so too does intrasocietal stratification into rich and poor, rulers and ruled. In other words, the internal structure of a society reacts to what goes on outside, as we saw in the case of the Yanomamö. Our rising standard of living, the voluntarily small families of the middle class, and the sometimes huge ones of the rich, depend on the "over"-population of "under"-developed countries. Just as the owner of capital appropriates the surplus-value of the worker, so do dominant nations reap the value produced by subordinate ones.

This makes it seem as if the impetus for political development always comes from somewhere else and, in a sense, it does. For each system, be it a culture or a domain within a culture, is in perpetual interaction with others, with which it forms larger ones. The sources of change for any culture therefore lie in processes of interaction between systems. Politics involves intercultural relations; the economy involves relations between culture and nature; and both involve relations between private and public, between personal and political. These are also the sources of cultural evolution, the subject of the next chapter, in which we will see that the sources of inequality, transformed, become those of equality.

VII.

Space, Time, and Process:

Cultural Evolution

Tomato Worms and the Birth of Humanity

What have always fascinated me about human history are transitions. The beginnings of something genuinely and qualitatively new contain exploding energies and unforeseen possibilities. I like to imagine them taking place as single great events. Several thousand years ago, a man or woman out collecting wild barley for dinner flashed that seeds planted one season would provide food for the next; many thousands of years earlier, an apelike precurser of *Homo sapiens*, played with the clean-picked thigh bone of a recently devoured antelope, and, in an idle daydream, suddenly saw it as a tool (or a weapon, as in Kubrick's *2001* vision); even earlier, on a clear morning, a young female ape gave birth to the first *Australopithecus*, and thus began the long process of human biological evolution.

It is, however, only in imaginary hindsight that these personages and acts burst forth so dramatically on the scene. In reality, each slowly developed from almost imperceptible, mundane changes. For example, the human species' characteristic continuous dependence on tools follows logically on other species' occasional use of them. Chimpanzees will often look for termite sticks, twigs which they strip, lick, and insert into termite hills, so as to attract the insect that they can then eat. The first humans to farm full-time were unknowingly completing a process begun thousands of years earlier by nomadic foragers, who, in the spring, scattered the seeds of wild, edible plants to increase their food supply the following summer. Or, again, the first cities grew gradually out of earlier ceremonial or trading centers, which had themselves begun as, perhaps, ordinary agricultural villages at important crossroads.

Of course, in absolute time and space, I suppose that there must have been a first *Australopithecus,* a first permanent garden, etc. but to the apes and, later, people alive at the time, they could not have seemed very remarkable. And, on reflection, these "firsts" don't seem so important in and of themselves. What is significant and amazing is the process of change itself, and the fact that many small shifts in state culminate in entirely new forms.

Since human life follows the pattern of all life, the anthropological model of the evolution of human beings and human culture is based on the biological one: It is a sequence of development which moves forward by continuous steps. At different points on the continuum, sharp breaks in patterning emerge; these represent new levels of organization, or transformations from one to another structure. In biology, these levels represent species; in anthropology, they are culture types, or levels of integration. The Yanomamö and the Nuer, for example, represent one level of integration, the contemporary United States and the Soviet Union another. Like the phylogenetic sequence of life forms, the sequence of cultural transformations mirrors their temporal order of emergence. Both sequences also reflect the universal tendency of matter to integrate at increasingly higher degrees of organization with increasingly higher concentrations of energy.

Although biological and cultural evolution are not identical in mechanics or processes, humans, even with their dependence on culture, are still biological creatures. As interpreted by evolutionary theory, formulated by the nineteenth-century British naturalist

Charles Darwin, fossil remains and the anatomy of living monkeys, apes, and humans reveal that *H. sapiens* evolved from nonhuman primates through processes which were initially biological but rapidly gave way to interacting biological and cultural ones. According to Darwinian theory, evolution proceeds by natural selection, in which those species best adapted to their environment survive and reproduce, and the others die out. Reproductive success is the criterion (used also by ecological theory) of, in Herbert Spencer's phrase, the "survival of the fit." The mechanism of biological evolution, as discovered by the nineteenth-century monk, Gregor Mendel, is the gene; recent twentieth-century biology shows genes to be complex protein molecules that govern the ability of individual organisms to adapt.

Let me convey this with a trivial example: As I was picking tomato worms off my tomato plants one summer, it struck me that I was getting rid of only those I could see, the ones on top. The others, crawling underneath the abundant foliage and camouflaged by their green skin, survived my depradations and lived to reproduce. The "fitter" worms, in other words, were those that happened to be out of my line of vision. If, then, there were some gene for feeding off lower branches, that gene would have been selected for: Its frequency in the worm population would have risen, just as that of the upper-branch-feeding gene would have decreased; and there would have fewer upper-feeders and more lower-feeders the next year.

Biological evolution is, however, a great deal more complex. The "feeding-place gene" is inherently improbable not only on the basis of the evidence (there was no reduction in the upper population the next year), but also on the basis of genetic action. Each gene actually controls only minute aspects of each organism. Each individual organism, therefore, contains thousands of genes. Each act or behavior is, conversely, controlled by many genes. Furthermore, Darwinian theory explicitly excludes some great Tomato-Worm-Picker in the Sky which/who selects and thereby causes evolution. The path of natural selection is, with respect to the affected species, haphazard, not goal-oriented.

Its direction does, however, make sense in terms of the interaction of organism and environment. The environment does not select one-sidedly; an organism reciprocally selects for its own niche. Organism and environment are, therefore, partly independent systems and partly integrated, and can thereby cause one another to change. In terms of each system alone, the changes appear to be accidental, but when the interaction of both systems is taken into account, the lawfulness of their behavior emerges, for the cause and therefore the explanation lie in their interplay, as in deviation amplification. All life forms are continually interacting with others and therefore changing; the raw material of change, or evolution, is genetic diversity. If we speak in terms of a species and its environment, the changes in the environment come from (1) the action of the plants and animals inhabiting it and (2) climatic and geological changes. Genetic mutations, which occur randomly in the members of every biological species, give the species potential to change. Most mutations weaken the organism's power of adaptation and kill off the affected individuals before they can reproduce. But some mutations may, in certain circumstances, be advantageous: They may increase the survival chances of the affected individuals, who will then reproduce in larger numbers, replace the others, and come to constitute the new population. The survival of a species depends on such variation even though, paradoxically, in surviving, the species will become different, for its appearance and behavior will have changed.

Five million years ago, the fortuitous interaction of environmental and genetic changes in eastern and southern Africa created a situation like this, in which were born together a new ecological niche and a new species ancestral to our own. Called *Australopithecus africanus,** it emerged from a series of tiny mutations that enabled tree-dwelling apes to walk upright, to see farther than four-footed apes, and to develop a finely tuned coordination

* There is some debate about the proper nomenclature for fossil remains; some physical anthropologists would classify *Australopithecus* as a member of our own genus *Homo,* though of a different species. There are different philosophies behind each choice; I use here the most generally accepted terms.

between their eyes and their hands, now freed from walking. These skills were probably neutral in the forests, neither adaptive nor maladaptive. But grasslands were replacing the forests; under the new conditions, these traits became advantageous and, in turn, selected for, as some apes came to use the previously unoccupied habitat. Although australopiths were born through biological change, they survived and developed through the interplay of biological and cultural processes: They were only four to five feet tall and lacked the stamina to travel as far and long as four-footed competitors. Though not members of our species, these bipedal creatures with opposable thumbs and vulnerable viscera shared with *H. sapiens,* the biological possibility and necessity of tool use. Tools helped them to dig out or cut down vegetation (which formed the bulk of their diet), slaughter game, and protect themselves from predators.

A new mechanism of evolution, culture, had thus appeared on the natural scene, and nothing has been the same since. Then, as now, though subject to natural selection as a biological adaptation, it was neither produced nor acquired genetically. Its permanent transformation of the material world was its most observable process, and tools its most tangible product. Its creation and perpetuation took place in the context of social relationships, which were creations themselves. In part, the raw material of human evolution, like the genes of biological evolution, still lay in the individual. Some tools were used and made by individuals; the learning necessary to use tools took place within the individual; and sometimes, individuals invented new ones. But, as the locus of human evolution was the multiindividual gene pool, i.e., the population, so was that of cultural evolution the group. The acquisition of many tools and their use required cooperation; the learner needed a teacher; and social relations often stimulated inventions. The unit of evolution, therefore, came also to be the social structure in which the individual lived.

Social life is not unique to the genus *Homo.* Ants and lions are social. So are chimpanzees, even more so. Even among plants, in some species, the individuals that stand in clusters have more chance of survival than single plants, because grouping provides, for example, greater protection from wind. But the human means of adaptation, culture, which comes from socially constituted intelligence and creativity, not only enables humans to survive and reproduce, but also has even altered biological processes. For example, contrary to the belief that humans' greater intelligence initially brought about their technological superiority to other animals, current anthropological thought holds that an expansive intelligence followed on the effects of tool use. After *A. africanus* appeared, biological and cultural evolution became mutually reinforcing. Since tool use conferred an adaptive advantage, it became selected for; in turn, this increased the adaptive success of upright posture and flexible hands. Australopiths came to be selected for, or so we infer from the increase and spread in its population. At the same time, *A. africanus* was not so intelligent, as far as we can tell. Although absolute brain size is only a weak indicator of intelligence, brain size relative to body size is a stronger sign. As inferred from the cranial capacity of fossil skulls, *A. africanus*' brain averaged 500 cubic centimers, as contrasted with an average 1450 c.c. for contemporary *H. sapiens*. This tripling of brain size far outstrips the change from four or five feet to five or six feet in height. Thus, it was only in the intervening 4 million years between the two that human intelligence developed; once in existence, of course, it gave humans an astronomically greater advantage over other species and enabled them to make the whole earth into their niche.

Culture, then, in the form of tools and social life, as much as biology and environment, created human biopsychology. Human intelligence includes not just "smarts," or knowledge, but a new way of thinking. Changes in brain size involved changes in brain structure, in the neurological system, and therefore in the psychological potential for social and cultural behavior. Tool use selected for those individuals who had the type of mind to learn it. But the type of mind that can see the relation between a piece of stone, a plant, and the filling of an empty belly is also a kind of mind that can think about the future and can create.

Creativity, too, probably came to be selected for: Archeological excavations have revealed a geometrical increase in tool variety beginning perhaps one to two million years ago. Tools were found in association with the skeletal remains of *H. erectus,** the descendants of australopiths. These pithecanthropines, nearer ancestors of *H. sapiens,* had undergone further biological evolution. Anatomical changes in the pelvis enabled them to walk longer distances. The brain capacity had grown to an average 1000 c.c. and had probably changed structurally as well.

Population increase, a mark of adaptive success, had pushed early *H. erectus* out of east Africa and on to north Africa, Europe, and East Asia. Late *H. erectus* populations had adapted creatively to the new, colder environments, for they knew how to make and control fire; we can assume that those groups that did not learn to use it died out, since no culture has appeared without it. It enabled them to transform many new environments in turn. Their increased stamina in walking also enabled them to expand their niche and to hunt cooperatively the big game of these more northerly areas. Encountering new environments, it is likely that only those who dealt with new environments creatively survived and reproduced.

The utilization of new ideas, however, depends on their being expressed, which in turn requires a system of communication capable of dealing with the imaginary, the abstract, the future. If ideation were adaptive, then so too would be a means to express and shape it. This process probably interacted with changes in the vocal apparatus of *H. erectus,* which, concomitantly with certain neuro-anatomical changes, made possible a nascent human language (or languages).

It is likely that language had immediate survival value. First, it would have redoubled creativity, for it carries the potential for new things in its ambiguous symbols and thus embeds novelty in

* In the intervening years, *A. africanus* was succeeded in different areas by new forms, such as *A. robustus* and *H. habilis.* New data on fossil remains are of course always emerging, so no final sequence of stages can be offered. For this reason, as well as exigencies of space, I do not discuss the stages in great detail.

everyday life. We do not ordinarily think of creativity as an everyday, social act. But, like language, which though spoken by individuals is yet a social phenomenon, creativity is a process that feeds on contact. In between the solitary moments of inspiration in which some creations emerge, the inspired, or mad, scientist or artist socializes with others either in her/his head or in actuality. And her/his work is inspired by the problems of its time and culture, as indeed, is the less exalted creativity which runs through everyday life and therefore underlies human survival.

The second reason that language would have been selected for is its function in everyday life. For, by mediating social relations, it would have enhanced the already effective adaptive value of social life. The continuity of social relations required abstractions like social rules, traditions, and moral systems, which linguistic symbols can encode and make accessible. Human language thereby permits the formulation, articulation, and transgenerational transmission of complicated forms of social behavior. And, reciprocally, complicated social forms themselves would have selected for the further development of communication (as continues to occur in extrasomatic, technological communications systems now).

The continued growth of complex social structures depends on their conferring selective advantages on the species. For a society of pithecanthropines to have been adaptive, its integration, even with a population of only, say, twenty-five, must have progressed beyond that of nonhuman primates. For example, even though chimpanzees cooperate in the care of young, the organization of status hierarchies, and territorial defense, each adult is responsible for feeding her/himself. Humans, in contrast, revolutionized the natural world, for they shared food on the basis of shared responsibilities and labor. This division of labor must have brought immediate evolutionary success, because it would have increased the efficiency of the food quest: If, on the basis of generalized reciprocity, the giving of goods or services without stipulated object or time of return, the males of a group hunted game and the females collected vegetables, and if all foraged in different areas, then someone was bound to catch or find some food; it would have been unlikely for all to have failed. All, then, would always have at least a little to eat and more people could survive.

Whereas genetic variation is the raw material of biological evolution, the raw material of cultural evolution is culturally devised: The human division of labor lessened the risk of failure by introducing diversity. Just as genes are built into and integrated within the individual organism, so with the division of labor in society: It parcels functions among differentiated structures and mutual responsibilities among different groups, and unites them by the same means. Sharing food and sharing work, in other words, are opposite sides of the social coin. The division of labor created not merely more, but more diverse ties among individuals; it required and occurred at the same time with the development of integrative exchange.

The increase in the intensity and interdependence of social life could not have happened had people not been somehow persuaded to participate in these new structures. The growing social complexity would, in other words, have been reciprocally enabled by final psychobiological changes which mark *H. sapiens.* If they had not occurred in *H. erectus,* or in the neanderthal variety of *H. sapiens,* who emerged by 100,000 years ago, they had certainly taken shape by between 40,000 and 60,000 years ago. By then, full-fledged humans inhabited many areas of the Eastern hemisphere and had begun to emigrate to the Western one, or the New World.

Of these mental changes, the one most relevant in this context is the self-awareness that enables the individual to relate her/himself to the group and to feel the commitment on which social integration depends. The establishment of social connections among individuals requires each to *identify* with others; this process depends on the ability to see how one's self simultaneously resembles and differs from the other's. We know that identification and commitment operate with both conscious and unconscious processes, and that, in turn, the soil in which social relationships root and grow is made of unconscious impulses toward and away from society, as well as conscious choices of action. We do not know the reason for, or mechanism of, the emergence of this split human psyche, though the problem attracts speculation. I would suppose that consciousness is what has evolved primarily during human and cultural evolution, and that there has been some natural and cultural selection for a split between it and the unconscious. But since we have survived so far with this split, to say that it is adaptive does not really explain anything, but is only to acquiesce in its existence.

To tie all this together into a neatly sapient package, individual insight into self, and the communication of one's thoughts and feelings about self and other, form the content of social integration and become possible only with language. It is also through language that the individual is persuaded to participate in society, for it is through language that humans are enculturated. Persuasion is institutionalized in systems of socialization: Born with little innate sense of how to survive and no physical ability to do so, human young are open to what their elders tell them to do. They are also open to something else they need, the assurance that what they are doing will be good for them and others; this is what convinces them to be willing to participate. Adults provide this by telling the young legends and histories that contain moral validations of their way of life, of their individual lives, and therefore of themselves.

By the time of the emergence of *H. sapiens*, culture probably contained full-fledged ideological systems, centering on moral systems that described, prescribed, and celebrated social life. Through them, children learned about their past, planned for their futures, and became adult participants in functioning social structures. Through social structure and cultural ideology, humans came to be morally bound to care not only for the young, but for the old and weak, in a way nonhuman primates do not. *H. sapiens's* control of the physical environment made this possible. And all this made possible survival and adaptability unprecedented in the natural world.

Space, Time, and Process

"Energy and the Evolution of Culture"

Gregory Bateson, a leading contemporary anthropologist, has recently said that whereas biological evolution proceeds by eliminating its mistakes, cultural evolution is fatally cumulative; human life is threatened by its own past. That which has enabled us to create culture is that which lets us retain our errors. Our abilities to remember, through writing and myth, what we become aware of and to forget only through the severity of psychological repression or political terror, may undo us. We have survived so well because our consciousness and our symbolic language have fueled our creativity. Our memories mean that culture does not have to be reinvented each generation; children add to what their parents know, and human adaptive potential among other species is thereby exponentially increased. But the same abilities also keep our errors alive, if not in material reality, then in people's minds.

Because we are conscious of ourselves, we know, or think we know, what is happening to us. Our self-awareness reveals things, like the atomic bomb, which make us wonder whether we ought to trust our interpretations of reality. Social observation uncovers patterns like millennia of sexual or political inequality that make us ask whether we can do anything at all to change them. Are we subject, we ask, to some preordained destiny (or to its modern counterpart, the operation of systematic principles that follow laws beyond our control)? Can we decide to fashion the world according to our beliefs, memories, and fantasies, and have it come out right? Can we go beyond our knowledge of destruction?

In a way, the question is whether people can escape the limitations of their culture. All ideology, of course, trains people to think that they can't; culture becomes (the best) destiny. Ours teaches us to believe in both fate and free will. It encourages us to submit ourselves to the fate of our upbringing. Yet it also condones cultural relativism and condemns the binds of ethnocentrism. It values change and the realization of individual will, though it blocks both. These emphases may bring about its transformation.

Evolutionary change has this double-edged character. What seems unchangeable eventually changes, and what seems to prevent it from changing has another side which enables it to do so. So it is with consciousness. The other side of Bateson's pessimism is the human ability to know one's own consciousness and cultural ideology, and, in knowing them, to take control. The cultural or personal selectivity of our observation does not enslave us. Nor need memories do so. Humans have the unique ability to know their past and present, and map out their futures. Though they also have the unique burden of self-doubt, arising from failed plans of action, the burden of memory permits the skills of self-correction.

Could there not be an interaction between evolutionary necessity and individual culture choice? I am raising here the problem of a conscious change of consciousness. Our consciousness, which is the immediate source of our decisions and actions, is indeed produced by culture, in interaction with the unconscious. But consciousness also produces culture. And, even more important, it is part of the evolutionary process. It both takes shape through and shapes natural selection.

Consciousness does not shape the evolution of culture without mediation, or by our mere will alone. There are, indeed, constraints within which the construction even of utopias must work. The major fate to which we are subject, according to the late theorist L. A. White, consists of two general trends: The evolution of culture involves an increase in (1) the amount of energy available to, and produced by human culture, and (2) the degree of integration, or organization, of social life. These trends are mutually reinforcing. The production and transformation of energy underlies biological and social life. Culture appropriates energy, in the form of plant and animal food, and uses it to recreate organisms and social relations, by expending energy in the creation of tools and social relations. Different energy sources provide lesser or greater amounts of energy. The earliest human societies depended on human labor enhanced by tools. The domestication of plants and animals brought the first great leap in amount of energy produced, for it enabled humans to control the reproduction of their energy sources. Subsequent increases came from the harnessing of wind and water, and the next qualitative jump was the use of fossil fuels in the industrial era.

Human history is not just the story of increasing energy. Energy use takes different forms, and each succeeding form contains forces impelling it toward change. The amount of energy captured depends on organization as well as on technology. The greater the energy potential, the more the organization necessary to tap it. For example, tool use enhanced *A. africanus's* chances of survival, but the refinement and specialization of assemblages of tools, or "tool kits," intensify only with the social structure characteristic of *H. erectus.* The society-wide division of labor itself increased energy capture: Just as it made it more likely that someone would bring food home, so it increased the probability that everyone would. But the social integration necessary to hold the division of labor together, like enculturation, rituals, and, perhaps, the institution of head man, entailed work and therefore required energy to be carried out. Hence, the more energy, the more integration was possible and necessary; the more integration, the more energy which could and must be captured.

These two trends have in part to do with advances in thermodynamic efficiency. For example, the division of labor, by preventing duplication of effort, saves energy for use elsewhere. In the long evolutionary run, this energy has been devoted to the growth of organizational complexity, i.e., increases in the number of parts of a society, their specialization, and their interdependence. The greater the diversification and interdependence, the more elaborate must be the institutional means for coordinating them. In other words, an increase in social integration means, concretely, the growth of specialized apparatus of control or of governing administrative structures. And this, as much as energy growth, has characterized cultural evolution.

White's theory of *universal* (in Steward's terms), or *general* (the label of Marshall Sahlins and Elman Service), *evolution* applies to the phenomenon of culture as a whole, and not to any one culture in particular.* Therefore, it does not preclude the possibility that two cultures with different energy and organizational levels, such as that of the Yanomamö and that of the United States, can coexist. The theory simply proposes a general, fundamental relationship between energy and social integration that frames the human experience. This proposition underlies our hypothesis about change and allows the construction of cross-cultural types, categories that organize and summarize our knowledge of cultural variation. The types also represent the levels of integration which in turn reflect the sequence of cultural-evolution as reconstructed by most anthropologists.

If we look at the archeological and historical records, we can synthesize from cultural continua all over the world a few levels of integration, each of which signals twin changes in energy capture and organizational complexity. The simplest is the band level of integration, in which dispersed bands of twenty-five to fifty people survive through a foraging adaptation, a domestic or a lineage mode of production, production for use and a basic division of labor according to sex and age. The major form of energy capture is human labor, enhanced by simple machines like the bow and arrow or the digging stick (used to dig root crops). Social integration is minimal, decentralized, and egalitarian. The physical coercion is rare, since individuals can be relied on to community's size allows social control to be carried out by face-to-face mechanisms like persuasion, ridicule, and ostracism; live up to personal obligations of kinship. The band, unsegmented except for families, is the maximal unit of continuous social cohesion; foreign relations between bands and intermittent, depending on seasonal or other occasional needs, such as the use of

* Steward characterized White's (and V. G. Childe's) evolutionary theory as universal to distinguish it from the unilineal schemata of nineteenth-century anthropology, which in effect proposed that all cultures must go through the same stages of evolution. That this is not the case is evidenced by the ability of Native American cultures to assimilate to Euro-American culture without going through, let us say, a feudal stage. Steward disagreed with both theories; I discuss his *multilinear* theory below.

another's water resources. Archeological remains afford us little knowledge of what ideology or individuality might have been like. But from contemporary foragers, we might infer supernatural beliefs and shamans whose personal mystical gifts can cure illness by mediating between human and spirit worlds.

This type of society represents not only the simplest, but the first human form of energy capture and of social integration. Although it characterized all human populations from their beginnings until about 10,000 years ago, it has, by now, all but disappeared. Bands are today found only in marginal areas where they have retreated from or been pushed by cultures with higher levels of energy capture and organization. Historically, their place was first taken by societies at the tribal level of integration, those which had adopted domesticated plants and animals. Later, both band and tribal societies suffered the expansion of the next two more complex levels of society, chiefdoms and states.

To explain how each step occurred, we have to shift our sights to specific cases and add the theoretical perspective of specific evolution, as developed by Sahlins and Service. General and specific evolution are different aspects of the same process. But where *general evolution* refers to overall changes in culture as a panhuman phenomenon, *specific evolution* refers to culture at the second level of abstraction, to actual sequences of development in particular areas. General evolutionary processes have to do with adaptive advances characteristic of the whole human experience. The processes of specific evolution have to do with adaptive changes in response to particular, local environmental changes that may or may not parallel general advances. In other words, a particular culture that develops later than another is not necessarily more advanced; for example, the ancient Han empire of China was more complex than the later feudal kingdoms of Europe.

Specific evolutionary processes, then, involve diverse adaptations to diverse situations, rather than advances per se. Specific evolution returns us to ecological theory and to considerations of political relationships between cultures. Let us examine one specific sequence, in the Middle East, of one general evolutionary advance, domestication. This will exemplify the theory of general and specific evolution and will also show how levels of integration change.

The domestication of plants came about under conditions of population pressure, the use of marginal resources, and diverse ecological niches. Within an area stretching from present-day western Iran, across the confluence of the Tigris and Euphrates Rivers into Iraq, lie four contiguous, contrasting environments: the central plateau of Iran, the intermontane valleys of the Zagros mountains, the Assyrian steppe, and the Mesopotamian alluvial desert. Foraging populations lived in this area by at least 40,000 years ago; they were nomadic, but each had a home base in one or another zone. By around 12,000 years ago, in the zone of the valleys, or "hilly flanks," population density began to increase, and people therefore began to spread out. Some began to colonize areas which, though on the margins of the valley zone, were nevertheless familiar, because the local ecological adaptation had been based on regional diversity: All groups used all four zones, moving from desert up to mountains and down again as they hunted the seasonally migrating game, harvesting on their way the wild grain ripening in altitudinal sequence. They also traded interregionally, for each region produced different, desirable natural resources. Turquoise and copper, for example, were carried from Iran to Assyria, and natural asphalt was brought back.

Archeologists hypothesize that the pioneers tried to control their new environments by attempting to recreate the plant life with which they were familiar. For example, they may have taken wild wheat and barley seeds from the hilly flanks and sowed them in their new home. This process, involving selective pressures from both the physical and human environments, and combining with mutations, caused the evolution of new strains of grain that were suited not only to the physical environment but to the human one of domestication. For instance, the new varieties were probably easy to harvest without loss of seeds. The first experiments with cultivation must have been only a small part of a society's adaptation; for example, like the Siriono, a twentieth-century

Bolivian foraging band society, they may have dropped their grain in one season and returned in another to harvest it; in the meantime, they would have hunted wild sheep and goats and gathered other vegetation.

In short, a very diverse ecological niche supported them until complete sedentary domestication developed, probably between 12,000 and 10,000 years ago. Full dependence on dometicates would have emerged only when, logically, agricultural production could be the major support and foraging something to fall back on. Reliance on domestication would also have depended on, and have had to wait for, the development of cultivable strains, the clearing of sufficient land for production, and the growth of a social structure compatible with sedentary life. For when people must live year-round in one place, as they do when they have full-scale agriculture, they can, for example, no longer resolve interpersonal conflicts in the manner of foraging bands, by threatening to abandon the offender during a seasonal population dispersal, or by doing it. Ways to resolve conflicts while keeping injured parties in the same place must develop, and these usually involve more specialized structures of social control, such as unilineal kinship and lineage elders.

The whole process, then, occurred gradually, not in a lightbulb flash. Nor did any one, as far as we can tell, consciously intend to create domesticated plants or the sedentary adaptation and social structure that followed. Instead, like any adapting population, they tried to maintain a constant relation to their environment, and in so doing, changed. In trying to keep things as they were in the "old country," the pioneer populations created a new environment for themselves, and so changed the world. From 10,000 years ago forward, full dependence on domesticated plants, the *neolithic revolution,* became a reality. It permitted the domestication of sheep and goats (because one can't keep animals for long unless one can feed them) and the establishment of permanent villages. The former foreshadowed a later source of energy, the draught-power of plow animals; the latter, the future growth of urban society and centralized government.

Domestication also precipitated a veritable explosion of creativity. Around 7,500 years ago, new strains of grain were developed; new plants, like lentils, and new animals, like pigs and cattle, domesticated; and new crafts invented. Villages in varied ecological areas began to specialize somewhat in the food they produced; full-time specialized nomadic pastoralist societies were able to form in symbiosis with full-time farmers, with whom they traded stock products for grain. And trade of all kinds grew, with perhaps even a few merchants who specialized in interregional trade.

Some theorists, like Childe, have hypothesized that this development of new technology and specialization could not have occurred without an increase in leisure time, and that this leisure was in turn made possible by the surplus produced by domestication. As we have seen, surplus is socially, relatively defined; furthermore, domestication and its surplus themselves required considerable inventiveness, as we have just seen. The argument is a bit chicken-and-eggy. Childe's position seems simple and therefore attractive. But it reduces to a mechanical determinism and therefore requires correction. He presumes that preagricultural societies had no leisure, and that therefore leisure, when it first appeared, was empty, and so could be filled by inventing. This assumption comes from industrial capitalism, where people work very hard to get leisure, and think that they have more than preceding generations. Now, it is true that the amount of leisure time available to the working class has grown since the difficult early industrial era. From this, our cultural ideology infers a linear increase, with industrial capitalism providing the most leisure because it is the latest, and therefore more "evolved," stage of evolution.

But recent anthropological studies, according to Sahlins, suggest that some people in the earliest human cultures may have had the same, if not more leisure than most of us have now. In fact, not only industrialism but also agriculture involve more, and more arduous, work than foraging and horticulture. Foragers, for example, have a lot of leisure time and use much of it in the form of sleep and sex, the rest in talk, ceremony, and tool repair. The postdomestication creativity, then, like domestication itself, probably emerged from the effect of population pressure on previously existing technological possibilities, and not from empty leisure. As we will see below, specialization indeed depended on surplus production, but it emerged from previous forms.

Domestication was, in any event, a successful adaptation, even if measured only in the strict ecological terms of reproductive success. The initially rapid growth of population at first caused no major changes as had the last population increase: This was because population density is relative not only to geographical space, but to the cultural space of energy capture. What, for example, would have been a large population for a forest-dwelling ape to support, was small for *A. africanus* who had tools to get food. High population pressure for *A. africanus* was low for *H. erectus* who had a division of labor. So it is here. Domestication so increased energy capture that a much larger population could be supported in the same area.

In fact, at this point, the once marginal areas might even have been underpopulated and might have attracted population. This was because, although cultivation yielded more energy, it required that more energy be consumed; since the major source of work energy was still human labor attached to simple machines, more people were necessary. But about 7000 years ago and thereafter, even these areas became overpopulated; people moved outward, some back to the hilly flanks, others to lower areas of southern Mesopotamia where the next evolutionary advances would occur and where the bases for these advances, the fabrication of metal objects and the invention of simple methods of irrigation, were being developed.

Domestication took place independently two or three other times in geographically, historically, and genetically unrelated populations (in North China, Central America, and, perhaps, West Africa), in what is called convergent evolution. In the New World, for example, the archeological record indicates a similarly gradual transition from food-collecting to agriculture, with a continued dependence on a varied resource base and an end result in permanent villages. The type of society that developed following this advance was also similar. In each case, the amount of energy harnessed per capita per year had increased over the previous adaptation, and correlated with a way of being and living that is called the *tribal level of integration.*

We infer from contemporary tribal cultures, like the Yanomamö or Gouro, what these first ones must have been like. Based on extensive, rather than intensive, use of resources and labor,* tribal modes of production (for use-value primarily) resemble the lineage, village or domestic modes and are integrated by reciprocity and redistribution. Competitive trade in commodities, however, may be carried out between societies, as we saw in the case of the Gouro, and as probably developed between the Middle Eastern regions. Some form of kinship including, perhaps, a marriage alliance system, organizes social relationships and political integration; descent principles may form clearly bounded segments, all similar in structure and function. Integrative mechanisms, like the Nuer kinship-territorial system, enable the whole society to coalesce if necessary, but otherwise hamper no one. No individual yet has coercive power over any other; if individuals differ in rank, the differences are ephemeral since leaders get their power by redistribution.

Some theorists, notably Morton Fried, have argued that *tribe* is a misnomer for these cultures or for this level of integration, because it implies an organized society whose cohesion is based on a hierarchy of leadership and presents itself to the outside as a solidary, uniform unit. Fried asserts that such a cohesive society, and the notion of it, are the products of the world view and treatment accorded by states to indigenous colonized peoples. This level of integration might more properly be thought of as consisting of autonomous villages (as among the Yanomamö or the Nuer), which had no paramount leader or unifying structure

* The difference between extensive and intensive agriculture is the amount of land used, and what makes the difference is technology and labor organization. Intensive systems, such as irrigation agriculture (see below), or plow agriculture, which fertilizes with the manure from draught animals, permit the same productivity on a relatively small area as results from a larger area with swidden and other extensive horticultural systems. Not all technologies can, however, be applied to all soil types, so tropical forest cultivation, for example, would not benefit from the plow.

until interactions with colonists forced them to develop hierarchical government.

Although the causes and effects were the same in each case of this general evolutionary advance to the tribal level, the independently evolved paths were, in Steward's term, *multilinear:* that is, each varied according to local differences in natural resources. In the New World, for example, the process began about 2,000 years later than in the Old World, partly because *H. sapiens* occupied the New World later, entering by the Bering land bridge between 60,000 and 30,000 years ago, and spreading down to the southern tip of South America by 10,000 years ago. Pastoralism did not develop there partly because herd animals, like cattle, sheep, or goats, were not indigenous to the New World. This altered later evolutionary paths: In contrast, in the Old World, pastoralism was not only an early village specialization within a trading network, but it came eventually to flavor a major portion of the cultural scene. It grounded the ecological adaptation and the political integration of the nomads of Central Asia and of the Saharan and Arabian deserts. Their chiefs ruled thousand of people, controlled millions of stock animals, and often exacted tribute from the oasis and desert-edge towns on whose fruits, vegetables, and grains they depened.

But that gets us ahead of the story. The evolutionary changes we have seen so far, the emergence of band and tribal levels of integration, of foraging, and of domestication, have had to do with interactions between the human and the physical environments. The next set of changes begin with the same processes, but end with the addition of intercultural interactions. After domestication, tribal societies underwent *adaptive radiation.* In new environments, the population of any species tends to grow until it reaches external checks: built-in, or homeostatic, limits develop later. We may assume that the tribes, in first adapting to the new environment of domestication, did the same. The new energy went first primarily into population and later primarily into organization. When their populations grew beyond the bounds of the newly created space, they then moved into and transformed many other regions with their new powers and were, in turn, transformed into systems which were culturally more differentiated in subsistence base, kinship organization, and belief systems.

What transformed them into more highly structured or integrated systems was contact with other social systems. Within a given adaptation, if population growth reaches a point of confrontation between communities or societies, it creates a new kind of environment, a social one, to which each must adapt by means of new social forms. We have seen one such neolithic adaptation in the Nuer's absorption of the Dinka, which both managed the confronted society and continued to allow expansion. But if the structures of two expanding, contiguous communities are equally matched, the energy of at least one of them will have to go into the development of yet more integrative forces that may, in turn, give it a competitive edge. If, for example, the Nuer had met an equally, or more powerful structure, there would have been a standoff, until one or the other developed a more centralized organization. In fact, this may have been happening to the Nuer when they faced the British colonialists, as the emergence of prophets among them may indicate. But any structural change was inhibited when the British deprived them of guns (which their control over gun manufacture and superior governmental structure enabled them to do).

In any event, to return to the distant past, archeologists hypothesize that in the Middle Neolithic, the population increase eventually resulted in intra- and inter-community conflicts. Their resolution entailed the origin of socio-economic inequalities, institutionalized leadership, and a centralized government run by political specialists. The specific conflicts arose not where domestication originated, but in lower Mesopotamia, where, between 7,500 and 5,000 years ago, devices had been created to use the annual floods in river valleys to water the fields of nearby communities. These inventions may have been taken up because population increase necessitated more effecient use of the constant water supply. Irrigation enabled these communities, though still linked to other agricultural and specialist villages in a trade network, to produce more than others. At first, the irrigation technology probably was shared by the members of one community, and perhaps even by a few communities on the basis of kinship and marriage ties.

But the initial (and subsequent) population increases could also have led to (and resulted from) a reorganization of rights to water (which was becoming scarce in relation to the increased population pressure) both within and between neighboring communities. The first restrictions would probably have limited access to water to members of a community, perhaps by means of such inheritance rules as corporate lineage control of water. Even tighter restrictions might have emerged, protecting corporate community ownership of water by preferential community endogamy. Since an endogamous rule would have dissolved earlier affinal bases for intercommunity problem solving, some concomitant multicommunity political structure must have developed simultaneously, particularly since the irrigation works themselves would have become objects of conflict. This development is suggested by archeological investigations which show that after the invention of the first irrigation canals, great multicommunity waterworks eventually came to be built.

Whatever the actual course of events, this leap in integration, like that in domestication, must have gradually developed on the basis of several pre-existing relationships. In particular, archeological research indicates that the earliest specialized buildings probably were temples. This suggests that religious leaders were the earliest full-time, non-food-producing specialists supported by a whole community. Indeed, in contemporary tribal cultures, if there is someone who is differentiated from others, that person is a priest, like the Trobriand garden priest, or shaman (who is as often a woman as a man). Tribal priests or shamans are part-time religious figures who support themselves by working like anyone else. A full-time priestly (or any other) specialization would require the provision of subsistence from surplus production. This might have been the first formally unequal use for a surplus, a departure from its role as a hedge against disaster and a generator of prestige in a system like the Kula.

At first, priests would not have been very powerful; they

probably would have depended for their continued social support on their success in cajoling rain from the heavens. But in combination with irrigation technology, religion and its officials would have provided the foundation on the basis of which a full-scale theocratic power structure could have developed. In competition with another community, even a fledgling power structure must have been selected for, because it would have raised the productivity on which it also depended. Under a system of use-production, a central authority can increase the amount each household produces. Like the Trobriand chief, or big-man, going on Kula, a leader could, for the purposes of transacting with or defying another village, exhort his people to devote just a little extra energy to a common effort, to plant more, or to make more artifacts, so as to support the construction of better irrigation works or the prosecution of successful battles over shore-line.

A political structure, in other words, developed at the point when the cultural environment became a selective force. The Middle Eastern archeological record is a silent but eloquent witness to the rapidity of its growth: Simple village shrines or temples mushroomed into large, elaborate structures, or ziggurats. From a position of dependence, priests moved into a position of power and then of wealth; leaders were buried in great tombs with ornaments of precious metals brought from far away, while the simple burials of most of the population reveal their continued modest, if not marginal, existence. Palaces housed full-time bureaucrats who kept records with newly-elaborated writing systems, oversaw long-distance trading expeditions, conscripted labor to build and maintain canals, roads, and palaces, and collected taxes in kind to finance all these activities by feeding those who carried them out.

By 5,000 years ago, the state level of integration had thus appeared in the area between the Tigris and Euphrates Rivers, with the characteristics described in Chapter VI, a centralized, specialized administrative structure; a division into two major endogamous groups, the few elite and the many masses, distinguished by their differential access to life-sustaining goods and services; a monopoly on coercive force; territorial sovereignty;

the control over writing and therefore long-distance communication, and over the codification and creation of history and myth, belief and knowledge. In the case of the first archaic or preindustrial states, like the Mesopotamian ones, or of the convergent instances in Mesoamerica and India, the urban elite run the government and most of the masses are rural food producers. While the peasants may continue to produce mostly for their own use in the domestic mode, they are nevertheless affected by the mode of production integrated by state redistribution. For example, the Mesopotamian theocracy took goods, like grain and tools, and services, like labor, from the peasants and transformed them into things that were necessary to keep life as the people knew it going. In Mesopotamia, cities developed simultaneously with the state and continued, in addition to the elite bureaucrats and priests, government-supported craftsmen who produced subsistence technology as well as luxury goods.

One view has it that these services were the government's return for the use of the peasants' labor and products, since any administrative work logically requires energy and therefore surplus. This would be correct if the government returned everything it took. But it did not. The elite, in their governmental roles, kept some for themselves. Sometimes, as in Mel Brooks's conception of Robin Hood, they "stole from everybody and kept everything." They either consumed what they took directly, eating the food and using the artifacts; or transformed it into commodities through trade, thus beginning the process of capital accumulation; or turned it into precious metals and fine fabrics, consuming conspicuously. The ancient elite, like those in contemporary states, thus had privileged access to wealth and other luxuries like education, as well as to power. They were, nevertheless, interested in providing the peasants with some level of care and protection because, first, they had to ensure a high level of food production to feed themselves and to finance trade, and second, protection was and is one ideological device to persuade people that the elite merit their position.

By 5,000 years ago, the most powerful social organization of humans in relation to resources and to other cultures ever to appear in human history had already evolved. It was the prototype for the contemporary Euro-American class structured system, as well as for the Soviet system, although these capitalist and socialist states themselves emerged only with the next great leap in energy (the use of fossil fuels) and in the organization of production (industrialism). The development of the state represents a push toward greater integration of society, and is, all told, an adaptive advance. The state is a politically unified structure that contains a great deal of ecological and social diversity; such diversity empowers it to withstand natural and social disasters. It can coordinate the activities of thousands of people engaged in different tasks in distant places by regulating time (e.g., official or fiscal calendars, daylight savings time, etc.), linking space through the construction of transportation networks, and uniting people's consciousness by celebrations shared either in person or, now, through electronic media (presidential inaugurations and resignations).

The ordered diversity stimulates production, for the state ensures and integrates the flow of goods and services by means of government-controlled money, marketplaces, and capital markets (or the buying and selling of factors or production, including tools, land, and money). These transactions take place, in archaic, or preindustrial states, in marketplaces, e.g., bazaars, where people may buy not only the means of production, but also consumption goods. These transactions rarely take place in the same locales in industrial states. The regulation of both is necessary for the successful cohesion of a state and the survival of its populace, because the markets and market-exchange play a major integrative role, particularly in the cities. They permit prosperity to increase because they can absorb any surplus rural population (such as people disinherited because of population pressure-induced scarcity of land). This population constitutes the labor force for specialized production. The market transacts not only labor, but also surplus agricultural products; it is the means by which specialists get fed, and the peasants in the hinterland get currency to pay taxes and to buy urban craft products. Finally, the market is the structural counterpart to the beginnings of alienable labor: It is the place where labor-power can be sold and where people can sell it in return for wages.

The state rules city, village, and market through "territorial sovereignty." This enables the state to allocate access to resources among its constituent communities, and therefore to divert the expenditures of energy from local squabbles to continued production. A uniform codification of law links up residentially or ethnically diverse populations; specialized government branches like those for tax collection, war making/peace making, and the judicial process; and higher and lower levels of organization, from local to central governments.

Like other levels of integration, the state competes successfully against lesser ones. It allows for a larger population; but, more importantly, its structure strengthens it politically and militarily. Apart from intimidating others with its might, it can also defeat and then absorb whole other social units; it may even allow them to retain their original level of integration, granting them semi-autonomy in return for tribute, military aid, and so on, as in the case of the U.S. Commonwealth of Puerto Rico. Or, finally, states can create international systems of control that allow other nations their political autonomy, but hold them in economic dependency; such is the relations of the United States to Brazil, or of the Soviet Union to Poland.

The question that has always plagued theorists of the origin of the state is how its inherent inequality could first have emerged. At the tribal level of integration, no one is more powerful than anyone else, but suddenly, in the state, there are very clear differences in wealth and political strength. The archeological record does not tell us why people would have accepted the unequal division of power and the exploitation to which they were subject; it records only that they did so. We are forced to speculate.

According to one view, the state came into existence because it was adaptive, that is, because it enabled larger populations to survive than had been possible under other levels of integration, and people's will or consciousness had nothing to do with it. It is true that the state was adaptive, but as we have seen, adaptation explains only why something remains, not why it appears. Although it also is true that human will cannot change overall adaptive processes or directions of evolution, we nevertheless should not dismiss individual processes. One of the problems of cultural (and biological) evolutionary theory is its omission of the relation between evolution and human action. To ignore this relation is to deny the importance of the unequal distribution of power in our own society and to acquiesce in the contradictions in our own cultural ideology: On the one hand, power is seen as something that is purely a matter of personal control and individual efforts; on the other hand, it is seen to lie fatefully out of our individual grasp, assigned, as it were, by the "wisdom" of evolution to some morally neutral state.

If the anthropological investigation into cultural evolution is an extension of human self-awareness and is one way of finding out who we are, then anthropological theory must confront the issue of power in terms not only of its social genesis, but also of its meaning to us as individual, conscious actors with the capability, will and desire to control, if not destinies, then our own lives. If, reasonably, we assume that most people are sufficiently intelligent that they cannot be fooled into accepting their own exploitation, then we must postulate something else.

A second theory is that inequality came about through conquest, with the vanquished society becoming the lower class. Later states did indeed conquer others in the course of imperial expansion, absorbing new peoples either as members of one lower class or, as in the Middle East, as members of occupationally specialized ethnic groups, all subject to the governing elite but not forming a homogeneous underclass. Other theories suggest a kind of trade-off: In return for administration of irrigation works, which would guarantee continuity of the food supply, and therefore economic security, peasants would cede power to a bureaucracy of priests. But this seems to me to attribute to them a kind of foresight that people rarely have, and a rationality that, unfortunately, they lack; indeed, if people knew that much about social control, they could have avoided exploitation.

No, what we need is to see how the potential for power can lie in a structure whose internal dynamic snowballs and catches people up so that, even if they are not fooled, they have little or no choice in what happens. Now, we have no direct information for Mesopotamia or any other early state on how this happened, though Robert McC. Adams provides suggestive speculation. We must therefore infer from ethnographic cases in which we find social structures and processes which look as if they were en route from tribe to state. Such cases have been called the chiefdom level of integration and have been found in, for example, Hawaii and other Polynesian Islands at the time of the European exploration of the Pacific. Each specific instance, of course, is not to be understood as a "missing link," but as a social system in its own right. Following Sahlins, the general dynamics of this level of integration suggest a course of transition from, say, a culture like the Trobrianders' to one like ours.

Chiefdoms, like states, exist in ecologically diverse areas. There are differences in access to strategic resources within the population, but the lines of power are more vague because everyone in a chiefdom is kin to every one else. Instead of a division into two, there is a continuous series of ranks. Unilineages are ranked according to the birth order of their founders, and individuals according to lineage membership and birth order: The firstborn sons of firstborn sons rank higher than the line of secondborns, who are superior to thirdborns, and so on. This minute division of prestige is validated in genealogies.

The paramount chief of such a kingdom is a full-time political, or administrative specialist who has material, political, and sacred power, and can get people to obey him in part because of his ritual power (such as his ability to tolerate mana). But they have a claim on him, because he is kin to them. He may, therefore, not exploit them, and he must redistribute generously. He need not redistribute everything, but when he asks for labor or goods, he must justify what he takes in terms of their welfare, not, as in the state, only by words, but also by deeds. Although their production feeds him, his royal retainers, and his family, and underwrites trade for luxury goods, he must make sure that the producers eat in case of famine, get the trade goods they need, and are rewarded for services rendered to him. The kinship relationship is thus a structural and ideological device which prevents the development of absolute differences and exploitation within the system.

Chiefdoms are notoriously short-lived, which is why there may be no material remains of them in Mesopotamia or other areas where the state first developed. In particular historical circumstances, they either tend to fall apart into smaller societies, much like the chiefdom of vassals and feudal lords in Europe, or to coalesce into larger, more solid states, as, we infer, took place in the Old and New Worlds, India, and Southeast Asia in separate, specific evolutionary lines. Structurally, chiefdoms always tend to balance precariously between their previous tribal equality and the full-fledged inequality of the state.

Their conditions of emergence are the same as those of any new level of integration. They lie in changes in the relationship between populations and resources, and may have taken the form either of conflicts between expanding communities, or of the increased organizational needs of a long-distance trading network (e.g., something like the Kula, or the trade among Middle Eastern neolithic communities). The chiefdom's structure is clearly transitional between tribal and state levels. All people in them are kin, but some kin are more equal than others, because some are more closely related to the chief; given this, the chief's sacred status enables him and his close kin, who are also the administrators, to see themselves and be seen as different in kind from all others and therefore, eventually, not their kin(d). Kinship and use-values still regulate production at the household level, but household production comes to depend on government-organized irrigation, trade, and so on; since the chief and his retainers administer them, they can easily take control of the wealth and power offered by this "Asiatic" mode of production.

Power comes to be transformed among different domains, from domestic to political, economic to social. Like the big-man, the chief still gives goods away, but, since royal status confers rights to wealth, he and the other elite keep some of the production for themselves. And, since, conversely, the display of wealth also validates rights to royalty, and, since, as we saw in Chapter VI, conspicuous consumption is one of the easiest devices known to state and nonstate society alike for getting people to fear and accept another's authority, it is easy for royalty to take a little more and return a little less, spending some on awesomely terrifying temples like those of the ancient Mexican ceremonial center, Teotihuacan. Like the big-man, the chief can stimulate production beyond the household level and create a society-wide economy among ecologically diverse areas, but he can do more with less risk, for he is a sacred personage. Whereas the big-man exploits his followers at the peril of their desertion and his consequent fall from power, the chief's followers desert at their own peril, because they depend on him for his relation to the world of the sacred. Finally, the rulers' withholding comes to be less and less noticeable or, at least, missed, since increased technological and organizational efficiency raise productivity. It is but a small step from there to the rulers' exploitation of their former lowly kin, now incipient peasants.

I think the balance tips under conditions of population pressure in relation not necessarily to physical but to organizational space, in inter-societal relations. This happens when chiefdom meets and competes with chiefdom. People require a centralized administration to carry out most of their economic activity, and to construct an ideology sufficient to align the activities of diverse individuals and groups. Administrative rules and activities are so complex and time-consuming that only full-time specialists can carry them out; and these circumstances become obvious, so that one group, the elite, can take advantage of their superior access to strategic resource to consolidate their power and overtly to validate their *coup d'état* in ideology, while those whose access is limited can only watch helplessly. Or, if they silently acquiesce, then they are merely acquiescing to a power over which they never had any control, the power of their gods incarnate in a priest or a divinely right king. For religious belief and ecclesiastical hierarchies have been two of the more powerful means of consolidating state power once it has crystallized.

A Journey Barely Begun

Just because the state is the most adaptive social system so far known does not mean that it's the best. But, although no society has been perfect so far, in some ways it is an improvement over earlier ones. The band society was also adaptive, but life in it could at times be very harsh for everyone; even though those who survived infancy may have lived to ripe old ages, infant mortality was high, and old people were sometimes left to die alone in the desert or tundra. The survivors may have had things that we have lost, like a certainty about who they were, based on a sense of integration between self, culture, and the natural world. But they also knew less about these things and had fewer choices about them. They certainly had fewer material riches. Although one may say, as a student once said in trying to justify the existence of underdevelopment, "You never miss what you never had," I'm not too sure that this is the case. I would bet that foragers longed for things they didn't have, even if they, like ourselves, couldn't always name what they wanted.

It seems to me that one of the characteristics of evolution is the continuing clarification of that which human culture is capable of providing, but which it still lacks. In no society, for example, at no level of integration, has the position of women ever come close to being satisfactory. The levels of integration, as progressive as they may be in energy capture, social cohesion, and standards of living, do not show a linear improvement in the status of women. I do not really know what accounts for this, any more than I am entirely certain about the origins of other inequalities. Therefore, I do not know for sure what needs to be changed. But shadowy suggestions are emerging, as from the theory of sex/gender systems. They include, most especially, radical shifts in the most fundamental and global of all social relations which frame the context not only of growing up and rearing children, but of everyone's everyday life. These shifts mean that there can be no liberation of women without the liberation of men, and of children, and of parents, and, indeed, of every other present and future self-aware status group in every culture. It also means that when these changes occur, there will also be great changes in consciousness, in ways of seeing, experiencing, and evaluating the universe.

Just as a permanent equalization of the sexes entails total change within a culture, so things cannot change in only one part of the world. General evolutionary theory, along with theories in other disciplines, implies that we have now reached the stage when there are no isolated cultures. In principle, no culture ever was isolated. When domestication developed, it spread by "diffusion," or borrowing, from one local population to another, and eventually affected the whole world; but as far as we know, it took 1,500 years for it to move even from the Middle East to ancient Greece. The effect of capitalism is qualitatively different, for it managed to take over the world in 500 years. And, in the future, given the rapidity of our transportation systems and the immediacy of our communication networks and the incorporating scope of the state, there will probably be only one world system, and the next change will not only be total, but relatively instantaneous.

At any one time, then, general evolutionary stages are accurate descriptions of all human culture, but they do not necessarily describe every individual culture. This is because, at any one moment in history, there will be one dominant level of integration, though not a single stage. Rather, in the past as at this moment, many different kinds of culture coexist. But one type prevails, just as one mode of production does in an economic system. Depending on the level of integration, dominance may also mean domination. Thus, 100,000 years ago all cultures were at the band level, so the band was the dominant form. But no band could dominate, in the sense of taking over other ones.

However, the increase in organization which typifies cultural evolution pushes towards inclusion and domination, as we can see in the adaptive patterns of the tribe and the chiefdom. By 5000

B.C., agriculture had developed in a sufficient number of areas so that all living populations were influenced by its productivity and by tribal organization which took many different but equivalent forms. By 3000 B.C., the state level of integration had likewise begun to alter the shape of cultures and their interrelations. Even if some societies remained preagricultural bands, and some tribes did not become chiefdoms or states, yet the higher level of integration affected all within reach, and had indirect repercussions on the rest, drawing some cultures in and pushing others out. With the European Age of Exploration and Industrial Revolution came the long-lived colonial absorption-domination of much of the world by a few expansive mercantilist and later capitalist empires.

Finally, at A.D. 2000, there exists an organization of culture that concretely has world-historical effects on all living and future generations, incorporating in one and the same system many societies. This world-system came about because of the development of a late stage of capitalism, monopoly capitalism, which is enabled by its organizational potential, and forced by its internal dynamic, to control, or at least, influence, the whole world. This means that there can be no developed countries without underdeveloped ones, and vice versa. Both are parts of one inter- or multi-national (or intercultural) structure; contemporary capitalists exploit not so much the working class of their own political unit, or country, as those of other autonomous political units. These states, in turn, exist in a hierarchy of power; there can, in other words, be no Third and Fourth Worlds without First and Second ones.

Economic power is easily transformed into political power, and this will be the driving force toward a single political system. This will be the next great leap forward in organization, in the direction in which human evolution has been tending. It will involve the integration of all life-support activities in one system of power and decision-making. This leap cannot happen without some form of socialism; it cannot happen until the best of capitalism can be separated from the worst, until its full productive potential can be realized without exploitation, and until individual self-realization becomes coextensive with societal integration. World political organization cannot occur until human beings can make the riches of the earth and of human labor available in the measure of their abundance to all human beings in the measure of their abilities and their needs.

It may be that this leap will involve a homogenization of all environmental adaptations and all cultures, but I doubt it. We have seen that evolutionary survival depends on diversity. Those species and cultures with the most adaptive potential have been those that are least specialized and most generalized, the most diverse and heterogeneous. Although less successful in any one environment, generalized species can inhabit more environments than others.* This all-round adaptability sets human species apart from all other life forms; humans are a more generalized species than others. In ecological terms, increased cultural organization means increased ordering of diversity. In other words, natural diversity has been culturally recreated, first, in the division of labor, and secondly, in the organization of the state. Perhaps its third recreation might be in a world organization of distant, differentiated, but integrated environmental and cultural systems.

As I conceive this process, it is analogous to what Marx said the pattern of change would be in economic systems: A change in structure could not occur until the fullest potential of the material forces of production had been realized, and the fullest potential can be realized only through the realization of all possible permutations of the social relations of production. At that point, the old relations of production become fetters on new technological possibilities and their productive potential. We already have the possibilities: One world culture could include many variable energy sources, "elbow grease" and fossil fuels, wind and water, the sun and the atoms; we also have technology

* Specialized species are those which do well in one environment. Being very well adapted, they have more difficulty in surviving environmental change. This is, incidentally, why there can be no survivors of the earliest human cultures, and is the reason for there being no living australopiths. As the conditions of their existence altered, the specialized ones died out and the generalized ones changed.

which might permit their integrated social use. Silicone chips make possible the manufacture of miniaturized computers and communication systems. Such media of information retrieval and communication would permit the coordination not only of ecological, but of cultural diversity, for they would allow decentralized control and more direct, individual creation of ideology.

This means that, just as a monolithic ecological adaptation would be unnecessary (as well as maladaptive), so would there be no need for cultural monotony. Human beings require some manageable, proximate group with which to identify, some group they can name and describe in terms of values and customs and beliefs. Even now, in the United States, ethnicity, always a major residential and occupational unit, is crystallizing as a significant political unit. Ethnic groups often are politically conservative, but that does not mean that they must always be against change. Our historical experience shows that as valuable as centralization may be, it must be countered by a force which protects the political nonprofessionals from the potential rapacity of the specialist administrators. Ethnic groups may be one such countervailing force.

One final dimension of increased culturally ordered diversity is heightened individuality. An implication of Chapter V's discussion of sex roles and psychological development is that we ought no longer to speak of the individual, or even of two types like male and female. Different gender types are possible, just as there are many types of personality or character. Capitalism has historically allowed for more variation in individual personality, consciousness, and choice than any hitherto preceding sociocultural form. Any world system, in providing for all other diversities, will have to incorporate this one as well, for the development of extreme individuality under later capitalism is something which cannot and will not be forgotten.

The realization of differentiated technology and personal style requires a fundamentally new social system which allows for both integration and decentralization, order and diversity, social progress and individual autonomy. The solution to this sociocultural problem lies not in technology but in power. The cultural form of matter's evolutionary increase in integration is the progressive inclusion of more and more systems within the same one.* Sometimes, this inclusion has taken the form of domination, by one culture over others, by culture over nature, by culture over the individual. But domination produces conflict, and conflict produces change. Dominated cultures have revolutions, those who don't die of pollution attack its makers, and under-nourished psyches drop out and fight back.

In the formulation of the Marxist-structuralist anthropologist, Jonathon Friedman, cultural change happens when there are contradictions both within and between systems. Conflict, then, arises intrasystematically, as from capitalism's contradictions between private ownership and socialized production, its promised equality and its structured inequality. Conflict also emerges when the relations between systems become strained, as when the rising profits of a dominant nation prohibit wages sufficient for the reproduction of the workers of the dependent nation; as when production goals deplete the energy sources on which they depend; as when the state's integration of diversity requires the demolition of individuality. Change therefore emerges from intersystemic interactions of conflict, which, seen from a wider perspective, fall *within* one system.

At such a point, change must occur, or all will die. But cultural change does not happen unconsciously, as it were, without the mediation of human will, awareness, action. It therefore involves the exercise of power, of decision making, of choice. If this is the case, and if anthropology is to comprehend it, then anthropology, like any ideology, must change so as to describe and prescribe the conditions of its own existence, even if it becomes totally transformed in doing so. It must include within it an understanding of power, of the individual, and of the simultaneous autonomy and dependence of systems with respect to one another. Just as the individual's view of the world is not

* And it takes longer to describe each succeeding stage, not because we are culturally closer to, and therefore myopic about, each, but because each is more inclusive and therefore more complex.

entirely consciously created, but is uncontrollably formed by unconscious and cultural processes as well, so a culture is not fixed by its ecological adaptation, social structure, or overt ideology. Anthropological theory must, then, accept structured indeterminacy, one source of which is subjectivity. Choice, therefore, exists within cultural process. The political, practical problem is to integrate this diversity and choice into new action and structure. The theoretical problem for anthropology is to show how people can choose freely and create meaningfully within the constraints of the material, structural, and symbolic forces which forge human experience.

We change in the same way that other species do: Simply by living, they alter their environment and force themselves to evolve into something different. But we also are different from other life forms, for we have a consciousness that makes us act. One of the quirks of human action is that things never come out quite the way we planned, and we still don't understand exactly why. All we can do is try. And, curiously, we are unable to do anything else; even our inaction will affect our future. Indeed, by not acting, we make a choice to validate the status quo. But the status quo will not remain; it must change and be changed, not only for the sake of morality, but for the sake of survival. We will be the agents of its change. We all are conscious individuals who, both because of and in spite of our cultural conditioning, can know what we want and can have the satisfaction of acting to create it, even if we don't know whether we will succeed. For otherwise, why do anything? Perhaps that is what human nature is all about—an impulsion to do, to search for an almost forgotten past or a future not yet named, to create order out of the chaos in the mind, in culture, and in nature.

Suggestions for Further Reading

For each chapter, I first refer to general surveys on main issues, then to a few more detailed works. I do not provide references for each culture mentioned but only for those discussed in some detail. For the most part, I have restricted myself to recent, generally available works, listing soft-cover editions where possible.

INTRODUCTION AND CHAPTER I

The best brief philosophical introduction to anthropology is Eric R. Wolf's *Anthropology* (1964, Prentice-Hall, Englewood Cliffs, N.J.). I have borrowed my title and some general perspectives from C. Wright Mills, *The Sociological Imagination* (1959, Oxford University Press, London). *Reinventing Anthropology*, a collection of essays edited by Dell Hymes (1969, Pantheon, New York), considers the relations between anthropological theory, moral judgments, politics, and the structure of academic anthropology; see, for example, Wolf's "American Anthropologists and American Society," pp. 251–263. The fullest textbook is Marvin Harris's *Culture, People, Nature* (1975, Thomas Y. Crowell, New York).

The Anthropological Imagination

Two classic works by Émile Durkheim, *The Rules of Sociological Method* (1895, repr. 1938, S. Solovay and J. Mueller, trans., Free Press, New York) and *Suicide* (1897, repr. 1951, J. Spaulding and G. Simpson, trans., Free Press, New York), formulate the premise of twentieth-century social science that individuals' actions are social facts. Two popular anthropological treatments of the same proposition, from contrasting points of view, are Ruth Benedict's classic study of culture and personality, *Patterns of Culture* (1934, repr. 1961, Houghton-Mifflin, New York), and M. Harris's cultural materialist essays, *Cows, Pigs, Wars, and Witches: The Riddles of Culture* (1974, Random House, New York). Alexander Alland, Jr., in *The Human Imperative* (1972, Columbia University Press, New York), readably refutes theories that emphasize the instinctual component in human behavior (e.g., those of Robert Ardrey, *The Territorial Imperative* [1965, Dell, New York] and Konrad Lorenz, *On Aggression* [1966, Harcourt Brace Jovanovich, New York]).

The number of books on field research grows constantly. Hortense Powdermaker's *Stranger and Friend* (1966, Norton, New York), an account of fieldwork in four different cultures, both narrates her personal experience and explains her professional goals and results. Pertti J. Pelto, *Anthropological Research: The Structure of Inquiry* (1970, Harper and Row, New York), discusses field techniques from a professional point of view. On philosophical issues and problems of scientific research theories, hypotheses, and objectivity, see Ernest Nagel, *The Structure of Science* (1961, Harcourt, Brace and World, New York).

Theories of the mutual creation of individual and culture are usually found outside of anthropology, for example, Herbert Marcuse, *Eros and Civilization* (1955, repr. 1962, Vintage, New York). See, however, Stanley Diamond, "Anthropology in Question," in Hymes (1969), pp. 401–429, and Bob Scholte, "Toward a Reflexive and Critical Anthropology," Hymes (1969), pp. 430–458.

Suggestions for Further Reading

Chapter II

The most comprehensive history of anthropology and anthropological theory is Marvin Harris, *The Rise of Anthropological Theory* (1968, Thomas Y. Crowell, New York), with its emphasis on the growth of cultural materialism. More recently, Fred W. Voget, *A History of Ethnology* (1975, Holt, Rinehart, Winston, New York) gives a less partisan view. See also chapter 1 of Robert F. Murphy, *The Dialectics of Social Life* (1973, Basic Books, New York) for a rapid, wry overview.

Lewis Henry Morgan's great work on the Iroquois, based on his field research, is *League of the Ho-de-no-sau-nee, or Iroquois* (1851, Sage and Bora, Rochester); his *Systems of Consanguinity and Affinity of the Human Family* (1870, Smithsonian Institution, Washington, D.C.) summarizes the data from the questionnaires he sent out to verify his evolutionary theories. Some of J. J. Bachofen's evolutionary ideas may be found in *Myth, Religion, and Mother Right; Selected Writings* (1871, repr. 1967, Ralph Mannheim, trans., Bollingen Series 84, Princeton, N.J.).

Sir E. B. Tylor's definition of culture comes from page one of *The Origins of Culture,* part 1 of *Primitive Culture* (1871, repr. 1958, Harper Torchbooks, New York, two vols.). A. L. Kroeber and Clyde Kluckhohn survey the many meanings and connotations of the concept of culture at both levels of abstraction in *Culture, A Critical Review of Concepts and Definitions* (n.d., Vintage Books, New York). British social anthropological views of the concept are found in Raymond Firth, *Elements of Social Organization* (1961, 2nd ed., Beacon Press, Boston) and S. F. Nadel, *The Theory of Social Structure* (1957, Cohen & West, London). For the ethnoscientific position, see Charles O. Frake, "The Ethnographic Study of Cognitive Systems," in *Cognitive Anthropology,* edited by Stephen A. Tyler (1969, Holt, Rinehart, and Winston, New York), pp. 28–41, and Ward H. Goodenough, *Description and Comparison in Cultural Anthropology* (1970, Aldine, Chicago). The symbolic structuralist view of culture can be found in Clifford Geertz, *The Interpretation of Cultures* (1973, Basic Books, New York).

My views on the importance of everyday life have been influenced by Erving Goffman, *The Presentation of Self in Everyday Life* (1959, Doubleday-Anchor, New York), and Peter Berger, *Invitation to Sociology: A Humanistic Perspective* (1963, Doubleday-Anchor, New York).

Franz Boas's collection of essays, *Race, Language, and Culture* (1940, repr. 1966, Free Press, New York) contains the classic discussions of the anthropological understanding of its title subjects. For an up-to-date account of the facts and theories of racial variation, see Alexander Alland, Jr., *Human Diversity* (1971, Columbia University Press, New York). On ethnicity, see, for example, *Ethnic Groups and Boundaries: The Social Organization of Culture Difference*, edited by Fredrik Barth (1968, Universitetsforlaget, Bergen/Oslo); on cultural imperialism, see Mina Davis Caulfield, "Culture and Imperialism: Proposing a New Dialectic," Hymes (1969), pp. 182–212. On language, see John Lyons, *Introduction to Theoretical Linguistics* (1968, Cambridge University Press, Cambridge).

Attempts at typologies of culture include: L. H. Morgan, *Ancient Society* (1877, repr. 1963, Eleanor Burke Leacock, ed., Meridian Books, Cleveland and New York): Robert Redfield, *The Primitive World and Its Transformations* (1953, Cornell University Press, Ithaca, New York); Julian Steward, "The Economic and Social Basis of Primitive Bands," in *Essays in Anthropology Presented to A. L. Kroeber*, edited by Robert H. Lowie (1937, University of California Press, Berkeley), pp. 331–345. See, too, E. Durkheim, *The Division of Labor in Society* (1893, repr. 1933, G. Simpson, trans., Macmillan, New York).

F. Boas 1940 and R. H. Lowie, *The Crow Indians* (1935, repr. 1956, Farrar & Rinehart, New York), state the historical particularist positions on theory and methodology. A strong relativist position can be seen in Benedict (1934).

On the idea of paradigms in science, see Thomas S. Kuhn, *The Structure of Scientific Revolutions* (1970, University of Chicago Press, Chicago), 2nd ed. For the original anthropological paradigm, see Clark Wissler, *Man and Culture* (1923, Thomas Y. Crowell, New York), pp. 73–77. Later examples are George P. Murdock et al., *Outline of Cultural Materials* (1965, HRAF Press, New Haven), and *Notes and Queries in Anthropology*, (Routledge & Kegan Paul, London), the research guide of the Royal Anthropological Institute, updated annually.

M. Harris, *The Nature of Cultural Things* (1964, Random House, New York) sets forth an etic method; Goodenough (1970) and Franke (1969) present emic methodology.

CHAPTER III

Pelto 1970, chapters 1–4, lucidly discusses the problems of selective observation. Gunther S. Stent, "Limits to the Scientific Understanding of Man," *Science* 187 (March 1975):1052–1057, considers the neurological basis for selective observation.

A. R. Radcliffe-Brown's classic collection of essays, *Structure and Function in Primitive Society* (1952, Free Press, Glencoe) introduces structural-functionalist theory, as does Nadel 1957. Bronislaw Malinowski, *A Scientific Theory of Culture* (1944, University of North Carolina Press, Chapel Hill) presents his nonstructural "needs" functionalism. Talcott Parsons's dense *The Social System* (1951, Free Press, Glencoe) represents the American sociological version of this theory. Robert K. Merton made the now standard distinction between "Manifest and Latent Functions," in *Social Theory and Social Structure* (1965, Free Press, New York), rev. ed., pp. 19–84.

A brief overview of all varieties of structuralism is Jean Piaget, *Structuralism* (1970, Channinah Maschler, trans., Harper and Row, New York). General considerations of anthropological structuralism are found in Murphy 1973 and Edmund Leach, *Rethinking Anthropology* (1961, Athlone Press, London). The best introduction to Claude Lévi-Strauss' ground-breaking but difficult work is *The Savage Mind* (1966, University of Chicago Press, Chicago); see too *Structural Anthropology* (1963, 1965, Claire Jacobson and Brooke Grundfest Schoepf, trans., Basic Books, New York), two vols., which contain essays spanning his career. A. F. C. Wallace's views on shared contrasts in communication are set forth in *Culture and Personality* (1944, 2nd ed., Random House, New York). Symbolic structuralism is exemplified by Geertz 1973; E. Leach, *Political Systems of Highland Burma* (1954, Beacon Press, Boston); and Victor Turner, *The Forest of Symbols* (1967, Cornell University Press, Ithaca, New York).

Stanley Aronowitz discusses colonized leisure in *False Promises* (1973, McGraw-Hill, New York).

Introductions to Marxist theory are: Anthony Giddens, *Capitalism and Modern Social Theory* (1971, Cambridge University Press, Cambridge); Richard C. Edwards, Michael Reich, and Thomas E. Weisskopf, *The Capitalist System: A Radical Analysis of American Society* (1972, Prentice-Hall, Englewood Cliffs, N.J.). A good selection from Karl Marx's and Frederick Engels's writings is *The Marx-Engels Reader*, edited by Robert S. Tucker (1972, Norton, New York). The most accessible works, and those most relevant to the considerations here, are K. Marx's "Introduction" and "Preface," in *Contribution to a Critique of Political Economy* (1859, repr. 1904, Charles H. Kerr & Co., Chicago); F. Engels, *The Origin of the Family, Private Property, and the State* (1884, repr. 1972, Eleanor Burke Leacock, ed., International Publishers, New York); and K. Marx and F. Engels, *Manifesto of the Communist Party* (1848, repr. 1948, International Publishers, New York). Different attempts to develop a theory of consciousness deriving from the Marxian one include Peter Berger and Thomas Luckmann, *The Social Construction of Reality* (1966, Doubleday-Anchor, New York); Max Horkheimer, *Critical Theory; Selected Essays* (1968, repr. 1972, Matthew J. O'Connell and others, trans., Seabury, New York); Marcuse (1955); and Jean-Paul Sartre, *Search for a Method* (1963, Hazel E. Barnes, trans., Vintage, New York).

CHAPTER IV

Two good, general discussions of social organization are R. Firth (1961) and R. H. Lowie's classic *Primitive Society* (1920, repr. 1961, Harper Torchbook, New York), revised into *Social*

Organization (1948, Rinehart, New York) (in which he virtually created the topic of voluntary associations or, as he called them, sodalities).

B. Malinowski's field research exhortations are found in chapter 1 of *Argonauts of the Western Pacific* (1922, repr. 1961, Dutton, New York).

Status and role receive comprehensive treatment in *The Study of Man,* by Ralph Linton (1936, Appleton-Century-Crofts, New York) which also discusses ideal and real culture, and Berger (1963). An interesting structural analysis of soap operas and American society is Susan Bean's "Soap Operas: Sagas of American Kinship," in *The American Dimension,* edited by W. Arens and Susan P. Montague (1976, Alfred Publishing Co., Port Washington, N.Y.), pp. 80–98.

Robin Fox's conversational *Kinship and Marriage* (1967, Penguin, New York), with its orientation toward alliance theory, is the best introduction to this subfield. Ira R. Buchler and Henry A. Selby, *Kinship and Social Organization* (1968, Macmillan, New York) is the best professional overview. The original structuralist analysis of kinship is C. Lévi-Strauss, *The Elementary Structures of Kinship* (1969, James Harle Bell, John Richard von Sturmer, and Rodney Needham, trans., Eyre and Spottiswoode, London), rev. ed. Self-teaching manuals of kinship theory and terminology are Ernest L. Schusky, *Manual for Kinship Analysis* (1972, Holt, Rinehart, Winston, New York), 2nd ed., and *Variation in Kinship* (1974, Holt, Rinehart, Winston, New York). G. P. Murdock, *Social Structure* (1949, Macmillan, New York), which inaugurated modern cross-cultural statistical research, systematically discusses and correlates types of descent principles and terminology. On kinship among the rich and powerful of the United States, see, for example, Michael Merlie and Edward Silva, "The First Family: Presidential Kinship and Its Theoretical Implications," *The Insurgent Sociologist* 5 (#3) (1975):149–170. On kinship among the poor, see Eliot Liebow, *Tally's Corner* (1967, Little Brown, Boston); Michael Young and Peter Willmott, *Family and Kinship in East London* (1962, Penguin, New York), rev. ed.

Fred Eggan's essay, "Social Anthropology and the Method of Controlled Comparison," *American Anthropologist* 56 (1954): 743–763 describes and illustrates the comparative method.

Chapter V

Two excellent ethnographies of Greek communities are Ernestine Friedl, *Vasilika: A Village in Modern Greece* (1962, Holt, Rinehart, and Winston, New York), and J. K. Campbell, *Honour, Family, and Patronage* (1964, Oxford University Press, Oxford). See too my own shorter pieces "Social Stratification in a Greek Village," in *City and Peasant: A Study in Sociocultural Dynamics,* edited by A. L. LaRuffa, et al., *Annals of the New York Academy of Sciences* 220 (6) (1974):438–495, and "Only on Sundays," *Natural History* (1971) 80:52–61. On Greek curing and magic, see Richard and Eva Blum, *The Dangerous Hour* (1970, Chatto & Windus, London).

On the study of the dominated by the dominators, see William S. Willis, Jr., "Skeletons in the Anthropological Closet," Hymes (1969), pp. 121–152.

A. F. C. Wallace's *Religion: An Anthropological View* (1966, Random House, New York) is the most systematic, thorough modern treatment of its subject. E. Durkheim's theory of the collective unconscious is set forth in *The Elementary Forms of the Religious Life* (1912, repr. 1915, J. W. Swain, trans., Allen & Unwin, London), along with his idea of society as the object of religious celebration; the notion of sacred/profane appears there and in Henri Hubert and Marcel Mauss, *Sacrifice: Its Nature and Function* (1899, repr. 1964, W. D. Halls, trans., University of Chicago Press, Chicago). B. Malinowski's theory that religion functions to reduce anxiety is developed in his essays in *Magic, Science, and Religion* (1948, repr. 1954, Doubleday-Anchor, Garden City). On science as a social phenomenon, see Berger and Luckmann (1966) and Kuhn (1962).

V. Turner, *The Ritual Process: Structure and Anti-Structure* (1969, Aldine, Chicago) is a lucid application of symbolic structuralism to puberty and other ceremonies. Arnold Van Gennep,

Suggestions for Further Reading

The Rites of Passage (1908, repr. 1960, Monika B. Vizedom and Garielle L. Caffee, trans., Routledge & Kegan Paul, London) is a classic exposition. Descriptions of Australian puberty rites can be found in Baldwin Spencer and F. J. Gillin, *The Native Tribes of Central Australia* (1899, repr. 1963, Dover, New York).

The best survey of psychological anthropology is Robert A. LeVine, *Culture, Behavior, and Personality* (1973, Aldine, Chicago). The psychoanalytic theories on which this subfield is based are covered in Sigmund Freud, *A General Introduction to Psychoanalysis* (1920, repr. 1963, James Strachey, trans. and ed., Hogarth Press, London), Standard Edition, vols. 15–16. A. F. C. Wallace (1974) discusses the subfield more abstractly. On the incest taboo, see Fox (1967). On the Oedipus complex, see Freud (1920). B. Malinowski discusses the matrilineal complex in *Sex and Repression in Savage Society* (1927, repr. 1955, Meredian Books, Cleveland and New York).

Gayle Rubin's Freudian, structuralist, and Marxist synthesis discusses the issues of incest, gender, and sex roles in "The Traffic in Women," in the excellent collection edited by Rayna Reiter *Toward An Anthropology of Women* (1975, Monthly Review Press, New York), pp. 157–210. Margaret Mead's *Sex and Temperament in Three Primitive Societies* (1935, Mentor, New York), and *Male and Female* (1949, repr. 1955, Mentor, New York), treat sex role variations cross-culturally. E. Friedl, *Women and Men* (1975, Holt, Rinehart, and Winston, New York) attempts to establish the conditions of equal sex role status in foraging and horticultural societies. Karen Sacks's "Engels Revisited: Women, the Organization of Production, and Private Property," is another good cross-cultural study, and is found in a second valuable anthropological collection on women edited by Michelle Zimbalist Rosaldo and Louise Lamphere, *Women, Culture, and Society* (1974, Stanford University Press, Stanford). This volume also includes Nancy Chodorow, "Family Structure and Feminine Personality," pp. 43–66, and Sherry B. Ortner, "Is Female to Male as Nature is to Culture?" pp. 67–88.

Mary Douglas presents a structural analysis of dichotomies, taboo, and pollution in *Purity and Danger* (1966, Routledge &

Kegan Paul, London). M. Mauss, *The Gift* (1924, repr. 1954, Ian Cunnison, trans., Free Press, New York) sets forth the theory of exchange as the integrative mechanism of human culture. Sol Worth, "Toward an Anthropological Politics of Symbolic Forms," Hymes (1969), pp. 335–366, discusses the relationships among control over symbols, the creation of ideology, and political power. Jules Henry poignantly analyzes American economy, society, and psyche in *Culture Against Man* (1963, Random House, New York).

CHAPTER VI

The best anthropological consideration of the origin of political and economic inequalities is Morton Fried, *The Evolution of Political Society* (1967, Random House, New York). There is, however, as yet no adequate brief summary of the subfield of economic anthropology. Marshall Sahlins's essays on use-value economies are collected in his Marxist-substantivist work, *Stone Age Economics* (1972, Aldine, Chicago). Harold Schneider, *Economic Man: The Anthropology of Economics* (1974, Free Press, New York) presents the formalist view of economic systems. The article creating the substantivist position and setting forth the three integrative types of exchange, "The Economy as Instituted Process," by Karl Polanyi, in *Trade and Market in the Early Empires,* edited by Polanyi, Conrad M. Arensberg, and Harry Pearson (1957, Free Press, New York), remains worthy of study.

On Marxist economic thought, see the suggestions given for Chapter III. A long popularization is Ernest Mandel, *Marxist Economic Theory* (1962, repr. 1970, Brian Pearce, trans., Monthly Review Press), two vols. On anthropological definitions of economy and of "mode of production," see Maurice Godelier, *Rationality and Irrationality in Economics* (1966, repr. 1972, Brian Pearce, trans., Monthly Review Press, New York) and Sahlins (1972). Claude Meillassoux's study of the Gouro, *Anthropologie économique des Gouro de Cote d'Ivoire* (1964, Mouton, Paris) is available only in French, but the data are summarized and his interpretations criticized by Emmanuel Terray, *Marxism and Primitive Societies* (1969, repr. 1972, Mary Klopper, trans., Monthly Review Press, New York).

Paul Bohannan created the concept of spheres of exchange in "Some Principles of Exchange and Investment Among the Tiv," American Anthropologist 57 (1955):60–70. E. Wolf's *Peasants* (1966, Prentice-Hall, Englewood Cliffs, N.J.) gives more information on markets and peasant economic systems. For an earlier model of Sahlins's domestic mode among peasants, see A. V. Chayanov, *The Theory of Peasant Economy* (1930, repr. 1966, Daniel Thorner, Basile Kerblay, and R. E. F. Smith, eds., Irwin, Homewood, Ill.).

A. P. Vayda and R. A. Rappaport survey the subfield of cultural ecology in "Ecology: Cultural and Non-cultural," in *Introduction to Cultural Anthropology,* edited by J. A. Clifton (1968, Houghton-Mifflin, Boston), pp. 476–498. Julian Steward delineated the subfield in "The Concept and Method of Cultural Ecology," reprinted in *Theory of Culture Change* (1955, University of Illinois Press, Urbana, Ill.), pp. 30–42. Eugene P. Odum, *Ecology* (1963, Holt, Rinehart, and Winston, New York) briefly introduces biological ecology. Paul Collins's "Functional Analyses in the Symposium 'Man, Culture, and Animals,'" in *Man, Culture, and Animals,* edited by Anthony Leeds and A. P. Vayda (1965, American Association for the Advancement of Science, Washington, D.C.), pp. 271–282, provides the thermostat model. Magorah Maruyama describes "The Second Cybernetics: Deviation-amplifying Mutual Causal Processes," *American Scientist* 51 (1963):164–179.

The introduction to *Political Anthropology,* edited by Marc J. Swartz, Victor W. Turner, and Arthur Tuden (1966, Aldine-Atherton, Chicago) surveys the subfield of political anthropology. My discussion of domains of power is based on Sahlins (1972), chapters 4–6. On the origin of ranking, stratification, and the state in relation to access to strategic resources, see Fried (1967). State-level modes of production (feudal, "Asiatic," hydraulic) are discussed in Karl Wittfogel, *Oriental Despotism,* (1957, Yale University Press, New Haven), and in *Sur le "mode de production asiatique,"* edited by Roger Garaudy (1969, Centre d'Études et de

Recherches Marxistes, Paris). Max Weber's discussion of legitimacy can be found in *Theory of Economic and Social Organization* (1947, repr. 1964, T. Parsons, ed., Free Press, New York), pp. 324–340. For Parsons's own discussion of consensual power, see "On the Concept of Power," *Proceedings of the American Philosophical Society* 107 (1963):232–262, as well as the introduction, Swartz et al. (1969).

Two sources on the power structure in the United States are C. Wright Mills, *The Power Elite* (1956, Oxford University Press, New York), and G. William Domhoff's *Who Rules America?*, (1967, Prentice-Hall, Englewood Cliffs, N.J.). On the role of international political and cultural structures, see, for example, André Cunder Frank, *Capitalism and Underdevelopment in Latin America* (1967, Monthly Review Press, New York).

CHAPTER VII

My discussion of human biological evolution is based on Bernard G. Campbell, *Humankind Emerging* (1976, Little, Brown, Boston). A popular treatment is John Pfeiffer, *The Emergence of Man* (1972, 2nd ed., Harper and Row, New York). Loren Eisely, *Darwin's Century* (1961, Doubleday-Anchor, New York), is a well-written history of evolutionary theory, and Alexander Alland, Jr., *Evolution and Human Behavior* (1967, Natural History Press, Garden City) explains the theory simply but completely. Peter Kropotkin, *Mutual Aid* (1972, orig. 1914, Paul Avrich, ed., New York University Press, New York) discusses cooperation and competition as of equal evolutionary importance.

A dated, but still exciting sweep of cultural evolution is V. Gordon Childe, *Man Makes Himself* (1951, Mentor, New York). Kent Flannery discusses the emergence of Old World domestication in "The Ecology of Early Food Production in Mesopotamia," *Science* 147 (1965):1247–1256. A comprehensive synthesis for the New World is William T. Sanders and Barbara J. Price, *Mesoamerica: The Evolution of a Civilization* (1968, Random House, New York).

The concept of levels of integration was first worked out by

Suggestions for Further Reading

J. Steward in "Levels of Sociocultural Integration: An Operational Concept," in his 1955 collection, pp. 43–63. Elman Service, *Primitive Social Organization* (1962, Random House, New York) presents another version of the four levels. Leslie A. White's essays on energy and cultural evolution are collected in *The Science of Culture* (1949, Grove Press, New York); his narrative of cultural evolution is *The Evolution of Culture* (1959, McGraw-Hill, New York). J. Steward, in his 1955 collection, considers multilinear evolution in chapters 1 and 11. M. Sahlins and E. Service attempt to unify Whitean and Stewardian theory in *Evolution and Culture* (1960, University of Michigan Press, Ann Arbor), which presents their theory of specific and general evolution. See too Fried (1967).

On the influence of population pressure on innovations in social structure and technology, see Ester Boserup, *The Conditions of Agricultural Growth* (1965, Aldine-Atherton, Chicago). Sahlins (1972), chapter 3 discusses the origin of chiefdoms through intensification of production.

Bryan Clarke discusses diversity as the basis of evolution in "The Causes of Biological Diversity," *Scientific American* 233 (1975):50–61. On the incorporative character of late capitalism, see Paul Baran and Paul Sweezy, *Monopoly Capital* (1966, Monthly Review Press, New York). On the embryonic world system, see Immanuel Wallerstein, "The Rise and Future Demise of the World Capitalist System: Concepts for Comparative Analysis," *Comparative Studies in Society and History* 16 (1974):387–415. For a discussion of the coequal roles of technology, social organization, and consciousness in determining change, see Don E. Dumond, "The Limitation of Human Population: A Natural History," *Science* 187 (1975):713–721. On intra- and intersystem contradictions, see Jonathon Friedman, "Marxism, Structuralism, and Vulgar Materialism," *Man* (1974, n.s.):444–469.

Index

Abstract thought, 146–147, 236
Adams, Robert McC., 257
Adaptation, 165, 256, 263–264
  and adaptive radiation, 249
  (*See also* Ecology, and ecological adaptation)
Adulthood, 4, 78, 81–82, 104, 107–108, 156, 158, 162–164, 176
Affines, 112, 114, 121, 126–127, 130, 134, 208, 251
Africa, 29–30, 112, 117, 216, 235
Age, 47, 128, 203, 242
Aged, 26, 109, 225, 260
Age-sets, 134–135, 156
Aggression, 163–164, 175
Agriculture, 45–46, 187, 230, 245–248, 262
  irrigation, 248, 250–252, 256, 258
  swidden, 190, 206
  (*See also* Domestication)
Albania, 34
"All in the Family," 131
Amulets, 139–140
Ancestor worship, 156
Animal ancestors, 20, 45
Anthropology, xiii, 19–24, 63, 265–266
  cognitive, 23
  cultural, xiii
  physical, xiii, 29
  social, 23
  sociology of, 36–43
  symbolic, 23
  (*See also* specific schools of)
Arapesh, 171–172
Archeology, xiii, 234–235, 242–244, 247, 250–252, 255

Index

Aronowitz, Stanley, 80
Art, 44, 171
Arunta, 157, 176
Australia, 44, 50, 157, 188
Australopithecus, 229–230, 232–235, 241, 247, 263

Bachofen, J. J., 20
Band society, 242–143, 249, 260–262
Baptism, 155
Barbarism, 46
Barter, 197
Basseri of South Persia, 46
Bateson, Gregory, 239–240
Beliefs, 32, 138–143, 145, 149, 152–153, 176–177, 224
Bemba of Rhodesia, 30
Benedict, Ruth, 43, 161
Berger, Peter, 24, 86
Big-men, 218, 222, 252, 258–259
Binary perception, 72–74, 122
Biology, 29–31, 72, 156, 160, 163–164, 171
  and evolution, 229–235, 237, 239, 256
  and kinship, 111–113, 118, 121–122, 127, 169, 193
Birthdays, 156
Bisexuality, 168
Blacks, 29, 131
Blue bead, magical, 148–149
Boas, Franz, 21, 161
Body, 144, 152
Bolivia, 244
Botswanaland, 33
Brain size, 25, 234–235
Brazil, 41, 44, 118, 210, 223, 255
Bride-service, 124
Bride-wealth, 126, 191–192
Britain, 34, 117, 250
Brother-in-law bond, 120–121, 124
Bureaucrats, 179, 220–222, 252–253, 256, 264
Bushmen, 33

Cafeteria, used as field research sample, 55–70, 74–78, 88, 92, 94, 96
Capital, 201
Capitalism, 19–20, 58, 64, 75, 80, 84, 89, 92, 167, 182, 184–185, 198, 200–202, 204, 211, 222, 246, 254, 261–262, 264–266
Caste system, 221, 223
Castration, 166
Caucasians, 30
Causality, 69, 92, 95, 209
Ceremony, 32, 139, 141, 145, 149, 155–157, 176, 215–216, 221, 230, 246, 259
Chagnon, N., 119, 208
Change, social, 15–18, 52, 65, 67–69, 83–85, 87–88, 92–93, 95, 146, 209–210, 242
  (*See also* Evolution)
Chayanov, A. V., 195
Cheyennes, 37–38
Chicago school symbolic structuralism, xvi
Chiefdoms, 46, 116, 126, 141, 165, 214–218, 225, 243, 249, 252, 257–259, 261–262
Childe, V. G., xiii, 242, 246
Childhood, 78, 81–82, 104, 107–109, 112–113, 141, 156–157, 162–164, 167, 174, 261
Childrearing, 2–4, 157–159, 171–172, 174, 188
China, 38, 156, 243
Chodorow, Nancy, 171
Chomsky, Noam, 73
Christianity, 140–142
Cities, 163, 230, 245, 253–254
Civilization, 46
Clans, 114
Class structure, 52, 70, 84–85, 88–91, 93–94, 109, 132–135, 213, 218–219, 223–224, 227, 254

Clubs, 103–105, 107, 132, 135
Cognatic relatives, 114, 117, 119, 129
Collective consciousness, 143
Colleges, 89–91, 93, 107, 132, 186
Colonization, 117, 210, 221, 248–250, 262
Commodities, defined, 185
Communication, 9, 26, 34, 79, 89, 91, 139, 146–147, 152–153, 169, 224, 235–236, 252–253
  (*See also* Language)
Comparative method, 133–136
Conflict in society, 28, 51, 85–89, 92–94, 102, 149, 179–180, 265
  and shortage of protein, 208–210
Consanguineal relatives, 112, 114, 125, 127
Consciousness, 82–84, 86, 95–96, 162–163, 224, 237–240, 265–266
Consumers, 177–178, 182, 186, 198, 202, 253, 259
Contradictions in society, 28, 84, 88, 92–93, 108, 142, 145, 151, 153, 163, 265
Contrast, 72–73, 76–80, 93, 122
Corporations, 66, 103, 114, 132, 182
Cousins, 129–130, 133
Craftsmanship, 9, 191, 203, 216, 246, 253–254
Creativity, 16–17, 27, 41, 184, 234–236, 239, 245–246
Critical Theory, xvi, 86
Cults, 141–142, 149
Cultural materialist school, 24
Cultural model, general, 79–80, 82
Cultural relativism, 41–43, 50, 239
Culture, xi, xv–xvii, 6–15, 19–43, 88–89, 92, 96, 139–140, 156, 159–164, 169–170, 173–174, 203–205, 233–234
  categories of, 81
  and evolution, 205, 228–266
  ideal, 109–111
  and intercultural structures, 51–53
  and nature, 72–73, 207, 228
  paradigm of, 48–53, 88
  patterns of, 28, 49–50, 64
  pure, 156
  reality of, 57, 109–111, 204
  and society, difference between, 23, 27
  specificity of, 13–15
  types, 43–48, 230, 242
Cultures:
  advanced, 46–47
  complex, 47–50, 53, 165, 177, 224
  maintenance of, 65–66, 69, 71
  primitive, 46–47, 51, 87
  simple, 47–50, 53, 66, 165
Customs, 148

Darwin, Charles, 37, 162, 230–231
Death, 155–156
Defoe, Daniel, 1, 8
Descent, 113, 117, 119–121, 125–127, 131, 133, 135, 169, 248
  bilateral, 129, 132
  cognatic, 129
  matrilineal, 20, 30, 44, 113, 118, 131, 166–167, 215
  patrilineal, 30, 44, 113–121, 188, 193
    temporary suspension of rules of, 118
  unilineal, 118–119, 245, 257
  (*See also* Kinship; Lineage)
Deviation-amplification model, 209
Dialectical materialism, 86
Dinka, 118, 241
Diplomacy, 215–216
Diversity, 254, 259, 263–264
Division of labor, 179, 184, 190, 193, 198–200, 236–238, 241–242, 247, 263

Index

Divorce, 110
Domestication of plants and animals, 187–190, 243–247, 249–251, 261
Domestic cycle, 108
Domesticity, 125, 127–133, 214–215, 217, 220
Douglas, Mary, 173
Durkheim, Emile, xii–xiii, 46, 143
Dyadic structures, 82, 103–104, 107

Ecology, xv, 15, 24, 216, 263–264
  and ecological adaptation, 182, 203–211, 217, 231, 235, 249
  and ecological niche, 204–205, 207, 232, 234–235, 244–245
Economic Man philosophy, 175
Economic structure, xvi, 48–49, 66–70, 84, 86, 88–89, 92–93, 112, 125, 130, 133
  distribution, 182, 185, 189, 195, 211
  exchange-values, 185–186, 190–191, 197–198, 201–203, 214, 220–221
  male dominance of, 171–172, 175–176, 178
  market exchange, 187, 191–192, 194–203, 212, 214, 224, 254
  and power, 180–205
  production, 93–94, 182–183, 207, 254, 259, 263
    control of means of, 47, 194–195, 212, 218–219, 221
    material forces of, 85
    social relations of, 85
  production, modes of, xvi, 184–186
    "Asiatic," 221–222, 258
    domestic, 87, 195, 199–200, 215, 222, 242, 248, 253, 258
    feudal, 222
    hydraulic, 222
    lineage, 189–195, 212, 214, 242, 248
    village, 189, 191–192, 194, 212–214, 248
  property ownership:
    in common, 114, 190
    private, 66, 84, 167, 184, 198, 201, 219
  reciprocity, 187, 189, 195, 258
  redistribution, 187, 195, 221, 248, 253, 257
  scarcity, 183, 211, 219
  services, sale of, 198
  subsistence, 45–46, 191, 195, 197, 201, 216, 218
  substantive, 187–188
  surplus, xvi, 200–201, 214, 218–219, 226, 246–247, 251, 254
  use-values, 185, 188, 190–192, 196–197, 201–203, 214, 226–227, 248, 252, 258
Ecosystem, 204
Ecuador, 41
Education, 89, 93, 160, 224, 253
  (*See also* Colleges)
Egypt, 165
Elders, 32, 117, 190–193, 195, 211–214, 245
"Electra complex," 168
Elite culture (*see* High culture)
Emic viewpoint, 95–96, 109–112, 130–131, 133, 152, 210, 218
Employers and employees, 69–70, 77, 105, 201–202, 224
Enculturation, 26–27, 38–39, 41, 91, 163–164, 174, 177, 238, 241
  (*See also* Socialization)
Endogamy, 132, 251
Energy, 205–206, 240–243, 245, 254
Engels, Frederick, 84
Epistemological status, 73
Esthetics, 145, 149

Index

Ethnicity, 29, 31–33, 36–38, 55, 70, 88, 91–92, 106, 109, 130, 132, 135, 223, 264
  and occupational specialization, 33, 221, 256
Ethnocentrism, 39–41, 47, 86, 90, 149, 159, 173, 239
Ethnography, 21–22, 48–50, 52, 102, 109
Ethnoscientists, 23
Ethos, 145, 151, 158
Etic viewpoint, 95–96, 109, 111, 131, 133, 210, 215
Evans-Pritchard, E. E., 23, 112–113, 117
Evil eye, 137–141, 143, 152–153
Evolution, xiii-xvii, 7, 15, 17–21, 46, 52, 85, 140, 144, 146, 162,
  convergent, 247
  multilinear, 242, 249
  specific, 243–244
  universal (general), 241, 243–244
Exchange systems, xvi, 47, 64, 175–176, 180
Exogamy, 119, 132, 165, 169–171, 192
Exorcism, 137–138, 142, 144, 149–150, 157, 164

False consciousness, 86, 95
Families, 103–105, 112, 116, 158, 164, 166, 168–170, 180, 184, 222, 227
  extended, 128, 131–132, 195
  nuclear, 27, 45, 104–105, 107–110, 112–113, 119–120, 124, 127–131, 133–134, 166–167, 175
  of orientation or of procreation, 107
Feminism, xvi, 87, 91, 168, 174
Feudal system, 92, 184, 221, 243, 258
Feuds, 115–117, 119
Fieldwork, 12, 14, 19, 21, 39–40, 43–45, 49–51, 99, 103, 139, 154–155
  (*See also* Cafeteria, used as field research)
Firth, Raymond, 23
Foraging, 33, 45, 50, 187, 189, 230, 242–247, 249
Fortes, Meyer, 23
Frake, Charles, 23
Frankfurt School, xvi
Freud, Sigmund, xvi, 162, 166–171
Fried, Morton, 24, 248
Friedman, Jonathon, 265
Friendships, 77, 104
Functions, 67–69, 71, 75, 96, 113

Geertz, Clifford, 23, 83, 145, 148–150
Gender, 3, 35, 166, 172, 180, 193, 264
  (*See also* Sex)
Genealogies, 193, 257
Genes, 29–30, 164–165, 231–233, 236
Genesis, 8
Geniuses, 161
Godelier, Maurice, 182
Goffman, Erving, 24
Golding, William, 1
Goodenough, Ward, 23
Gouro of Ivory Coast, 188–201, 206–207, 211–212, 222, 226, 248
Governmental structure, 117, 217, 245, 250, 254
  (*See also* State, the)
Graduation ceremony, 157–158, 186
Greece, 12, 32, 34, 40–41, 100, 137–145, 148, 151, 176–177, 186–187, 195–200, 206, 210, 218, 220–222, 224

Index

Greek Orthodox church, 140–142, 149, 155
Groups, social, 69, 81–82, 84–85, 112–113, 126
  mechanical vs. organic, 46

Halloween, 141
Harris, Marvin, 24, 95–96, 208, 210, 219
Hawaii, 165, 257
Henry, Jules, 177
Heroes, 150
Heterosexuality, 168, 178
Hierarchy, 84, 142, 150–151, 157, 188–190
High (elite) culture, 22, 89–91
Historical materialism, 84–86, 88, 95
Historical particularism, 43
History, 46–47, 87, 242, 253
  pre written, 87
Holism, 18, 22, 24, 28, 49–50, 53, 63–64, 84, 88, 181
Homeostat, 207–210, 249
Homo erectus, 235, 237, 241, 247
Homo sapiens, 14, 25–26, 72, 204, 229, 231, 233, 235, 237–238, 249
Homosexuality, 91, 104, 168
Horkheimer, Max, 86
Horticulture, 187, 190, 246
Households, 128, 134, 142–143, 167, 171–172, 175, 188, 195–197, 199–200
  (*See also* Domesticity)
Housewives and housework, 5, 100, 185, 188, 226–227
Hubert, Henri, 143
Humanities, the, 17
Human nature, 1–6, 159
Hunting, 187–188, 194, 213–214

Ideology, xiv, xvi, 23, 74, 84–86, 88–90, 92–93, 95, 102, 108, 110, 136, 145–146, 148–153, 158, 160–162, 168–178, 181, 198, 223–225, 238–240, 259
Iliad, 210
Illness, 144–145, 243
Immigrants, 30, 37, 89, 90–91, 93, 135
Imperialism, 33, 47
Inca empire, 46
Incest taboo, 130, 164–167, 169–171
India, 253, 258
Indians (*see* Native Americans)
Individual, and relationship to culture and society, 6–13, 15, 18, 24, 27, 41–42, 64, 76, 82–83, 86, 100, 142–143, 148, 150–152, 170, 181
Industrialism, 19–20, 80, 187–188, 203, 226–227, 246, 254, 262
Inequality, 68–69, 84, 87–89, 171, 179–181, 223, 255–256
Infant, experimental isolation of, 1–6, 8, 16
Infanticide, 120, 165
Inheritance, 119, 132, 213, 223, 251
In-laws, 44, 112, 120–124, 128–129
  (*See also* Kinship)
Institutions, 22, 67, 74, 92, 103, 106, 108, 112, 134
  formal, 102
  informal, 102–105
Integration, 176–177, 179–180, 232, 236–238, 240–243, 248, 251–252, 254–255, 257–258, 260–262
Intelligence, 25, 73, 160–161, 234
Intuition, 110, 173
Iroquois, 20
Islam, 32, 140
Israel, 32
Italy, 143

Jamaica, 34
Japan, 221

INDEX

Jivaro of Ecuador and Brazil, 41
Judaism, 32, 37, 140, 142

Kalahari Desert, 33
Kindred, 129
Kinship, 20, 27, 44–45, 47, 66, 70, 87, 111–135, 169–170, 179, 192–194, 197, 200, 207, 222–223, 242, 248, 257–258
  and non-kin groups, 127, 134–135, 215
  classificatory terms of, 122–123, 129
  (*See also* Descent; Families; Marriage)
Knowledge, 138–139
Kroeber, A. L., 26
Kula Ring, 96, 215–218, 251–252, 258
/Kung, 33, 188
Kypria, 210

Labels, 69–70
Labor (*See* Work)
Lactase, ability to produce, 30
Language, 22, 29, 32, 35–37, 82, 115, 139, 147, 152, 235–236, 238
  (*See also* Linguistics)
Laws, 31, 47, 66, 117, 181, 224, 255
Leach, Sir Edmund, 83
Leisure, 79–80, 103, 177, 184, 226, 246–247
  (*See also* Play)
Leopard-skin chief, 116, 126, 214
LeVine, Robert A., 161
Lévi-Strauss, Claude, 73, 149–150, 169
Liebow, Elliot, 131
Life crises, 155–156
Life-styles, 218–219
Lineage, 113–121, 123–127, 132, 135, 167, 189–193
  corporate, 114–115, 128, 193, 251
  major, 115
  maximal, 115, 117
  minimal, 114, 117
  minor, 114
  (*See also* Descent; Kinship)
Linguistics, xiii, 23, 33–34, 36, 72–73, 130
  (*See also* Language)
Locke, John, 161
Lord of the Flies, 1
Luckmann, Thomas, 86

Magic, 12, 138, 140, 148–149, 154
Maine, Sir Henry, 20
Malinowski, Bronislaw, 21, 50, 100, 138, 166, 168
Mana, 141, 165, 257
Marcuse, Herbert, 86
Marketplaces, 33, 216, 225, 254
Marriage, 5, 20, 31–32, 44, 89, 109–110, 114, 118–130, 132, 135, 145–146, 148, 151, 156, 165, 167, 169–170, 192–193, 197, 207, 211–213, 216, 248
  and forbidden matches, 124
  and inbreeding, 164–165
  and love, 112, 118, 125, 128–129, 132, 134, 169
  monogamous, 112, 128, 178
  negative rules of, 121
  place of residence after, 124–125, 129–131, 215
  plural, 120–121, 128
  positive rules of, 121, 130
  (*See also* Endogamy; Exogamy)
Maruyama, Magoroh, 209
Marx, Karl, xii, 37, 84, 162, 200, 263
Marxism, xiii, xv–xvi, 22–23, 83–96, 140, 182–183, 193, 200, 202, 211, 221, 223, 265
"Mary Hartman, Mary Hartman," 131

Mass media, 224–225, 254
Materialism, 10
Maternal instinct, 171
Matrifocal households, 131
Matrilineage (*see* Descent, matrilineal)
Matrilocal residence, 131, 215
Mauss, Marcel, 143, 169, 175
Maximizing, 186
Mead, Margaret, xi, 171
Meillassoux, Claude, 188, 194
Memory, 161, 162, 239–240
Men, 5, 28, 40–41, 72–73, 87, 120, 123–124, 143, 151–153, 156, 159, 167–171, 194, 227, 236, 261
(*See also* Sex roles)
Mendel, Gregor, 231
Merchants, 191–192, 196, 199, 246
Mesopotamia, 247, 250, 253, 257–258
Mexico, 216, 250
Middle East, 29, 243–244, 248, 252, 256, 258
Migration, seasonal, 45, 206, 210, 244
Military, 9, 200, 223–224, 255
Mind, 144, 161
-matter dichotomy, 15–18, 23, 181
Money, 66, 70, 185, 197–199, 214, 254
(*See also* Wealth)
Mongoloids, 30
Morality, systems of, 16–17, 22, 26, 38, 41–42, 85, 108, 125, 139, 143, 224, 238
Morgan, Lewis Henry, 20, 46–47
Mother-in-law avoidance, 44, 124
Mundugumor, 171
Mutations, 232, 244
Myth, 8, 44, 118, 150, 193, 224, 239, 253
Nadel, S. F., 23
Nationality, 29, 31–34, 38, 51–53
Native Americans, 8, 20–21, 37–38, 52, 242
Natural selection, 231, 233–234, 236, 238, 240
Nature, 72–73, 156, 173–174, 205–207, 228
Nazi Germany, 28
Negro "race," 30
Neo-evolutionary schools, 24
Neolithic revolution, 245
Neolocal residence, 129–130
Neurology, 25–26
New Guinea, 171
New World, 247, 249, 258
Nineteenth-century social theorists, 9, 19–20, 24, 37, 45, 86, 160, 242
Nomads, 246, 249
Nuclear family (*see* Family, nuclear)
Nuer of the Sudan, 30, 44, 46, 112–119, 125–128, 133–135, 156, 187, 189–190, 193, 206, 214, 230, 248, 250

Objectivity, 13, 150, 162
Object-relations school, xvi, 170
Observation, 16
detached, 38–39, 42, 109–110, 162, 173
and intuitive knowledge, 110, 173
selective, 55–61
Odysseus, 8
"Oedipus complex," 164, 166, 168–169
Ontology, 82
Operationalism, 73
Organization, social, xiv, 240–243, 263
(*See also* Integration, social)
Ortner, Sherry B., 73, 173–174
Ottoman empire, 33, 196, 221

INDEX

Parenthood, 109, 112–113, 123, 157–158
  and parent/child sex taboo, 165–167
Parsons, Talcott, 71, 224
Pastoralism, 46, 187–188, 249
Patrikin, 115–116, 118–119
Patrilineage (*see* Descent, patrilineal)
Patrilocal residence, 124
Peasant societies, 195, 259
Personality, 160–166, 171, 207
Pithecanthropines, 235–236
Play/work dichotomy, 76–81
  (*See also* Leisure)
Polanyi, Karl, 187
Political structure, xvi, 31–33, 36, 46, 68–70, 84, 88–89, 91, 112, 116, 119–121, 124–125, 127–128, 132, 135, 141, 145, 148, 153–154, 165, 167, 171–172, 176–178, 180–182, 193–194, 214–217, 251–252, 257, 261–264
  international, 227–228
  and legitimacy, 223–224
  and ranking, 217
  (*See also* Governmental Structure; State, the
Polyandry, 120
Polygamy, 120
Polygyny, 120, 126–127
Polynesia, 141, 165, 257
Population size, 36, 207–210, 227–228, 235, 247, 249–251, 254–255, 259
Positivistic empiricism, 10
Power, 9, 15, 45, 68, 70, 84, 88–90, 92–93, 116–117, 125–127, 133, 165–166, 169, 171–172, 174, 176, 179–181, 192, 195, 201–202, 211–225, 253, 255–256, 262, 264–265
  and coercive force, 45, 47, 116, 181, 223–224, 242, 248, 252
  consensual, 224
  and loyalties, 117, 127, 217–218
  official, 222
  and prestige, 120, 125, 212–213, 215–219, 222, 251–252, 257
Priests, 45, 215, 251–253, 256
Private/public dichotomy (*see* Public/private dichotomy)
Process, notion of, xvii, 7, 11–13, 15, 51–52, 92
Procreation, 119, 125, 128, 160
Production (*see* Economic structure, production)
Protein, absence of, 208–210
Psyche, 159–160, 162, 164, 168
Psychic structures, 73
Psychoanalytic theory, xvi, 162–164, 166, 168, 170
Psychology, xvi, 159, 161, 163–164, 169, 181, 209–211
Psychosomatic, 144–145
Puberty rites, 134–135, 151, 155–157, 171
Public/private dichotomy, 142, 147–148, 151–152, 173–174, 214–215, 217, 219–220, 225, 227

Race, 29–31, 36–37, 55, 58–59, 70, 84, 88–89, 91–92, 130, 132, 135, 160, 221
Radcliffe-Brown, A., 65, 87
Rappaport, R. A., 209
Reality, 57, 60–61, 148, 152, 174
Reification, 10–11, 18, 27, 37, 50, 52
Relationships, social, 4–5, 9–10, 25, 28, 42, 46–47, 62–75, 77–78, 81–82, 233
Relatives (*see* Kinship)
Religion, 28–29, 32, 36, 45, 109, 112, 132, 135, 137–145, 148–152, 155–156, 224, 260
  (*See also* Priests)

INDEX

Repression, 163, 170, 239
Research (*see* Fieldwork)
Revolution, 29, 85, 265
Rhodesia, 30
Rites of passage, 155–159
Ritual, 141–143, 145, 150–158, 171, 176–178, 183, 193–194, 215–216, 221, 224, 241
Robinson Crusoe, 1
Rockefeller family, 132, 222
Roles, 101–103, 107, 112, 122, 164, 171, 180
  (*See also* Sex roles)
Royalty, 133, 165, 222–223, 225, 259–260
Rubin, Gayle, 168–169, 173

Sacred, the, 116
  sacred/profane dichotomy, 143, 151–152, 173
  sacred symbols, 148, 150
Sahlins, Marshall, 24, 195, 216, 241, 243, 246, 257
Salvage ethnography, 21
Samoans, 48
Savagery, 46
Science, 11, 13, 17, 60–61, 138, 140–141, 143–144, 149
Self:
  awareness of, 162, 180, 237–239
  integrated sense of, 170
  splitting of, 176–178
Service, Elman, 24, 241, 243
Sex, 47, 128, 134–135, 159–160, 163–172, 174, 180, 193, 246
  taboos, 124, 164
  (*See also* Bisexuality; Gender; Heterosexuality; Homosexuality; Incest taboos)
Sex roles, 3, 35, 109, 120, 128, 143, 166, 171–172, 178, 190, 203, 265
Shamans, 243, 251
Siblings, 109, 113, 120–124, 129, 210
Sickle-cell anemia, 29, 164
Siriono of Bolivia, 244–245
Slavs, 34–35
Soap operas, 99–102, 106–107, 109, 111, 131, 133–134, 227
  (*See also* "Somerset")
Socialism, 84, 204, 254, 262
Sociality, 6
Socialization, 27, 158
  (*See also* Enculturation)
Social life, 9, 233–234, 236–238
Social race, 31
Social sciences, 15, 17, 41, 153, 159, 181–182
Social structure, 106–107
Society, 6–16, 18–19, 23, 105–106, 110–111
  and culture, difference between, 23, 27
  maintenance of, 65–66
  (*See also* Cultures)
Socio-economic formations, 22–23, 85, 133, 250
Sociology, 19, 23, 71, 150
"Somerset," 101–102, 107–108, 130, 132–133
Soviet Union, 221, 230, 254–255
Spain, 143
Specialization, 33, 110–111, 176–177, 214, 216, 221, 246–247, 249–252, 254, 257, 259, 263
  (*See also* Division of labor)
Speech, 147
  (*See also* Language; Linguistics)
Spencer, Herbert, 231
Spouse, use of term, 129–130
State, the, 220–226, 243, 248, 252–258, 260, 262–263
Statistics, 106
Status, 101–105, 107–108, 112, 116, 122, 155, 164, 225–227
  ascribed, 223

Index

Status quo, 71, 84, 87
Stereotypes, 42, 70
Steward, Julian, 206, 241–242, 249
Strangers, attitudes toward, 116
Structural-functionalism, 65–66, 71, 81, 84, 87, 92–93, 95, 100, 136
Structuralism, xv–xvii, 71–83, 93, 95, 149–151, 162, 170–171, 182, 193, 265
Subcultures, 31–33, 37, 52, 88, 90–91, 132, 160–161
Subjectivity, 27, 82–83, 96, 150
Substantivism, 187
Sudan, 30, 223
Supernatural, 32, 139–140, 142, 144, 243
Superstitions, 140–141
Surplus production (*see* Economic structure, surplus)
Survival of the fit, 231–232
Symbolic analysis, school of, 83
Symbolic structuralism, xvi, 73, 83, 86, 149–150, 172
Symbols, 23, 27, 83, 147–152, 158, 165, 169, 171–175, 216, 224, 235–236

Taboos, 141
  (*See also* Incest taboos; Sex, taboos)
Taxes, 195–196, 200, 221–222, 225, 252, 254
Tchambuli, the, 171–172
Technology, 15, 47, 70, 144, 184, 203–204, 225, 241, 246, 263–264
Terray, Emmanuel, 193
Territorial boundaries, 31–33, 116–119, 125–126, 133, 136, 175, 192, 220, 225, 248, 252, 255
  sections, in Nuer communities, 116–117, 135
Thanksgiving, 141
Theory, xii, 13–15, 18, 48–49, 60–63, 111, 143
  and fact, 93–97
  (*See also* Marxism; Structural-functionalism; Structuralism)
Third World, 87, 221
Tiwi of North Australia, 44
Tools, 25, 47, 85, 229, 233–235, 240–241, 246–247
Totems, 45
Trade, 215–216, 218, 230, 245, 248–249, 252–253, 258
Triadic structures, 81–82
Tribes, 115–117, 134–135, 243, 248–249, 255, 261–262
Trobriand Islanders, 50, 96, 113, 160, 166–167, 215–217, 222, 225, 251–252, 257
Turkey, 12, 33, 221–222
Turner, Victor, 23, 83
Tylor, Sir E. B., 22, 24, 26–27
Typologies, 46, 48

Uncles, 166–167
Unconscious structure, 74, 82, 95, 163, 224, 237–238, 240, 265–266
Unilineage (*see* Descent, unilineal)
Unions, 135
United States, 28–29, 32–33, 37, 53, 66, 88–90, 218, 222–223, 225, 230, 255, 264
Universal patterns of culture, 49–50, 64
Us-them concept, 37–38, 50

Valentine's Day, 141
Values, 22–23, 136, 146, 148, 151, 162, 183
Vayda, A. P., 24, 209
Venezuela, 44, 119, 210
Violence, 117

Virilocal residence, 124–125
Vocational training, 90, 93
Voluntary associations, 134–135

Wallace, A. F. C., 79, 140–141
War, 92, 115–121, 194, 207–210, 214–216, 255
Wealth, 45, 84, 88–89, 218–219, 221–223, 225, 253
(*See also* Money)
Weber, Max, 150, 223
Wedding, 119, 126
White, Leslie A., 26, 240–242
Wilmott, Peter, 131
Wissler, Clark, 49
Witch doctors, 12
Witches, 141
Wolf, Eric R., 37
Women, 5, 40–41, 72–73, 87, 99, 120, 123–126, 131, 134, 143, 151–153, 156–157, 159, 167, 168–169, 171–176, 199, 212, 225–227, 239, 260–261
(*See also* Sex roles)
Work, 9, 66, 84, 176–178, 193–194, 199–201, 220
and alienation, 186, 188, 202–203, 220, 226, 255
-play dichotomy, 76–81
unpaid, 184–185, 226
World culture, a, 37, 106, 255, 261–264
World view, 139–141, 144–145, 151, 158, 183–184

Xerox, 36

Yam harvests, of Trobriands, 215–218
Yanomamö, 44, 119–127, 129–130, 133–134, 154, 165, 170, 206–210, 214, 216, 228, 230, 242, 248
Young, Michael, 131
Yugoslavia, 5

Zulu of East Africa, 46

About the Author

Muriel Dimen-Schein is currently Associate Professor of Anthropology at Herbert H. Lehman College (CUNY). She has published in *American Anthropologist, Annals of the New York Academy of Sciences, Ethnology,* and other journals. Her fieldwork includes research in a mountain village in Epiros, Greece, and a Navajo Reservation in Arizona.

Professor Dimen-Schein received her B.A. from Barnard College and her M.A. and Ph.D. from Columbia University.